THE GOOD LIFE OF WESTERN MAN

THE GOOD LIFE
OF
WESTERN MAN

William H. Marnell

HERDER AND HERDER

1971
HERDER AND HERDER NEW YORK
232 Madison Avenue, New York 10016

Library of Congress Catalog Card Number: 70-140236
© 1971 by Herder and Herder, Inc.
Manufactured in the United States

Contents

To John and Margaret Gill

Foreword

BY ARNOLD TOYNBEE

In this book, Professor Marnell offers an answer to one of the questions that human beings have asked themselves at all times and places. We may guess that our descendants will go on asking this question so long as the human race continues to exist. The question is fundamental, and therefore Professor Marnell's book is of perennial interest.

Professor Marnell holds that a human being's life is good in so far as he spends it on serving other people. For these, of course, his life is obviously good if he serves them well and truly; but it is also good for the genuine altruist himself. The altruistic side of his life-work, if there is such a side, will make him, too, happier because, to this extent, he will have fulfilled the purpose of human life. He will feel that his life has been good, and it will have been a good life in fact.

The equation of the good life with altruism has been made, with impressive unanimity, by all the higher religions and philosophies. The Christian aphorism "Whosoever will lose his life for my sake shall find it" was anticipated in action by the Buddha. He deliberately postponed his own exit into Nirvana in order to show to his fellow sentient beings the way that he had found. This is the main point of Professor Marnell's book, and on this ground he is surely unchallengeable.

An original feature of the book is the illustration of this main thesis in a series of imaginary life-histories of individuals

ix

in classical Greece and in the medieval and modern West. Professor Marnell analyzes his characters' motives. How far were these altruistic, and how far egotistic? And, in so far as these persons had altruistic ideals, to what extent were they faithful to these ideals in practice? The creation of imaginary characters is less difficult when one is placing them in the setting of his own society. Professor Marnell's eighteenth-century English and nineteenth-century and twentieth-century American characters are, not surprisingly, more convincing than his fifth-century-B.C. Athenians and his medieval Westerners. The high point of the book is the history of an imaginary American family, the Gardners, through five generations. The first Gardner founds the family's fortunes in Western Reserve. The fifth Gardner renounces wealth in the spirit of the Buddha and Jesus and St. Francis. Professor Marnell gives a dramatic unity to his epic by making the fourth Gardner fall in the Second World War at Monte Cassino, the birthplace of altruistic service in the Christian Western World.

Professor Marnell is a believer in the efficacy of "enlightened self-interest." He is concerned to show that Westerners who have sought wealth and power for themselves have not only benefited their fellow Westerners in fact but have been partly inspired by an altruistic ideal.

I find Professor Marnell's method of presenting his theme attractive, and I agree with it up to this point. Indeed, I think there will be few dissenters. There are, however, also some controversial features in the book: for instance, the limitation of the horizon to Western Man; the selection of the imaginary biographical illustrations; and the thesis that these examples of total or partial altruism are all to be credited to "individualism."

Professor Marnell's main point surely holds good for all men, not just for Westerners. He counts fifth-century-B.C. Athenians as Westerners. But their attitude to life was appreciably different from ours, and, having nevertheless admitted that the good life, as he sees it, holds good for them too, Professor Marnell has, so it seems to me, implicitly admitted that the same picture of the good life holds good for everyone.

In illustrating a thesis by examples, there is always the danger of selecting, in good faith yet misleadingly, a set of instances that support one's case. But discordant voices may impugn the case, and they are not silenced by being ignored. In Professor Marnell's series of records, two voices have, for me, been conspicuously left unrecorded. I miss the voice of the Periclean Athenians' ill-used and justly aggrieved Greek subjects. I should also be curious to hear the unrecorded voices of the Gardners' employees and of the pre-Columbian inhabitants of the American territories that the Gardners and their like helped to open up for settlers from the western end of the Old World.

Professor Marnell's most controversial theses are that individualism is a specifically Western characteristic; that it is a virtue; and that the good life, which is synonymous with altruism, has been a product of individualism.

It might have been wiser to analyze the meaning of the word individualism before giving it a charismatic connotation and placing it to the Western civilization's exclusive credit. Every living organism is an individualist; for to be alive means succeeding, partially and temporarily, in setting oneself up as a center of the universe and making the rest of the universe serve this pseudo-center's self-centered purposes. In this sense it is true that all—not only Western—human beings are inescapably individualists, even when they are striving with all their might to devote themselves and, if need be, to sacrifice themselves, to altruistic purposes. The potency, and the potential evilness, of a living creature's built-in individualism is attested by the unanimous verdict of all the higher religions and philosophies. Though they differ greatly in their interpretations of the nature of ultimate reality, they speak with one voice in their fundamental precept for human action. This precept is: "Let him deny himself." Your first task is to master, subdue, and eradicate your own self-centeredness.

This is, of course, a spiritual tour de force. Yet it is only in so far as we achieve it that we can fulfill the true purpose of life. The more dynamic a person is, the more forcefully his fundamental individualism will assert itself. This is obviously true of individualists in the conventional sense of ruthless contenders for power and wealth who pursue their egotistic am-

xi

bitions at the expense of their fellow men and of non-human nature. But a dynamic person can also be ruthlessly individualistic in the pursuit of an altruistic ideal. The Buddha deserted his wife and child. Jesus "dropped out" of his family. St. Francis, hippie-like, stripped himself naked and flung his fine clothes in his tyrannical rich father's face. Florence Nightingale pained her conventional-minded mother and sister. (Her father understood her, and the Buddha's father was eventually reconciled to the Buddha's dramatic repudiation of his heirship to his father's throne.)

If individualism is interpreted in this fundamental sense, then it is superfluous to note that altruists, too, are individualists and it is misleading to place their altruism to their individualism's credit. They are individualists because they are living creatures, but they are altruists, not because of their individualism, but in spite of it. They are altruists only in so far as they have managed to overcome their innte self-centeredness.

However, Professor Marnell does not use the word individualism solely in this fundamental and universal sense. He sees individualism as being, not a moral handicap, but a virtue, and he claims that this virtue is specifically Western. In his mind the word is, I suspect, loaded ideologically. The individualism that he is praising is a particular political and economic regime that he is tacitly contrasting favorably with socialism or communism. This comes out in his Epilogue. Here he notes that "the richness of an unopened continent" has not been the American people's exclusive asset.

There is a similar richness in southern Siberia, but the spirit of progress, opportunity, freedom, and service has never been allowed to meet the challenge. Somehow that spirit belongs to the instinct for the west, not the instinct for the east.

This passage throws a retrospective light on the book as a whole. Professor Marnell's equation of the good life with altruism is yoked together—unfortunately, in my opinion—with an apologia for the Western fraction of mankind, and then only for the fraction of this fraction that has happened to go west.

This *mystique* of the virtue of westwardness is an ancient phantasy. It is a version of the myths of the Land of Cockayne (ominous fancy word), Atlantis, the Garden of the Hesperides, and Elysium, yet in truth the people who have opened up "virgin" lands (i.e. lands previously inhabited only by "natives") have displayed the same vices and virtues, whatever may have been the point of the compass for which they have been heading. The winners of the West in North America are birds of a feather with the Russians who have opened up Siberia and with the Irish, Scottish, and English people who have opened up Australia and New Zealand. The Scottish and English settlers in New Zealand were as sincerely convinced of their own respectability as were the settlers from Connecticut in Western Reserve. But New Englanders and British and Irish and Cossacks would all have looked identically abominable to the "natives" whom they despoiled, evicted, and, in some cases, exterminated.

Professor Marnell is on the side of the angels in the main thesis of this book, but he is also on the side of the Westerners, and we Westerners are not really any more angelic than the non-Western majority of our fellow human beings. Under similar temptations, we all behave in similar unedifying ways.

Introduction

This is a book about the good life. It is not an attempt to define the good life but an attempt to determine what it has meant at key periods in the history of the western world. Like every attempt at the history of thought, its real purpose is to illuminate the thinking of the present day. The final spirit of a society can be most accurately determined by what it considers the good life. More soberly, the shortcomings of a society can best be understood in terms of the shortcomings of its concept of the good life.

The search for the good life is the constant preoccupation, however implicit in daily life and subconscious in daily thought, of both men and society. We have presented men and women living the good life in various periods of history as they and their particular ages conceived it. They are in the main fictional, and they are unquestionably idealized. Our attempt has been to depict the pattern and the fruits of success, not the agony of struggle, to present victory and not the battle, the goal and not the race course. It would be entirely naïve to suggest that people of any age have achieved it in substantial numbers or with comparative ease. It would be equally cynical to maintain that they have never done so. The good life is the hard life to attain and the harder life to maintain. The obstacles to its attainment are many, the highest hurdles to clear are in the human heart. Victory in the good life does not come at a point in time. It is a form of living, and the very recognition of the fact of victory in the quest for it comes slowly, often painfully, and victory itself may be disguised as disappointment or even as defeat. The good life is the life the Lord ordained, and the ways of the Lord are strikingly unconventional.

The search for the good life is perennial and unending. It exists today, it has existed in every age. Man is still the same forked being that he always was, with no natural defenses but his wits. He is also the same noble creature with a majestic destiny, if one is willing to accept the confidence and optimism that lie beneath every *memento mori* of the Middle Ages. His physical needs are precisely what they were in ancient Athens, medieval Chartres, Renaissance London, Paris of the Enlightenment, the Philadelphia of Benjamin Franklin, and the New York of J. Pierpont Morgan. In reviewing the concept of the good life held in ancient Greece, the Middle Ages, the Renaissance, the Enlightenment, and what might be cautiously labelled yesterday but with some hope that it is today as well, we do so because in the first four periods at least the concept is relatively clear-cut and philosophically founded. That there be striking similarities between views in these past ages and views held today is to be expected. Man, his needs, and his aspirations have not changed. The similarities, however, are only intriguing. The differences are important, because it is from the differences that we may perhaps learn.

PART ONE

THE CITIZEN

As Werner Jaeger demonstrated in Paideia, *there is one single and central concept that runs through Greek thought in the centuries of the ancient world. To the Greeks the aim of life is to create a higher type of man. Man has been born for the good life and the state created for the good life, but the good life is something each has to achieve and its achievement is the ultimate purpose for the existence of each. The Greeks believed that there exist certain natural and universal principles that govern life. Philosophy exists to determine them, the state exists to impart them, society exists to perpetuate them. The final achievement of Greek art is not the Parthenon, or the sculpture of Phidias, or the poetry of Homer and the drama of Sophocles. The final and supreme achievement of Greek art is Man. The starting point is the ideal, the ideal man and the ideal life. The nature of the ideal was refined and purified as the centuries passed; one cannot talk of the ideal of Greek culture except in terms of time and place. From Homer to Sophocles and Plato*

1

the entire moral and intellectual history of Greece is the history of a rising ideal of culture, a rising ideal of what constitutes the good life.

There is a stark, almost magnificent simplicity to the cultural ideal of Homer's Iliad. *Glory comes in battle and its meed is the praise of one's peers and a lion's share of the booty. It is simple as a winter landscape on the Manitoba prairie, this concentration on personal renown to the exclusion of every other purpose and ideal. Achilles is the first Greek aristocrat, lord of an aristocracy of the arm, the eye, and the foot. The Homeric ideal of the good life is the aristocratic ideal in its simplest form; there is something of Achilles in every aristocrat who lives by the ideals of his class.*

Centuries after Homer came Hesiod, and with him another concept of the good life. In it a certain moral leavening is apparent. It rests upon the life of the Greek peasantry, with its immemorial round of duties, its patient following of the sun as it rises from the bed of winter, renews life upon earth, mounts to the life-giving might of midsummer and autumn's harvest, and sinks again to the bed of winter. Man obeys Nature's dictates and receives Nature's bounty. Laboring man can find good and evil in himself, Hesiod maintained, nor is it without significance that Aristotle chose Hesiod as the text from which to expound his Ethics. *The good life is the life close to the soil, from which grows the physical harvest of nature and the metaphysical harvest of virtue. Through the centuries multitudes who have never heard the name of Hesiod have preached Hesiod's doctrine of the good life, and not an inconsiderable number have practiced it. Hesiod's concept is still the sadly nostalgic, old-fashioned, American ideal of the good life after the pastoral model.*

The dominant Greek ideal, however, was the civic ideal. Two Greek words summarize it, eunomia *and* isonomia, *effective authority and equal authority. Out of* eunomia *developed the authoritarian spirit, oligarchic rule, the stern self-sacrifice and stark city-state morality of Sparta. Out of* isonomia *developed the democratic spirit, popular rule, a high degree of self-sacrifice to be sure but also the cultivation of the individual. This was the*

2

ideal brought from Ionia to Attica and fostered to its richest development in the Athens of Pericles. Then as now it is one of the most exalted concepts of the good life, and one of the hardest to achieve. Solon, who did more than any other man to lay the foundation for it in Athens, says, "The hardest thing of all is to recognize the invisible mean of judgment, which alone contains the limits of all things." This invisible mean of judgment and the concept of proportion it implies became the central Greek explanation of the universe. In Athens the invisible mean of judgment separated in the individual Athenian the man and the citizen. An Athenian citizen was partly an individualist enjoying a degree of self-determination not to be matched until the appearance of the American frontier, and partly a member of the corporate body to which he owed his allegiance, his position in the world, and the best of his abilities. Let us consider in specific terms what this meant to the Athenian citizen of the period of Athens' greatness.

1.

Three Athenians

PHILO arose from his cot of straw and shook his *chiton* reflectively. Abstractly, he considered as his fellow creatures the myriads of winged and crawling things that never left his company day or night, but he was hardly ready to go the full Franciscan way and think of them as his brothers and sisters. After making sure that he would wear his *chiton* relatively unshared, he wrapped himself in it and fastened it at the shoulder with the Athenian equivalent of the safety pin. Next he put over his head an unshaped garment, his *himation,* which had a hole for his head and nothing more, except a certain capacity for draping itself around him as he stood or walked. On his feet he put thick foot pads held there by thongs, similar to those now worn by Americans in swimming attire en route to the beach. As he had no intention of travelling a long distance that day, he required no head covering. Since neither his *chiton* or *himation* had a pocket, he would remember to put some loose change in his mouth before he left the house. He then lit a wick which floated in a cruet of oil, creating not so much light as Milton's "darkness visible." His breakfast opened and closed with a sort of pudding, with fish in between and the ubiquitous olive. His other meals were distinguished from breakfast only by the time of day when

5

they occurred. He was then ready to leave his house of sun-baked brick and take upon himself the duties and responsibilities of the day. In any other age Philo would quite obviously have been a man sunk in unimaginable destitution, an object of religious compassion in the Middle Ages, of secular concern in the Renaissance, of fastidious disregard in much of the eighteenth century, and of civic responsibility today.

The great problem about Philo, as a matter of fact, would not have been to relieve his apparent destitution but to determine what his economic status actually was, and then an even greater problem would have been to indicate to him why it mattered. He might have been a very poor man, but he might also have been a very rich man indeed. The houses of the rich and poor in ancient Athens were as similar as the television sets of the rich and poor in America, and so were their diet and their dress. All three were abysmal by modern standards, but it is of no particular assistance to an understanding of the Greek concept of the good life to preen ourselves on the immeasurably greater comfort of our daily lives. The people that created the *Oresteia* was entirely capable of creating a stove, and the builders of the Parthenon could have built a house with inside plumbing. Before we can understand what the good life meant to Philo, we must free our minds of every concept born of the Industrial Revolution and fostered by the concept of progress. Philo would not have believed in progress, could the modern meaning of the term be made clear to him. He believed in stability. He would travel over the horizon of human thought, but he wouldn't move a foot out of his way to improve his standard of living. Indeed, the very use of the word *improve* betrays one. Improvement in that sense is a modern concept, not an ancient one. Philo was eternally eager for the new idea, endlessly devoted to the concept that challenged the previously accepted. St. Paul capitalized on that trait on Mars Hill. But there was nothing in Philo's life corresponding to what the modern world calls fashion. Indeed, he could comprehend no conflict between fashion and custom because he had no other criterion for daily life but custom.

Philo was what the modern democracies would call a politician, and what Athens called a citizen. He was automatically a member of the popular Assembly, along with the other 40,000 adult male citizens of his city of about a quarter-million inhabitants, and two or three days a month he attended meetings of the Assembly. Philo was somewhat more conscientious in this regard than the average, substantially less so than the completely dedicated. He never missed one of the ten regular sessions a year if his health at all permitted attendance, but he was a trifle cavalier about the extraordinary sessions which the magistrates so frequently called. There was no set quorum at the Assembly, but 6000 votes was agreed to represent the will of the Athenian people. Experience had demonstrated that at least one-seventh of the citizens of Athens could be counted upon to attend every session of the Assembly, regular or extraordinary, in the course of a year. As Pericles put it in the Funeral Oration, "We call our constitution a democracy because its working is in the hands not of the few but of the many."

Philo felt just a shade less conscientious about Assembly attendance this year than he had in the past, since the previous year he had done his service on the Council. This was representative government, not fully popular democracy, and Philo felt a considerable pride in the fact that he had had his year of full time service on the Council even though he owed the fact to chance and not to an electoral mandate. He was one of the 500 members chosen by lot to represent the ten tribes, and hence for an entire year was, so to speak, the one Athenian citizen in eighty who really kept Athens running. It was the richest year of his life, this year when he attended Council meetings on a daily basis. It was an experience which he could repeat once, but chance would hardly do that much for him at his present age. He was lucky to have been one of the two Athenian citizens in five who enjoyed for one year of their lives the richest experience an Athenian citizen could enjoy.

On this particular day Philo was reporting for possible jury duty. He might be called to serve in the higher court called the Heliaea, which theoretically was the same size as the Assembly and therefore composed of the same citizens. By Philo's

7

time it had been divided into a number of separate courts, but since no court had fewer than 201 jurymen, it was required that 6000 judges always be available. Philo was reporting this day as one of the 600 judges from his tribe. If selected by lot, he would be assigned to one of the several courts. This was an experience he always enjoyed. The magistrates handled the minor cases, and the ones that came before the judges invariably had their interest and sometimes their fascination.

Philo was available this day for court service since this was not his period for military duty. As he had reached the age of forty-eight, he had thirty years of service as a heavy-armed foot soldier behind him and twelve more to go. After he had reached the age of sixty, he would be free to give all his time to the Assembly and the courts, always with the entrancing possibility that Lady Luck might recall him for a sunset year on the Council. As a man of substantial means but not great wealth, Philo was a heavy-armed foot soldier. He could afford the rather expensive equipment necessary: helmets, breast-plates, gauntlets, and greaves were by no means cheap, but neither were they beyond the reach of a man in comfortable circumstances. Furthermore, the fact that he could afford to be a heavy-armed foot soldier entitled him to eligibility for the minor magisterial offices and so for a further enriching of his career.

In Athens military service was rewarded in the financial sense by the privilege of contributing according to one's means to the support of the Athenian armed forces. A full-blown plutocrat would have the privilege of outfitting and maintaining a ship in the fleet. He might ride to battle in his chariot, fight as befits a plutocrat while his charioteer held the bridle, and then ride back again. Naturally he paid a princely price for this privilege. A knight, and Philo was not quite rich enough to make this grade, would ride to battle on a horse and not in a chariot. Those less blessed by prosperity than Philo were light-armed foot soldiers and like him walked to battle, and those not fiscally blessed at all cheerfully rowed in the navy. In times of peace the standing army and navy were set at 6000 men, the consecrated figure that symbolized the Athenian people. Athens combined in an extraordinary fashion equality of rights with inequality of obligations.

There was something of the fine amateur spirit to Philo as he busied himself about the public concern and gave to the game all the resourcefulness of his ingenuity and all the means at his disposal. There was also something of the artist, as he extemporized the conduct of his city-state. The amateur has his set of values as does the artist, and they are never materialistic. It is the game that counts, or the creation, not what it costs in effort or wealth to create or win it. Philo would never think in terms of expenditure of effort or wealth as if it were a drain upon his physical and material resources. They existed to be expended. Therefore he trooped off with his thousands of compatriots day after day to the Assembly or the law courts, happily and totally oblivious of what other cultures would consider personal concerns. Being no less vocal than their modern sons and heirs, Philo and the others met in places of great tumult and confusion, and the success of the magistrates in getting and maintaining order was worthy of the race that produced Hercules. But they were amateurs and artists who gathered on the Pnyx for the meeting of the Assembly, or poured into the benches for the day's legal hearings. Philo had the love of the game that an amateur must have, the love of creating something—in his case a just, happy, and productive city life—that sustains the artist. Thucydides quotes Themistocles: "Indeed if we choose to face life with an easy mind rather than after rigorous professional training, and to rely rather upon native inspiration than on a State-made position, the advantage lies with us; for we are spared all the weariness of practising for future appointments, and when we find ourselves in the vein we are as happy as our plodding rivals. Let them toil from boyhood in a laborious pursuit after efficiency, while we, free to live and wander as we please, are ready, when the time comes, to face the self-same problems. For our trust is not in the devices of professional and material equipment, but in our own good spirits for city life." The plodding rivals were, of course, that unenlightened breed the Spartans. But the plodding rivals could also be the races of modern man. The good life of the ancient Greeks was the good life of their cities. The Greek cities had their problems, but not what we call the problems of the cities.

Since it is not recorded that Philo was fed by ravens, why was he free to live and wander as he pleased, living the life of an amateur politician and artist statesman? What presumably would be the quick and cynical answer of the man in the street who is totally innocent of Hellenic studies, that his wife did the work, is not without a strong measure of truth. The full truth was twofold, Phronime and Skythes, Phronime his wife and Skythes his slave. Philo had married Phronime after the leisurely fashion of ancient Greece, when he was thirty-two. She was fifteen. The difference in age gave Philo precisely the margin he needed for the proper training of his wife, a margin none too broad as he knew and as Rabelais attested for his own, much later age. It was not, of course, that Phronime had come to him without proper training. She came from a good, solid family of his own tribe, her father was his frequent associate in the Assembly, and Philo had investigated the girl herself quite thoroughly before he married her. Her prior training, naturally, had been greatly furthered by the fact that there was only one conceivable destiny for a girl of Phronime's background. She was born for marriage, trained for marriage, directed toward marriage, and she married.

Philo and Phronime had been married sixteen years, and Phronime was a veteran housewife. Every last detail of the household, the direction of the house slaves, all purchases, discardings, renewals, and domestic decisions were hers and hers alone. Every last responsibility about her sons was hers to bear until they were ready for their tutors. For this she was born, trained, and directed. She lived the life her mother lived before her, and her grandmother before her mother, and it was the life for which she trained her own two daughters. It was the only life she could really imagine, because it was the life dictated by custom and custom was the sole norm of human life. It was an indoor life, a secluded and unimaginably circumscribed life, but it was life as she and all the women of her background knew it. She was aware that there were women of another kind, indeed known as *hetairai,* "the other kind." They were men's playthings, but they could be men's challengers as well. Some of the fine minds of ancient Greece were lodged under the diligent coiffures of *hetairai.* Phronime did not have a fine mind, nor indeed would she have known precisely what a fine mind was. She was born, bred, habituated, and inured to a life that did not demand what the world calls a fine mind. Yet how should one characterize the mind that absorbs, holds, and attends to every final detail in the management of a home and does so with quiet competence and dignity? Some Greek women slipped their bonds, of course; one of the most human and delightful of the poems of Theocritus concerns two liberated suburbanites en route to a matinee. Phronime was not of their sort. Philo could safely neglect his house and home, because he knew it was not neglected. Phronime was at home.

Did the good life of Philo the amateur politician and artist statesman and the good life of Phronime the household presence merge and coalesce? One can only wish that one knew. Nothing quite so clearly reveals the shortcomings of literature as the search in it for life. Penelope was the model of the loyal and devoted wife but the circumstances of her married life, with its twenty years of separation, were hardly typical. Alcestis was an inspiration of wifely devotion and self-sacrifice, but there was something obviously theatrical about her giving up her life for her husband only to have Hercules wrestle it out of the grasp of Death. By definition one does not look for the good life in tragedy, and common sense dictates a wary search for it in comedy. The truth is that literature has very little to do with the ordinary lives of ordinary people, not even when it proclaims that such is its subject. A Greek Jane Austen would be a pearl beyond price, but there is no Greek Jane Austen. One can only assume that domestic happiness, the unvoiced pledges of affection, the tender symbols of devotion, the instinct for understanding and for sharing that have made marital happiness the very cornerstone of the good life in other ages and places were present as well in the lives of Philo and Phronime. It is simply that the record is silent on the point.

11

What was explicitly deemed the good life of ancient Athens and accepted as such by Philo centered on the city and not on the home.

Then there was Skythes. To say that Skythes was Philo's slave is technically correct, and vastly misleading. He was a slave, taken in battle when very young indeed, and brought into the home of Philo and prepared for the wide range of destinies that might well be his. Skythes had an extraordinarily quick mind for business, and an extraordinarily deft way of avoiding the lot of the second best in a business deal. Philo pondered the trait in the youngster Skythes, and marked him in his mind for serious matters. Skythes was now approaching forty. Philo owned a carting business between the Piraeus and the city, and a rather good piece of land for olive trees toward the west of Attica. Skythes managed them both, and managed them efficiently and well. This was his basic service, and Philo thought of him precisely as the owner of a modern business would think of his plant manager. Philo was an Athenian citizen and therefore moved in a totally different sphere from the one in which Skythes belonged, but he never thought of Skythes as his inferior in any sense except the political. In a decade something very significant had happened. Skythes contracted with several other citizens to transport goods for them, and was properly paid for the service. He also undertook the management of several farms close to Philo's olive grove. Skythes was very well paid for his services, and Skythes paid meticulously a commission on his earnings to his owner Philo. The truth that developed in the decade was that Skythes had come to have a larger income than Philo, and wealth has a way of affecting the spheres in which people move. Skythes held a position of substantial authority and power in the city, and he commanded the respect that went with the position. He did with fine competence and success what he was privileged to do as a slave in ancient Athens: he made an excellent living as a free enterpriser, and he made a good living too for his owner Philo who otherwise might have had a very meager living indeed. Skythes could act with this freedom because he was a slave. Had Skythes been a philosopher as well, the most disturbing thoughts about

12

life and its stations might have racked his brain, but fortunately for his peace of mind he was a businessman. He was married, one trusts with marital happiness—a strong component in his good life, but if literature is silent on that aspect of the lives of Athenian citizens, it is doubly silent where slaves are concerned.

The issue of freedom is always complicated by the issue of responsibility, as it was in the case of Philo and Skythes. The politics of Athens was the responsibility of Philo and the other citizens; the economy of Athens was the responsibility of Phronime and Skythes, of the other wives and the other slaves. In neglecting his home and business to do his full share in the work of running the city, Philo was doing the natural and normal thing. He was Aristotle's *politikon zoon,* a man oriented to public life. As such he was the sane, normal, companionable Greek citizen. As he bustled about the Assembly, took his turn at the courts, did his year in the Council, polished his gauntlets and greaves for a spell with the heavy-armed troops, he was leading the good life of an Athenian citizen. The Athenian who concentrated his attention on his home, his farm, and his business was abnormal and eccentric. He was *idiotes,* a man oriented to private life. It is interesting to note the progression of meanings of *idiotes:* a private person; a useless, anti-social, egotistic person; a monomaniac; an idiot. But none of this applied, of course, to Skythes. He was a slave, and therefore he was free to be a businessman. The supreme Athenian respect for politics and the total Athenian disrespect for economics found expression in all sorts of corollaries. That fact must be understood before one can even cross the threshold to enter an understanding of the Greek philosophy of the good life.

2.

Athens: The Principles of Life

RIGHT-THINKING Athenians like Philo did not believe in personal economic advancement; there were limits of which shrewd entrepreneurs like Skythes were well aware. If some *idiotes* acquired more land than was seemly, the city promptly redivided it. Athenians believed in proportion, not aggrandizement. Each Athenian citizen should own some land, an appropriate amount, and practically every one did. There was no tenant class in Attica; what few tenants there were worked land that belonged to the temples or the brotherhoods. Greek workmen belonged to associations of their crafts, but such associations bore utterly no resemblance to modern trade unions. Prices were fixed by immemorial and unchangeable custom, and the time workmen devoted to public business effectively prevented over-production. There was competition in Greek industry, but it was competition in skill and not in economic gain. Fixed wages were neither known nor desired, and fixed hours of employment would have produced a revolution. The citizen must be free to attend the Assembly and the law courts. It is very difficult to conjure up a modern parallel to the economic associations of ancient Greece. Perhaps the relationship among the doctors accredited to a hospital suggests its nature.

That amateur spirit which characterized the Athenians in their public life found in public fiscal policy forms of expression which would leave a modern Treasury official doubting his sanity. There were practically no taxes in Athens, and none on income or property. A tax is a legal imposition, and a legal imposition would be inconsistent with the status of an Athenian citizen. The citizen must be free to aid the city in the way he chooses. He may underwrite a play, equip a naval vessel, finance a musical contest, or erect a public building. Such free contributions were called *liturgies,* "public works," and it was the privilege of the free citizen to make them. This was the economic competition the Athenians understood and practiced with gusto. And yet the modern Treasury official, dedicated one suspects to the enrichment of the governmental tills by the drain on citizens' pockets, might ponder the significance of this fact: in Greece the wealth of the city was always greater than the wealth of its individual citizens. Polybius says that in 378 B.C. the total private wealth of Athens was only six times greater than the revenue which came to the city every year. The Athenians may have been amateurs in public finance, but they financed the most magnificent public buildings ever erected in the world.

Into his life as a citizen Philo fused all those sentiments and loyalties that in modern life cluster about the home, the church, the school, the neighborhood, the office, and the club. In the very opening paragraph of the *Politics* Aristotle says, "The city is the highest of all forms of association and embraces all the rest." The city gave Philo, Phronime, and Skythes the kind of efficiency they really desired, the efficiency that gives protection against the invader and justice among the residents. In his praise of city institutions Pericles puts justice first, and Plato has Zeus send Hermes to earth, "bearing in his hand Reverence and Justice to be the ordering principles of cities and the bonds of friendship and conciliation." Such was the Greek ideal of the good life as it worked out in practice. The characteristic which sets it apart from every other concept that has

15

emerged in western culture is the unmatched significance in it of the city. The Greek was, to a degree unimaginable at any other time or place, a *politikon zoon,* one who lives in a city and devotes himself to that city life in which public and private business merge and become indistinguishable. In his eyes politics, the business of a city, was the duty and the preoccupation of the citizen. Economic well-being was of vastly lesser importance and progress in the modern sense was a concept yet unborn. Hence the wonderful flexibility of Athenian life that made Athens the model city which the one hundred and fifty or so other cities really admired and emulated. The model of Sparta, oligarchic, militaristic, resting uneasily on serfdom, was another matter. Sparta represented an earlier stage in the development of Greek culture, a stage that locally underwent petrifaction. Athens was The City, and by its standards the standards of the other cities were set.

The difference between the Greek principle of city life and the modern comes down to the fundamental and profound contrast between proportion and progress as ideals. The Greek ideal of proportion in one sense really is the negation of the ideal of progress. It is easy, however, to overlook the fact that the ideal of proportion is entirely consistent with the ideal of qualitative progress. A man may become better without becoming richer and more comfortable. A city may become better without becoming larger and more prosperous. Athens became no larger than Providence, Rhode Island, but it influenced the entire course of artistic, literary, philosophic, and political history as no other city, not even Rome itself that at its finest absorbed and expanded so much that was Athenian, has ever done. The case for progress is not self-evident and beyond dispute. There is also a case for proportion.

Pericles rightly says of Athens, "I say as a city we are the school of Hellas; while I doubt if the world can produce a man, who where he has only himself to depend upon, is equal to so many emergencies, and graced by so happy a versatility as the Athenian." Such was the result of the good life as the Athenians conceived it, Rome learned from it, and to a degree that has varied with time and place the western world has never entirely forgotten.

There is a fundamental consistency to this ideal. It grows easily and naturally from the heroic age through the period of city-state development into the high noon of Athenian greatness, and is transmitted from Athens to Rome and there perpetuated with its basic principles unchanged. The men who held to its convictions and recorded them in literature had the courage of their convictions. The courage of one's convictions is not at all difficult to maintain when things are going well, but a very different matter in days that are bloody and troubled. The ancient ideal of the good life can be deceptive in this respect. It is so grave, so immaculate, so elevated above the trials and uncertainties, the doubts and fears of earthbound mortality. It is the subject matter of much that is immortal in the literature of Greece. One meets Socrates of the imperturbable serenity, Plato with his vision of Ideas as immutable truth, Aristotle who catalogued and numbered life's infinite variety. Yet Socrates fought in battle, Plato saw the crumbling of Athens, and Aristotle strove to train the half-tamed son of a Macedonian conqueror. Their ages were war-wracked and blood-stained, and had apocalyptic nightmares. Their wars are finished, the blood is dried, the nightmares vanished in the light of other days. There remain the defense of Socrates, the *Republic* of Plato, the *Ethics* of Aristotle. This is the literary philosophic record of the Greek ideal of the good life, and in a strange and striking way it remains consistent amidst all the differences of the philosophic schools. It is the concept of the good life as the life of virtue, the concept of virtue as dedication to one's fellow man, the concept of dedication as self-sacrifice to the welfare of the city. It is grave, immaculate, and elevated, but it is the concept of men who lived in war-wracked, blood-stained decades.

Quite as important to the distinctive nature of the classical ideal is what it does not include. The good life is not the life of material possessions, although material possessions are never despised by the Greeks and Romans and in their desired

17

forms are considered adjuncts to the ideal. There is something deliciously ironic in the fact that the philosophic school which held material possessions in the lowest regard is the school with which they are now universally associated, the Epicurean. The good life is not the life of artistic creativity or aesthetic enjoyment of the arts. This is the more intriguing in the light of the greatness of the classical artistic achievement. The good life was not the life that Aeschylus led, or Sophocles, Phidias, or Praxiteles, and Cicero led the good life when he saved Rome from Catiline, not when he wrote the *De Senectute* and the *De Amicitia*. The arts were esteemed, honored, treasured, but in no way identified with the good life. That identification, like the gradual separation of the good life from the life of self-sacrifice, was to be the work of the Renaissance.

Nor did the classical ideal of the good life rest upon religious convictions. The ancients had a mythology, but not a theology. The age of faith passed away in Greece at an early date, to be followed by an age of cults. Restless seekers moved from one to another, as whim and fashion dictated as well as unsatisfied yearnings of the human heart. Plato and Aristotle speak of God with reverence, but it is the sort of reverence with which one might speak of the farthest star in uttermost space, incalculable light years away. Reverence and awe may be attributes consistent with the religious attitude, but they are not religion.

The consequence was that the State had to assume in ancient thought much of the role assumed by the Church in the Christian order. Belief in natural law was a cornerstone of ancient thought, the sole foundation of Stoicism and a faith more eloquently expounded by Cicero, perhaps, than by any other believer in natural law. Whether one calls it God's law or Nature's law, however, makes little difference in the absence of a Church and a theology. It must be translated into statutes and its moral foundations must be explained and expounded, and in the ancient world no institution but the State could assume that responsibility. Hence the insistence of Plato and Aristotle that the State assume the full responsibility for the moral instruction and guidance of its members. The Christian world has passed through various stages in which the State was subordinate to the Church, the Church was an instrumentality of the State, and the State and Church were kept rigidly separate. Nothing in this experience is of much help to an understanding of the religious situation in the ancient world, where the State was the Church.

Consequently the classical ideal of the good life must be defined in terms without religious overtones or theological connotations. The good life is the life of virtue in which the mind directs the body, values are accepted in their proper scale, the lower self is sacrificed for the sake of the higher self, and man fulfills himself in the highest degree when he gives what is finest in himself to the service of his city. The ideal is entirely human, neither buttressed by religion nor motivated by it, nor does it anticipate a still better life beyond as a reward for its attainment here. The classical ideal of the good life is a totally secular ideal, but it is the noblest monument ever erected in the ancient world.

PART TWO

THE SAINT

*"Two loves have created two cities: love of self, to the con-
tempt of God, the earthly city; love of God, to the contempt of
self, the heavenly." In this simple statement by St. Augustine is
implicit the complete medieval ideal of the good life. Those
who lead the good life do so in the love of God and the contempt
of self, and their spiritual citizenship is not of this world. The
medieval ideal of the good life is not an earthly ideal nor is it
directed toward a temporal objective. There is no difference
among the ancient philosophies nearly so basic as the difference
between them all and that.*

*The composite medieval picture of the good life is a mosaic
of many stones and many colors, but pictured in it is always a
single, central image. There is the pattern of the good life in the
religious community separated from the secular world physically
and yet ministering to its needs. This is the pattern of the monastery as St. Benedict conceived it. There is the inspiring pattern
of the* poverello, *the pattern of St. Francis and the Franciscans,*

21

who lived in the heart of the world where that heart was in anguish and bled, and ministered to it. These will be our first concerns. Beyond the religious pattern is the great pattern of feudalism itself, the good life of the castle and the fief, as well as the good life of the secular clergy which was tangent to it. There is the pattern of chivalry in which everything that was best in the life of the castle coalesced, at least in principle, and in the finest spirits of the Middle Ages found embodiment. Beyond the good life of the feudal age is that newer and still developing pattern to which we must next address ourselves, the pattern of the town and specifically of the guilds which dominated town life in the medieval period.

It is, then a mosaic of many stones and many colors but it has a unifying principle. The good life is what St. Augustine said it was, the life that is led in the love of God and the contempt of self. Thus the single, central image before the eyes of those who would lead the good life, whether it be in a monastery, a city church, a castle crowning an outcropping of rock or a simple hut on the edge of the acorn forest, whether it be in a workshop in a town, a lazar house set off from mankind by warning signs and by fear itself, or one of those proto-factories already appearing in Florence and Antwerp, was always the image of the saint. By this image those who would lead the good life patterned their own lives. In the following pages we shall try to depict some of them as they led their own lives in reality, and then to see the image as it presented itself before the eyes of the spirit. In the Middle Ages, as in every period of human history, the gap between the ideal and the real was a major chasm, but in the Middle Ages as in every age there were those who tried to bridge it. The average men and women here presented are those who led the good life.

1.

The Monastery

ONE must be aware of the world from which the monks withdrew. It is difficult, even in the blood-drenched twentieth century, to envisage what the centuries of terror were like, those bleak ages when every horror that had seemed impossible came to pass, and nothing in life seemed secure but insecurity itself. Across the face of the Roman earth rolled barbarian wave after barbarian wave: Ostrogoths and Visigoths, the Alani, the Alemanni, the Burgundians, and from some black abyss of the East, the Huns. One tower of civilization fell and then another, and in one vast and cataclysmic crash Rome itself. The ultimate impossibility came in 410, with the instruments of the impossible, the Goths and their leader Alaric. When Rome fell, it was as if heaven and earth had passed away. It was as if Washington were to fall in this century to the North Koreans, or the North Vietnamese, or whatever the horde from the strange and fearsome East. St. Benedict was educated in the Niobe of nations, at the hour when "all is doubly night."

In this "double night" were two crying needs, one physical, the other intellectual. The first was to repair the ravages of war in the land itself and to rescue the pathetic human victims. The second was the less immediate but farther reaching one, to save what Europe had inherited from Greece and Rome.

23

These two needs gave rise to two types of monastic effort and two men of stature rose to achieve them, Benedict of Nursia and Magnus Aurelius Cassiodorus.

Midway between Rome and Naples, in the valley of the Garigliano, is a picturesque and isolated hill. On its summit in 529 there were a temple of Apollo and a grove sacred to Venus, and countryfolk in whom survived both paganism and a simple pagan devotion used to toil their way up the winding, stony path to the soaring summit beneath which lay the province of Caserta, the eastern plains, and a faint suggestion of dim blue at the far horizon, the Gulf of Gaeta. There they would lay their garlands at the feet of the Far Darter. Up the steep and stony path Benedict climbed with a select and tiny band. The temple was abolished and Apollo knew Monte Cassino no more. Where the temple had stood there rose two oratories, one dedicated to St. John the Baptist and the other to St. Martin, and the monastery of Monte Cassino came into being.

Far beneath Monte Cassino disaster continued to ravage Italy. Benedict and his monks could see the Roman and the Gothic armies harry the plains of Caserta, but they could also see the endless expanse of heaven in whose service they themselves fought. When the battle raged, the countryfolk who are always war's most pitiable victims still wound their way up the steep and stony path to a succor far more tangible than any Apollo could afford. When the battle ended, the monks filed down the mountain to bind up wounds, bring food and clothing to war's victims, calm the anguished and give promise to those sunk in despair. When the wars were over for the moment and the Goths triumphant, their king Totila, now lord of Italy and master of Rome, also climbed that long and stony climb to meet a man in whom he sensed that there was something different, something better, stronger, and more resolute than he had faced upon the scene of battle. The saint met the barbarian, and the barbarian bowed his head and took rebuke and instruction. At the end Totila fell at the feet of Benedict, asked and received forgiveness, and the first turn had been taken away from disaster and decay. The good life of ancient

Italy had been obliterated, but on Monte Cassino the pattern of the good life of the Middle Ages first began to form. Let us examine the pattern.

The sky is compact with stars, and the sky seems to move down to meet the mass of the mountain as it hunches up in the darkness. A bell sounds softly, a muffled figure moves through the dormitory where the monks sleep side by side, and shortly lights flicker and then move silently through the stone cold corridor to the darkened chapel. Presently the soft swell of chant arises, rising and falling as the swell rises and falls on a quiet day at sea, falling to silence and then rising again. For an hour or more the quiet tide of music ebbs and flows, and then the silence is complete. Lights again move silently through the stone cold corridor, again the dormitory is peopled, men twist shaggy bed coverings about them, and presently there are the night sounds of those asleep. It is now a bit after three in the morning.

At six the corridors are again peopled in the half-light of dawn, again the chapel filled, and once more the tide of song rises and falls. This time it is Lauds. Two other times the monks gather, for Vespers late in the afternoon and for Compline before they retire for the night. They do as the peasants of Cassino do, pagan or Christian. They rise with the sun and they bed with the sun. Night is broken at two for the Benedictines to sing vigils, but they have between eight and nine hours sleep each night. Except for the break their night's rest is that of the countryside.

It is forenoon now and the sun is strong with all the strength it has in south Italy down where the plain reaches the sea, where the air of the Appenines is far away and the winds from Alpine mountains do not reach until autumn is advanced. The rains have been heavy, the path down the mountain has been badly gutted, and they say the mud holes on the road to Caserta would mire an ox. Monks work silently and quickly, with primitive tools, but with the strong arm and leg muscles of the peasant stock from which they come. A gutted path is refashioned, mud holes are filled, and a road that was a nightmare becomes passable again. The people who travel the road

25

wonder at the silent men who toil without talk and, one half imagines, without rest. Why do they do it? No one pays them. No one forces them at the lance point. They are neither slaves nor criminals. *Laborare est orare,* they are said to murmur; work is prayer. The memory of Apollo fades, the story of the crucified Christ takes on a new meaning. A scholar passes by on his way to Capua, and he remembers quaint old Tertullian: "See how these Christians love one another." A shovel of dirt is thrown in, it is raked even with the rest; some rocks are set in place beside the ditch; they are banked with earth and their position strengthened. Slowly a better road emerges, one better graded and drained, one less likely to wash away the next time the Appenines thunder and the torrents roar down the hills. It is for us, the people say. "See how these Christians love one another." This was Benedict's way of amending disaster and decay. It is nature's way as well, a shovelful at a time.

At Monte Cassino the monks are simple laymen with brawny muscles who do the two things that they know, work and prayer, and have been taught that there is no essential difference between them when the work is for one's fellow man. Mass is seldom said there, only on Sunday and important feasts. The good life on Monte Cassino is a very simple life: the monks sing the praises of the Lord and do the Lord's work with their bare hands and the youthful muscles the Lord gave them to use in His cause while they had their youth and strength. They trust to Him for the rest. They sing His praises in the middle of the night and at dawn. They do His work in the morning and the afternoon. They eat His good food at midday in the summer, somewhat later in the winter: perhaps eggs or fish, two cooked vegetables, their salad, bread, and wine, but not meat. They have had their simple breakfast and they have their simple supper after vespers. They listen to collations read at sunset (not all of them can read), they sing compline, and go to bed. They have prayed somewhat over three hours. Those who read have done so in the afternoon while the others worked on the roads, the farm, or the vineyard, or perhaps fixed the broken axle or attended to the problem at the well, or went to the village where the illness was or the other village that had the fire. They have worked about six hours and their night's sleep is at least eight hours more. They have worked with their hands, minds, and hearts. It has been the good life. St. Benedict brought it into being.

Let us turn from Monte Cassino and the labor of simple lay-men to Viviers and the struggle to save learning. Magnus Aurelius Cassiodorus was the sort of man who so towers above those of his time and place that after his passing simple people might think a god had walked the earth among them. Born at Squillace, on the sole of the Italian boot, he brought to the barbarian conquerors of Italy the knowledge and the skills that centuries of culture had produced, and they did not know existed until they had conquered Italy and Italy had begun to conquer them. He handled the financial affairs of Odoacer. He ruled the western empire for Theodoric, and made fruitful alliances with the eastern. For fifty years he was the intellec-tual power behind the Ostrogothic throne, but his heart was deep in the south of Italy, deep in Bruttium where he had founded at Viviers a monastery after the model of Monte Cas-sino. After years of political magnificence, he retired for thirty years of isolation and comparative oblivion. The thirty years are incomparably more important than the others, for he es-tablished at Viviers the other Benedictine tradition, that of scholarship.

The work of Monte Cassino was done by groups of men; the work of the scholar is by nature solitary. Now the sun is hot with the pitiless heat of the Italian toe that points toward Africa. The monk in the cell has sung lauds and matins, and he has hoed cabbages and pruned vines. He has had his noonday meal, and he fights the good but unavailing fight against sleep. To his left is the ancient manuscript, with the frayed corner that is obliterated except for some bleached-out scratchings. God knows what those words are. The sheets crinkle and curl, and with the slightest pressure they break. Letters are crabbed and crammed, and somehow thought flows into thought with-out the aid of those salutary and blessed inventions, the comma and the period. He copies, and a great blob of perspiration

27

falls upon his sheet and crawls out in all directions. He mops it up and blows it dry, and copies again. He is not a learned man, God knows, but Cassiodorus knows best what is God's will and apparently it is God's will that this short, strong Calabrian peasant whom Cassiodorus has taught his letters should lay down the hoe and pruning hook with which he is thoroughly familiar and master this scrawny and awkward quill. And so he copies, and hardly knowing what he does, he saves civilization from disaster and decay. He is the forerunner of all the monks in all the monasteries of the western world who will preserve the treasury of Greece and Rome and transmit it to the modern age. But he does not know that. All he knows is that work is prayer, and it is God's will as revealed to him through Cassiodorus that he should do this particular work, and do it he will though sleep surge through him in waves, the letters swim and merge, and another blob of perspiration has just fallen on his sheet. The good life is not the easy life. That he certainly knows.

Some centuries pass and the world changes, but not entirely. A convent is agog, as well it might be, since tomorrow is the day for the bishop's annual visitation. He will come to hear complaints and if they are serious enough, to act on them. He expects the nuns to be tale bearers, and they expect to bear tales. The prioress hopes that the tales will be neither too long nor too serious, and she has good reason to hope that this will be true since she has done her level best and she has shrewd reason to believe that her convent will stand comparison with any in England.

She has been in the convent just a half century, since she is now an aged woman of sixty and was just ten, on the edge of maturity one might say, when she put on the veil. On the edge of maturity, since girls often married at twelve and nuns regularly took perpetual vows at fourteen. For a half century she has risen at two in the morning for Matins and Lauds, and risen again at six for Prime. Nothing has changed in this regard since St. Benedict led his followers up the path to the top of Monte Cassino. For a half century she has had her light breakfast of bread and wine after Prime, her main meal at noon (a somewhat flexible hour, with a tendency to creep in the direction of the morning), and her light supper after Vespers. Morning has been mainly for prayer and spiritual reading, in French or English since Latin was for strong, educated men. Afternoon has been for work, perhaps some cultivating of the vegetables in the convent garden in the warm months or even the raking of hay in the fields, likely the embroidering of vestments in the winter or the sewing of those little bands you put around a cut finger. You worked without talking, of course, but you had to communicate. Syon Monastery, it is said, had a code table of 106 signs. Put together the hands and wriggle the fingers; that was fish. To pull the little finger of the left hand with the right hand meant to milk the cow. Anyone might know that, but one had to know the code to know that to hold one's nose with the right hand and rub it with the left meant mustard, or to rub the left thumb with the right meant salt.

The convent had its problems, of course, and the prioress hoped the bishop might not be appalled by them. There was the matter of nuns staying up after Compline. That certainly made for drowsy Matins at two the next morning. Then there was the singing itself, the slurred and dropped syllables, the speeding up of what was not to be speeded up. It was well known that a special devil named Tittivallus collected these omitted syllables and presented them by the bushel basket to his satanic lord: "These are they who wickedly corrupt the holy psalms: the dangler, the gasper, the leaper, the galloper, the dragger, the mumbler, the fore-skipper, the fore-runner, and the over-leaper: Tittivallus collecteth the fragments of these men's words," one authority reveals. But at least this was an aristocratic convent and the nuns were ladies. One heard horrendous tales of tempers elsewhere.

The prioress had an enormous responsibility, not all of it spiritual. She had to be a business woman as well, and unless she was a very good business woman ends were hard to pull together. But she had her little worldly compensations. She had her own room and did not share the common dormitory; she had her cook and housemaid and her companion nun who attended her and provided for her needs (and reported to the bishop). This nun was called her chaplain and the office rotated to prevent favoritism. And she got off the convent grounds quite frequently, on business to be sure. She had responsibility, but she had compensations. There is reason to believe that the bishop was not too displeased by what he heard the following day.

Such was the good life of St. Benedict. A Benedictine monastery was a stronghold of peace and quiet in the turbulent early Middle Ages, but a stronghold from which men sallied forth to serve their fellow men. When St. Benedict climbed Monte Cassino, he climbed out of a Europe in ruins. He knew that civilization could be rebuilt only the slow, hard way by men of prudent wisdom and quiet, sober dedication. The Rule that he wrote is no less magnificent for its prudence than for its purpose; in most respects it was no more severe than the ordinary routine of secular living in his day and age. He established a common round of daily duties, none too onerous. He required the three renunciations that are external: poverty, chastity, and obedience. He balanced the active and the contemplative in the lives of his monks, and in their active lives he balanced the mental and the physical. St. Gregory in his *Homilies on Ezechiel* defined the two lives: "The active life is to give bread to the hungry, to teach the ignorant the word of wisdom, to correct the erring, to recall to the path of humility our neighbour when he waxes proud, to tend the sick, to dispense to all what they need, and to provide those entrusted to us with subsistence. But the contemplative life is to retain indeed with all one's mind the love of God and neighbour, but to rest from exterior action, and cleave only to the desire of the Maker, that the mind may now take no pleasure in doing anything, but having spurned all cares, may be aglow to see the face of its Creator; so that it already knows how to bear with sorrow the burden of the corruptible flesh, and with all its desires to seek and join the hymn-singing choirs of angels, to mingle with the heavenly citizens, and to rejoice at its everlasting incorruption in the sight of God."

In the instinctive Platonism of the Middle Ages there is a certain parallel present between Plato's guardians of the city and the medieval clergy. In Plato as in Benedict the distinction between the active and the contemplative life is to be found, as it is in St. Augustine along with his dictum that the mixed life is best. The difference is that in Plato the active life of the guardians and the contemplative life which is its reward are lived within the framework of this life; in St. Benedict the active and contemplative lives alike look to the life beyond. That is the basic difference between the concept of the good life of the ancients and the good life of the Middle Ages. But just as important is the difference between the Platonic "Do thy own duty" and the medieval "Do the duty of the station in life to which God has called thee." In Plato the good of the state is supreme; in medieval thought the good of the individual is supreme since the only ultimate good is union through salvation with God, and men are saved one by one. Thus there is a certain spiritual democracy that underlies the entire hierarchy of medieval society, a certain individualism present in its monolithic whole. Faith means faith in Christian doctrine and hope means hope of salvation, but love is the universal Christian virtue. Dante's Inferno is filled with those who failed in love. The perversion of love is pride and in the lowest pit of hell, buried in the eternal ice, are the monsters of pride: Judas, Brutus, Cassius, Satan. Out of the hatred of pride flow the Christian virtues: humility, obedience, compassion, renunciation. This is the philosophy of the good life in the tradition of St. Benedict.

Its manifestation, however, was a very different thing. It was a man mending a road, another man building a house. It was a nun sewing a garment or weeding a garden. It was a monk toiling over a manuscript, a prioress toiling over some household accounts. The monk mending the road may once have been a count, the nun sewing the garment may have been the daughter of a baron. But in the cloister they were all children of God living the good life as St. Benedict had prudently and wisely defined it.

31

2.

The City Street

ALL the children of God did not live in the cloister. The Benedictines sallied forth from their spiritual fortresses to minister to their fellow man, but they always sought the center again and indeed were bound to it forever. On the old Roman tower at Monte Cassino is a Latin inscription: *Inspexit et despexit,* "He saw into the world and he scorned it." Benedict and the sons of Benedict did not scorn the world for others, but scorned it for themselves. They lived to make the world a better place, but they lived out of the world to insure themselves a better destiny. It was a natural instinct that made them seek the mountain top, Monte Cassino, the Grande Chartreuse, or indeed Mount Equinox in Vermont where the American Carthusians have their isolated hermitage.

Then came St. Dominic and St. Francis. They were in the world and in a sense they were of the world, and in every sense they loved the world. They were utterly different the one from the other, and they were profoundly the same. As Dante puts it in the *Paradiso:*

> *One will I speak of, for of both is spoken*
> *In praising one, whichever may be taken,*
> *Because unto one end their labors were.*

But the instinct is always to speak, not of the great apostle of faith, Dominic, but of the great apostle of love, Francis. Dante speaks darkly of the beloved "reft of her first husband," who waited one thousand and one hundred years and more for the coming of her second lover.

> But that too darkly I may not proceed,
> Francis and Poverty for these two lovers
> Take thou henceforward in my speech diffuse.
> Their concord and their joyous semblances,
> The love, the wonder, and the sweet regard,
> They made to be the cause of holy thoughts.

There was in the life of St. Francis of Assisi an unimaginable freedom. What he had, the numerator of his life, was very little but the denominator of his life, his desires, was nothing. When the fraction was resolved, he had infinity. He had perfect freedom from every worldly desire, every worldly fear, every worldly misgiving, apprehension, and concern. He could range the world with a song upon his lips because in his heart there was room for nothing but love. Wherever there was sorrow and suffering, need and misery, Francis was present. The very lepers were his brothers in Christ, and he ministered to them. Francis preaching to the birds, Francis addressing brother fire, Francis praying on his death bed, "Be praised, O Lord, for our sister, the death of the body, whom no man may escape," is one of the strangest figures in all history, because the sanctity embodied in him is the rarest of all conceivable human qualities. He died with a song on his lips, just as he had lived. "I am not a cuckoo, to be afraid of death. By the grace of His Holy Spirit I am so intimately one with God that I am equally content to live or die."

Francis found Lady Poverty a widow since Christ died, and not only did he unite with her in spiritual union but so did the followers of Francis who came so quickly, mysteriously, spontaneously to his side. They also made their plea to Rome: may we have nothing. And they had nothing except their share of that mysterious serenity of spirit, that disturbing and profoundly radical set of values, even that song that was always

33

on the lips of Francis because, like the serenity and the values, it arose from the depths of his heart. What Francis not so much founded, since Christ had already done that, as brought back to a world that had lost it in the maze of worldly concerns was the good life in imitation of Christ. For all the charm, the quiet devotion, the transparent sincerity and piety of the book called *The Imitation of Christ,* its message is not exactly the imitation of Christ. The *Imitation* came from a monastery, and Christ did not live in seclusion. So with Francis. He was the most Christlike man that has ever lived, and if it be charged that the Franciscans were not worthy of Francis, it can be answered that Christians in general are not worthy of Christ. By and large the Franciscans strove to be worthy of Francis, and within the limitations of normal human frailities many succeeded.

To be worthy of Francis it was not necessary to think something new or to say something new. Francis never thought nor said anything new. It was necessary to be something new. St. Francis preached on the street corners. His subject was the conversion of men. Conversion was no mystical experience, no rapture the more enticing for the formless way it eddied through one's being. Conversion was giving up sin. It was giving up dishonesty, anger, lust, false pride. Conversion was giving back what one had taken dishonestly, ending that feud with one's neighbor, forgetting that other woman. But there were more than sinners to be converted. There were the just also to be converted, those who followed Francis on the path that leads not merely to righteousness but to perfection. This path led through the generosity of the Benedictines of Mount Subiaso to the little chapel called the Portiuncula and to the ten most glorious years of the Franciscans. It was at the Portiuncula that the immediate followers of Francis were something profoundly new, as the Apostles who were their models and their inspiration had been profoundly new.

The Franciscans were mendicants in a sense, and technically they are a mendicant order since they own nothing either corporately or individually, but before that they were a laboring order. Idleness was certainly not part of the Franciscan

34

creed. A brother was to carry on the trade he practiced before, but for payment he was to accept only the food he needed. If it was not adequate, he then might beg. To Francis money was not only the root of evil, but the passion flower itself. Furthermore, granted the purpose of the Franciscans, their very poverty was an asset. They could work among the poor because they themselves were the poor. They were wedded to Poverty, and the union was a happy one. There is a sense in which the poverty of the Franciscans was the precise opposite of asceticism. Aseticism suggests deprivation, and the Franciscans were marvellously rich. They had an overflowing abundance of freedom, happiness, and absence of worldly concern. Their very poverty helped them to fix their gaze upon the spiritual heights which only those who serve their fellow man in a spirit of total self-denial can attain.

The preaching of the Franciscans was marked by that same mysteriously rich poverty. There was no dogma in it, no theology, no subtlety of reasoning. It came from common men and it was addressed to common men. Francis's fishermen of Galilee were farmers of Assisi, with now and then a member of the nobility who had found the true nobility. They simply entered the order, and the entrance requirements were very simple. One gave what he had to the poor. It is even recorded that three notorious robbers became Franciscans. The entrance requirements for them were equally simple. They gave up dishonesty. It was a simple gospel the Franciscans preached: there is no true joy but the joy of perfection. But perfection is something that comes partly by contrition, partly by attrition, contrition for sins and attrition of self. There is a wonderful story in the *Fioretti,* the life of Francis and his disciples as the fourteenth-century imagination conceived it. Whether it is true in fact is not of the slightest consequence. It is profoundly true in spirit.

St. Francis and Brother Leo were passing one day from Perugia to the Portiuncula and St. Francis instructed Brother Leo how he should describe the perfect joy. If the Friars Minor are an inspiration to the world of holiness, that is not the perfect joy. If the Brothers rival the miracles of Christ, that is not

35

the perfect joy. If the Brothers have universal knowledge and talk with the tongues of angels, that is not perfect joy. If the Brothers convert every infidel in the world to Christ, that is not perfect joy. "Father, I pray you in God's name tell me in what consists the perfect joy," said Brother Leo. And St. Francis replied, "When we arrive at Santa Maria degli Angeli, soaked with rain, frozen with cold, covered with mud, dying of hunger, and we knock and the porter comes in a rage, saying, 'Who are you?' and we answer, 'We are two of your brethren,' and he says, 'You lie, you are two lewd fellows who go up and down corrupting the world and stealing the alms of the poor. Go away from here!' and he does not open to us, but leaves us outside shivering in the snow and rain, frozen, starved, till night; then, if thus maltreated and turned away, we patiently endure all this without murmuring against him, if we think with humility and charity that this porter really knows us truly and that God makes him speak thus to us, then O Brother Leo, write that in this is the perfect joy. . . . Above all the graces and all the gifts which the Holy Spirit gives to his friends is the grace to conquer oneself, and willingly to suffer pain, outrages, disgrace, and evil treatment, for the love of Christ."

In the ultimate analysis, the difference between the good life of St. Benedict and the good life of St. Francis is the difference between the prudently possible and the gloriously impossible. Both ideals became worn and tarnished and had to be subject to repeated renewal. The ideal of Francis was the higher, and it became worn and tarnished the more quickly; the ideal of Benedict was less lofty, but it wore better. The residents of the heavenly city can be as varied as the residents of any earthly city, and the good life of both Benedict and Francis is founded on the love of God and the contempt of self. In this we see one of the strangest and most mysterious links between classical antiquity and the Middle Ages, a link in what perhaps is the true chain that holds together mankind in all its ages.

Aristotle was the accepted philosopher of the Middle Ages, but just as behind Aristotle himself was Plato, so behind the formal Aristotelianism of the Middle Ages was an instinctive

Platonism. At the very heart of Platonism is the contrast between the senses and the thoughts, the body and the spirit. But monasticism rests upon the subjection of the senses and the body to the thoughts and the spirit. The rule of St. Benedict was prudent and possible, but all its prudent possibilities cannot disguise the fact that it rested on what for most people is the final austerity, the subjection and denial of what is physical to what is spiritual. Men were not meant by nature to live in monasteries, but to the men who live in monasteries and are happy there, nature is not God. The rule of St. Francis was paradoxically soaring in its very humility, even more contrary to nature than the rule of St. Benedict. But Francis, who is probably the supreme nature lover of all history, never thought of nature as other than part of God's creation and hence everything in nature his brother and sister. In both rules the mind directs the body, values are accepted in their proper scale, the lower self is sacrificed for the sake of the higher self, and man fulfills himself in the highest degree when he gives what is finest in himself to the service of his fellow man for the greater glory of God.

But this is to quote, until the very end, what we said of the classical ideal of the good life. The orientation has changed from earth to heaven, the ideal is no longer exclusively human but now rests upon religious belief, one no longer is a resident of a single city but rather a resident of two cities. George Santayana says in his *Reason in Religion,* "All history was henceforth essentially nothing but the conflict between these two cities; two moralities, one natural, the other supernatural; two philosophies, the one rational, the other revealed; two glories, the one temporal, the other eternal; two institutions, one the world, the other the Church. These, whatever their momentary alliances or compromises, were radically opposed and fundamentally alien to one another. Their conflict was to fill the ages. . . ." But when entire allowance is made for for the extent to which monastic withdrawal may have been based upon a sense of that conflict, a dread of its impact and a fear of its consequences, the fact remains that the monks came down from Monte Cassino to minister to their fellow man and the followers of Francis never scaled its summit. The best and noblest adherents of the good life in the Middle Ages never saw the two cities in conflict, but rather followed St. Augustine who drew a careful distinction between the heavenly city which is the city of God, the earthly city which is the city of the condemned, and the visible society on earth, the State, which is neither the one nor the other. The State is a state of pilgrimage, of pilgrims seeking their eternal salvation and aiding one another in the quest. As St. Augustine puts it in *The City of God,* ". . . the heavenly city uses earthly peace in this its pilgrimage; it preserves and seeks the agreement of human wills in matters pertaining to the moral nature of man, so far as, with due regard to piety and religion, it can; and it relates that earthly peace to the heavenly peace, which truly is such peace that it should be accounted and named the only peace of the rational creature, seeing as it is a most ordered and most concordant companionship in the enjoyment of God, and, again, in the enjoyment of one another in God." That is the true ideal of Benedict, Francis, the true and faithful followers of both, and the truly pious of the secular clergy who in the Middle Ages drew their spiritual inspiration from the regular clergy. Self-sacrifice and service to one's fellow man was indeed "the enjoyment of one another in God." Obedience to the first commandment and the other commandment were one and inseparable in the best religious thought of the Middle Ages. It was the city of the damned that was the implacable foe of the heavenly city, not the ordinary city of man on earth in which Benedict labored for his fellow man and Francis inspired him with the glory of the infinite. Let us now turn our attention to one form that the city of man took in the Middle Ages, the fief and the castle which was its pulsating heart.

3.

The Castle

THERE was a hint of something not quite darkness for the pines to stand against on the hills across the river to the East. There was a bar of undulating silver on the water, and the suggestion of a stir in the air. Then a cock crowed and a dog barked, and a man stirred uneasily on the bench where he lay huddled, stirred uneasily, yawned, stretched, and half rolled to his feet. He was ready for the day even as he stood erect. His coarse tunic fell easily into position as fustian will after the first few months of uninterrupted wear. He shoved a smouldering log a few inches and a mouth of red with jagged teeth of black leered at him from the cavernous fireplace. A shove to another log brought out sparks spitting in protest, and light enough to make half visible great cauldrons that hung from giant hooks like somber black globes in a necromancer's cave. The faintest hint of what to the shivering skin of faith might be warmth caressed him as he leaned into the hearth and coaxed a reluctant light onto a tallow dip. Now the eye of faith had light, as the skin of faith had warmth, and the barest modicum of either. But the man was used to the barest modicum of comfort, and so were the lord and lady whom he served.

The lord was a baron whose fief measured some three hundred square miles. The lady was the daughter of a count and by dowry a substantial part of that mileage came from her. The room was the hall of the *palais;* in the cultivated thirteenth century one no longer lived in the bleak, clammy, Stygian, monocellular *donjon* as people had in the dismal centuries gone by. The groom, who had slept on the bench outside the chamber of his lord and lady after the casual fashion of his age, had readied the hall for the day that now was clearly dawning. The logs had been stirred and the tallow dip lighted. The groom now would enter the chamber and help the baron dress. Already it was five o'clock and the day far enough along even for a man of the baron's advanced years (he was forty) and his lady who was eight years his junior to be abroad. The iniquitous practice rumored about the other barony on the west fork of the river far across the ridge, of sybarites lolling in bed until six in the morning, had no place in this well-ordered castle.

Since there had been no guests the previous night of a standing elevated enough to warrant a bed in the baron's chamber —sleeping room had been found for two monks, a clerk, and a merchant of Ghent whose news from the Low Countries merited for him a little more consideration than his worldly state—the groom had a simple task preparing his lord for the world and the day, as the maids did in preparing their lady. A monk chanted Matins for the lady, and perhaps for the maids had not their preoccupation with stays and braces inhibited devotion, as she and her husband were prepared for the chapel and for Mass. The baron and his lady had already put themselves in the frame of mind that devotion requires. On awaking they had made the triple sign of the Cross, said the first prayer of the morning, and reviewed mentally the good deeds appointed for them to do that day. The *Quatre Ages de l'homme* says that they should have repeated the list of good deeds three times before arising, so as to have it firmly in memory and to neglect no jot nor tittle. The baron and his lady, however, combined with good will an instinct for practical simplicity. One need not follow literally the precepts

40

of devout but notoriously unworldly clerks. And so, when dressed, they went to the chapel, heard Mass, and gave alms to those who knew from diligent experience that the moment of emergence from the chapel after morning Mass was the propitious moment for the outstretched hand. Then they took a brief walk in the garden which was the lady's demesne and delight, washed their hands in rose water, and had their simple breakfast of bread and wine. Their bread was white, since they were nobility, but their morning wine was as thin as that of the grooms and the maids.

The morning was for work, the evening for play. It was no small matter to be lord of a realm three hundred square miles in area, to be lord and master of its every last detail, solely responsible to the duke and beyond him to the king, and beyond them both to God, for its wise, righteous, and efficient management. Several other knights on whom fortune had not smiled sufficiently lived in the castle with the baron. They were his chief subordinates in the management of the fief. Under them were the chief servitors, the ones who managed and operated the farms, the cattle, the stables, and most important of all, who managed the peasants. The baron would consult them in the course of the morning, and he would find that each one was very much an independent lord in his own realm. As an experienced lord of a fief he would take independent talk, and even strictly pertinent back talk, from the master falconer which could lead to a private war if voiced by another baron. But each person of this little world, this intricate microcosm of the great world of the Middle Ages, had his proper, respected, and unchallenged place in it. It was a world that could not have operated were this not so. It fed itself, clothed itself, sheltered and warmed itself, guarded itself against nature, beast, and man. The woolen clothes it wore next to its skin unchanged through the long winter months had been fleece on the backs of its sheep, wool on the teeth of its carding machine, thread on the spool of its spinners, and cloth on the table of its tailors. The meat in its brine vats had been a calf in the pasture and the stall, and a hog in its acorn forest; a herdsman, a forester, and a butcher had brought it to

41

its present state. The bread it ate had been rye and barley in its fields, sown, grown, and reaped by its peasants, ground by its millers, stored by its cellarers, and baked by its cooks. In this world people handled cloth, meat, and other food, but not money. Even the baron handled little money, although of course the gift of money at Christmas and at Easter to every living soul, even to the last and least of God's beggars on the fief, was as the law of the Medes and the Persians that altereth not. The baron, wise and experienced man that he was, knew that his powers were limitless except where they were sharply limited by inflexible tradition. All this, this economy of dairy and dirt farming, of field and stream, of stable, granary, shearing shed, and brine vat was the baron's responsibility. And so the morning was dedicated to its supervision, to reports from its every sector, to problems and puzzles, sudden emergencies and predicted calamities. The problem was presented, the puzzle outlined, the emergency reported, and the calamity unveiled. Then the subordinate waited, whether he be belted knight or lowliest forester of the hog herd in the acorn forest, until the baron made his decision.

The baron had his three hundred square miles to supervise, but the baroness had her three hundred souls who lived in and about the castle, and they were her concern. In the immediate foreground was her retinue of maids, at least ten or a dozen young women off the farms who had been trained to do the household work. There was a great deal of cleaning to be done in the vast hall and the chambers of the *palais*. It is a serious mistake to think that the Middle Ages were not clean; they were clean, but not sanitary. The baroness had been taught cleanliness at the convent school she attended as a girl, along with her French and Latin, and her knowledge of the principal stars, the healing herbs, and the art of setting a broken bone. She bathed with great regularity, but drank water from a contaminated well. She supervised the cleaning of the *palais:* the rushes on the hall floor were replaced with regularity and the bird cages faithfully scraped out. She saw to it that the *palais* was clean by the standards of housewifery, and they were the standards of the present day minus what scientific knowledge has added to cleanliness.

The eternal and the endless work of women was the manufacture of cloth and the making of it into garments. Great bags of wool were brought from the shearing place in the *palais*. Then followed the cleaning, the carding, the weaving, the cutting, and the sewing. Slowly, painfully, laboriously, but steadily fleece was transformed into fustian, to be worn next to the skin all the long winter, to irritate it until the skin broke out in all sorts of skin rashes that became infected and ugly, and if bad enough were confused with leprosy and took on ominous overtones suggestive of the wrath of God. Little wonder that white, soft, clear skin is the attribute of maidens in the romances and *chansons de geste;* it must have been rare indeed in reality. But people had to be clothed and kept warm, and northern Europe can be brutally cold in winter and nowhere in northern Europe colder than in the great and draughty halls of medieval castles. Keeping three hundred people clothed and warm was foremost among the responsibilities of the baroness.

That she was hostess when there were guests to entertain, and that was almost nightly, one takes for granted. One also takes for granted that in the baron's absence her authority was complete: then it was the baroness who supervised the fields and the farms, the stable, the granary, and the shearing shed. But all this was in the ordinary course of human events. Private wars in the Middle Ages were ubiquitous and endless. War of any sort is not consistent with the good life, but it is consistent with life itself, and on occasion the baroness might have to supervise the defense of the castle against hostile attack, be certain that the towers were manned, the moats protected, adequate fire power ready to enfilade the open areas, and the boiling water and bubbling pitch ready for a last emergency. It is a matter of record that on occasion noble ladies did it more effectively than their absent husbands ever would have.

There is in this something profoundly paradoxical, yet very important to medieval life. The baroness would be legally a minor all the days of her life. She would be under the legal protection of her father until she married. Then she would pass into the legal custody of her husband. If both died, a brother or an uncle would become her guardian. If she became a widow and a substantial dowry would accompany her second marriage, that marriage would come promptly either at the insistence of some knight or conceivably at her own insistence. It is bad enough to be a wife and legally a minor, but it is worse to be a minor sister or niece in years of full maturity. And so the baroness, who supervised the feeding and the cloth- of a large immediate household and a little state of perhaps three hundred souls, who had entire responsibility for the running of a castle, the entertaining of an endless procession of guests, and always the full responsibility for everything in a little principality of three hundred square miles when the baron was away, and this could mean the ultimate responsi- bility of defense against attack, was a dependent minor.

The morning was for work, the afternoon and evening for play. The baron might hunt. Many of his rank had a passion for hunting, a passion compounded in uneasy measure from the thrill of peril which can be a part of man's intricate and composite makeup. It was much simpler and safer to face a mounted knight charging with spear in position than to face a wild boar with a boar spear as it suddenly charged from the brake. Hunting, the learned agreed, was good for the soul since it freed one from the sin of sloth. It was hardly good for the souls of the peasants whose crops were trampled and destroyed by the horses as they raced across the countryside, but the learned were not in full agreement as to what was good for the souls of peasants. Adversity can be made into a virtue when one draws the proper lessons from it, and the peasants had ample opportunity to draw the lesson of adver- sity during the hunting season. Or there was the elaborate art of falconry, the most aristocratic of all sports, with a ritual that put to shame modern skiing and golf. It was even prac- ticed in miniature indoors at elaborate banquets, where the prime surprise might be an enormous pie carried in with full pomp and then slashed open to allow the live birds inside to fly out and up to the rafters where they would be speedily and mercilessly cut down by the falcons the lords had brought to the dinner for the purpose. Far from being a bit whimsy, "Sing a song of sixpence" with its baked pie and its singing black-birds was standard entertainment for the king.

The baroness meantime could be busy in her garden, cultivating the roses, lilies, and marigolds, tending the vegetable garden where all the vegetables we know except the potato grew, or supervising the gardeners as they pruned the apple, peach, and pear trees in the garden. By and large, however, the baroness had less time for relaxation than her husband, and she even had some sense of guilt when she took the time for a game of chess. Chess was an aristocratic game, quite as much so as falconry in its very different way, but an aristocrat was certainly not above a game of backgammon and the ladies of the castle in their hours of relaxation might even play games now relegated to the nursery, games like blind man's buff. Socially smaller fry might while away the hours with tennis and billiards, tennis meaning handball and billiards a sort of field hockey.

In the evening came the hour of romance. A jongleur with a rich repertory of tales of Camelot and Arthur's knights, or Charlemagne and the twelve peers, of Julius Caesar, Alexander, or the Trojan War was in the castle. In the evening all would gather in the great hall, the baron and baroness on the elevated dias, the lesser lords and ladies about them, the squires and the pages, the maids, the cooks, the grooms, the whole world of the castle ranged about in an aristocracy of position and a democracy of spirit to hear the romance or the *chanson de geste* the jongleur would undertake. His performance would be punctuated by rest periods in which jugglers and acrobats would entertain, since a notable jongleur was not so much a man as a troupe. At last his performance would be over, his reward would be forthcoming, and the day would draw to its end. The baron and his lady would retire to their chamber, be disrobed, mount the massive bed, and submerge themselves in a billowing sea of feather mattresses, and have the curtains drawn about them to shelter them from the night air which everyone knows is poisonous. The children of the noble couple would retire to their lesser chambers, the maids would lie down for the night at a respectful distance from the baronial bed, and out in the hall the groom would huddle on the bench, pull a rough cloth about him, snuggle into it, reach out once or twice for a bit of final warmth from the dying fire, and give himself to sleep. Night would be far advanced, nine o'clock at the least, but the day had been rich and varied and the sleep of the just is one of life's rewards. Tomorrow would be today's repeated replica.

This was the Middle Ages in the castle and the fief, and there were hundreds of castles and hundreds of fiefs from the marches of England and Scotland, where the clans of ancient Celtic tradition contested the land against the encroaching castle, all the way to the distant East where the Magyars were sloughing off immemorial Asia and preparing for their European destiny. From Scotland to Poland and to Hungary was the land of the castle and the fief, the land of chivalry and everything it connoted. National boundaries meant nothing, and kings relatively little. The world of the Middle Ages was hundreds of little worlds, each self-contained, each self-supporting and self-sufficient. The good life was lived in the castle and the fief, and so was the evil life, the life of terror and of torture, and the life of endless war. The former continues to be our concern.

The baron, to simplify the range of medieval titles, was lord of the castle and the fief, its guardian, its inspiration, and its master. Naturally the concept of the good life in the castle and the fief begins with him. At the hour of his birth the nature of his future life, its responsibilities, authority, powers and privileges, was known, and for twenty-one years he was prepared for it. The first seven years he spent at home with his mother, learning obedience and the other lessons within his childish ken. The next seven years he spent at the castle of some lord friendly with his father, perhaps a respected vassal, perhaps his peer among the lords of the land, conceivably the duke if his father merited the honor, or even the king. The boy learned the way to act in the presence of his elders and superiors, how to enter their presence, how to conduct himself in it, how to leave it. He served as a page under the women of the castle, learned to obey without question, to be prompt, accurate, and reliable. He learned the rudiments of his religion and the foundation of the moral code by which he was to lead his entire life. He learned the lesson of cleanliness, as cleanliness was understood in the Middle Ages. When he was fourteen the women had taught him what they had to teach, and he was ready to pass under the instruction of men.

From the age of fourteen to the age of twenty-one he was a squire, although after the first four years he was more accurately considered a *demoiseau,* a little lord. Now he learned the manly lessons, horsemanship, the use of sword and lance, the arts of hunting and hawking. He learned the virtues as the men as the men of his age understood the virtues, and indeed it was by these virtues that he was to lead his life. The virtues of medieval knighthood were simple, concrete, and austere, and therefore very hard indeed.

The first virtue was prowess. He would have the ultimate authority in the years ahead, and therefore the ultimate responsibility, for defending the fief against the rapacity, treachery, and tyranny in which the age abounded. No time in the life of a fief was quite so perilous as the period when the old lord had passed into eternity and the young lord was taking over his appointed responsibility. Then if ever did rapacity, treachery, and tyranny have their hour, and the young lord must have been trained closely and well in the hard lessons of warfare to repel them. Underneath all the panoply of medieval chivalry, like a bedrock on which rested the courteous and admirable qualities, was the mailed fist, the studded pike, the brawn and the heart of the German warrior. Before everything else the young knight had to know what it meant to be *preudome,* a man of prowess. Unless you can beat the other man in battle, nothing is of consequence.

The young knight, however, would not fight alone. He would enter into his proper position in the elaborate system of the fief. He might be heir to the liege lord, but the liege lord himself was vassal to the duke, quite as truly as the lesser nobility were vassals to him. Loyalty was something owed and expected, the cement which held the fief together. He would have to learn what loyalty was, and why it had to be, and what it meant to be loyal in a world in which rapacity, treachery, and tyranny abound. He must be brave and he must be loyal.

The young knight would have a social position to maintain as well as a military position. The world in which he lived and moved would expect him to be generous. At this point one must voice that word of caution always necessary at the point of convergence between life and literature, history and letters. The clerks make the books, as the Wife of Bath lamented, and the viewpoint of the clerks colors the books and the lives of the clerks color the viewpoint. The life of the clerk was fiscally precarious, as was the life of the jongleur and the composer of the *chanson de geste*. They lived on the generosity of the aristocracy to whom they told their tales or for whom they wrote them. Hence generosity looms very large indeed in literature as a hallmark of the aristocracy. Generosity was the third virtue, honored in life perhaps as highly as it was extolled in literature, perhaps not. The viewpoint of the clerk and the jongleur affected the story, but the viewpoint of the story affected the way the listener thought. Life does imitate art: the generosity that was so emphasized a literary virtue was a living virtue as well. Indeed, it became the vice of extravagance as the notion grew out of it that it was unworthy of a knight to live within his means.

These are the simple virtues of the knight, plain and unadorned bricks for the foundation of the good life. They are the virtues of man to man: bravery, loyalty, generosity. Out of the relationship of man to woman and man to God arose the more subtle virtues, and then with a curious sort of reverse action, ideals that grew out of these latter relationships came to apply to the relationships of man to man.

The position of woman in medieval literature is very strange. Woman is the daughter of Eve, and she is the daughter of Mary. Woman is the source of man's downfall, and the source of man's redemption. In Chaucer's *Nun's Priest's Tale,* after the cock Chauntecleer has refuted at length and to his own entire satisfaction the viewpoint of his feathered wife Pertelote, a viewpoint which was rooted in what would now be

termed science, positivism, and similar damnable heresies, he
relaxes his intellectual austerity, beams upon her beauty, and
assures her, "Mulier est hominis confusio" (Woman is man's
ruination), and then, since Latin is beyond the female sex,
benignly translates for her, "Woman is mannes joye and al
his bliss." The view of Chauntecleer was precisely the view of
the Middle Ages; woman is man's ruination, and all his joy
and bliss. Nor should one apply to the juxtaposition the sort of
thinking often mislabelled Puritanism, and consider joy and
bliss synonyms for ruination. That was not the medieval way
of thinking. Woman was indeed Eve, man's ruination; and
woman was indeed Mary, all man's joy and bliss.

As time passed, woman became less and less the daughter
of Eve, more and more the daughter of Mary. In literature
the whole matter is indeed complex, because the code of
courtly love rested solidly on the concept that there is an
incompatibility between love and marriage. Courtly love is the
love of Lancelot for Guenevere, the sinful love outside the
marriage bond, not the love of Arthur for Guenevere, his
wedded wife. But literature and life are not identities. The
position of the baroness in the castle simply was too important
and the way she filled her position simply too admirable for
clerks to dismiss her as the daughter of Eve. Too many
lordly husbands and wives found love quite possible within
the framework of the judiciously arranged marriage, found
the heavy responsibility of managing a fief the strongest bond
of loyalty, found that generosity can be a more subtle thing
than the giving of material gifts, for love to be exclusively the
illicit convention of a school of poetry. Courtesy grew as a
virtue partly out of literature, to be sure, but mainly out of
life. One could hardly have the virtues a knight should have
toward his fellow man and not have a companion set of virtues toward womanhood, and husbands and wives in every
age are altogether too often in love, and loyal, faithful, and
devoted to each other, for the code of courtesy not to develop
out of life itself.

Then the code came to be extended into the other realm
which belonged to man alone, and developed into an elabo-

rate code of behavior that governed the relationship among lords, and especially their relationship in the mimic war of the tourney and the not altogether real war of the battlefield. Just as there was always something of warfare in the knightly play of the tourney, so there was always something of play in the knightly warfare of the battlefield. What other age in human history would have accepted the Truce of God, which forbade warfare from Vespers on Wednesday until sunrise on Monday? Or the Peace of God which in effect allowed warfare only in the dead cold of winter and the dead heat of summer, when it would interfere the least with the important occupations of plowing, sowing, and harvesting? To be sure, the Truce of God and the Peace of God were far from universally observed, but in what other period of human history would they have been thinkable? Courtesy was a strange, intricate, contradictory, fascinating virtue, but it was a virtue. Marital fidelity was part of it, and also marital infidelity. It was partly religious in its inspiration, and partly grounded on a mockery of religion. It started as a highly artificial code of conduct between the sexes, and ramified until it became a code of conduct on the field of battle. What is fundamental is that in all its strangeness, intricacy, and contradictory qualities courtesy was a great civilizing force. Bravery, loyalty, and generosity are virtues within the comprehension of barbarians, but one has to be civilized to understand, or even to misunderstand, courtesy.

The third relationship, that of the knight with God, gradually gave to the code of chivalry its most exalted meaning. The connection between knighthood and religious dedication came very slowly, and there was always in it a curious mixture of the idealistic and the pragmatic. The latter is the simpler and may be mentioned first. Fighting was the occupation and the avocation of the primitive knight when he first began to emerge from his fur-clad Germanic warrior forebear. The Church tried to curb the fighting instinct by such rules and regulations as the Truce of God and the Peace of God suggest. Its success was partial, and usually very partial. Courtesy also helped in this regard, since courtesy also was an amusing mixture of the idealistic and the pragmatic. It would be the gravest breach

50

of courtesy to attack an unarmed knight, partly because it would be taking an unwarranted advantage of a fellow aristocrat and partly because the danger of it would make a knight always stay in armor when on the road, and armor is hot, heavy, and excessively clumsy. Everyone benefited in comfort and ease of motion, as well as grew in moral rectitude, by the universally observed rule that an armed knight could not attack an unarmed one. There was always an element of play in medieval warfare, and hence that element of rules by which one must abide that is inseparable from sports. The more chivalric warfare became, the more comfortable, and the more chivalric it became to capture your opponent and hold him for ransom, the safer and more lucrative.

Knights however would fight, and therefore the Church tried to make their fighting as constructive as possible by directing their martial energies against the heathen and the infidel. Prussia was ideal for the purpose. It was not too far away and the Teutonic Order was gradually converting the Prussian heathen at the point of sword and lance. Invasions of the Moslem world were more difficult to organize and more elaborate to carry through, but the guerdon of glory was greater and the ultimate prize, Jerusalem, lay under the crescent. In the Crusades the fusion of courtesy and religion into what may be called religious chivalry reached at least its theoretical completion. Parenthetically, excursions against the Turks were learned by experience to be impractical. The Turk has never deemed warfare in any sense a game nor conducted it for anything short of keeps. By the late fourteenth century a knight might have made the Grand Tour of heathendom with lance and sword. Chaucer's Knight had fought in Granada, Morocco, Algeria, Egypt, Asia Minor, Armenia, Lithuania, and Russia, fighting always against the Moslem and the pagan. But he came fairly close to the end of an era.

Religious chivalry, however, was a reality as well as an ideal. Writers such as John of Salisbury went so far as to maintain that the military profession was of divine creation, and that the knights may fairly be considered as a secular arm in the service of the Church. The knight was a special servant of the Church, dedicated to keeping the faith, fighting to defend the Church and the right as a dedicated servant of God and the prince. There are two swords, said Stephen of Fougeres, the spiritual and the temporal, and the two orders must use them in harmonious defense of Church and State. Ramon Lull, who had fought the Moslems as a knight and served the Lord as a priest, considered knights as well as priests the anointed of the Almighty, the world's bravest, strongest, and most loyal in His service. Thus Roland dying but proclaiming his vassalage to God, and weary, heart-sore Charlemagne in the dust and ashes of Roncevalles heeding the call of the Pope and readying himself for one more weary, heart-breaking campaign against the infidel present in imaginative literature the simple embodiment of religious chivalry, as Perceval and Galahad dedicated to the quest of the Holy Grail embody it in a richer, more sophisticated, finely symbolic literature. It would be naïve to say that Philip of Valois, Edward the Black Prince, and Bertrand du Guesclin embodied the ideal in its perfection, but it would be cynical to say that they embodied it not at all. Like every ideal, the ideal of religious chivalry was only partially attained, but combined with courtesy it was the ideal that civilized the western world. Thus the dubbing of a knight was properly a religious ceremony, with the night of prayer at the altar that preceded it, the ceremonial bath before it which was a sort of renewal of the baptismal vows, the attendance at Mass before the candidate knelt at the feet of the bishop, was presented by his sponsors, given the buffet that still survives in the sacrament of confirmation, and so was knighted. He was solemnly dedicated to bravery, loyalty, generosity, courtesy, and chivalry, bound to defend his liege lord with faith and courage, to protect the defenseless and sustain the needy, to defend the faith and his fellow man, to revere woman as the daughter of Mary, and to follow all the days of his mature life the Christian ideal as that ideal was presented to men of his station in life. It was an austere ideal, and it is likely that few achieved it. But it is equally likely that many tried to achieve it, and it was not beyond the reach of the man of good will.

In a sense the code of knighthood was for the second estate what the code of St. Benedict was for the first estate, a code by which men of normal powers and good will could guide their lives. It grew fantastic as all such codes inevitably do, and its death knell sounds through the pages of *Orlando Furioso* and *Don Quixote*. But it is the death knell of the code that sounds through these pages, not the death knell of bravery, loyalty, generosity, courtesy, and chivalry. In the complete sense they are not yet born upon this imperfect earth.

This was the code by which our baron undertook to live. We are safe in the assumption which lies midway between naïveté and cynicism; by and large he tried to live by it. On occasion he failed, and on some occasions failed badly. When he failed he regretted it, did what seemed the appropriate penance, and promised to do better next time. When he succeeded, he felt a thrill of satisfaction which he knew was in itself a bit dangerous since it smacked of pride, but at least he savored the thrill. In short, he behaved in respect to the code by which he lived just about as men of good will in every day and age behave toward the code by which they live. If our thesis has any validity at all, it rests upon the fact that every age is to be judged by neither its saints and sages nor by its fools and villains, but by its average men and women of good will.

The relationship of the baron to his family was compounded of both authority and responsibility. His wife was a legal minor in theory, but she was such in practice only to the degree that her own character and temperament encouraged subordination. She had altogether too much responsibility herself, and commensurate authority, to be anything less than a junior partner in the management of the fief. Until they reached their majority the children of the baron were entirely under his authority, but the manner in which he manifested his sense of responsibility told much about him. His sons had to be given the long and careful training preliminary to knighthood, and over almost all of it he could exercise at best a remote control. On the other hand, he had direct control and responsibility for the education of the sons of certain of his peers. The education of his daughters was a lesser concern since he could trust the convent school to do it well, but their marriage was another matter. Marriage had to be arranged with meticulous care and as a devoted and responsible father with solemn obligations to his flesh and blood, he had to consider their spiritual well-being and happiness as well as the material soundness of the matches he arranged. Nor, indeed, was his responsibility in this regard ever ended. Death might at any moment put the custody of a widowed daughter back into his hands, or for that matter his mother, aunts, sisters, or cousins. To be head of an aristocratic family in the Middle Ages was to assume a responsibility at once undetermined and indeterminable, but neither light, transient, nor partial.

The relationship of the baron to the Church stood somewhere between his relationship with his peers and his relationship with his family. It was certainly no intellectual relationship. The baron assumed that the clergy knew theology as he assumed that his competent falconer knew falconry or, for that matter, as a good cook knew cooking. He needed a chaplain to attend to his spiritual needs just as much as he needed a falconer and a cook, and not in a totally different sense. His chaplain towered above his cook in social stature; where he stood in terms of the falconer tended to vary with the baron. It was the relationship with the bishop of the diocese or the abbot of the monastery that might pose the problem. By and large Church and State tended to be inseparable in the Middle Ages, but inseparable by the fact of parallelism rather than by the fact of identity as in classical antiquity. Translated into practical terms, this meant that wise and prudent barons knew the religious province and prudently stayed outside it, knew the secular province and jealously guarded its borders. Wise and prudent bishops and abbots did the same on their side of that invisible but very real line of division. The baron never questioned either the articles of faith or the absolute necessity for the Church and its spiritual ministrations, however much he may have questioned the sanctity and dedication of his authoritative counterparts of the cloth, or their ordained subordinates.

As always, it was his relations with his subordinates that

really tested the virtues of the baron. It would be a serious mistake, however, to imagine that nothing else determined those relations but the efficacy of the baronial virtues. There was a most elaborate hierarchy in the fief, and those subordinates in charge of the maintenance of the castle or the stables, farms, or forests, or in charge of supervising the peasantry, were themselves men of responsibility and authority, jealous of their own quasi-fiefs, living and working with one another on the terms that the facts of parallelism always dictate, and having the authority over their underlings commensurate with their responsibility. Each of these subordinates had a time-hallowed role to fill in the fief, a role that was handed down from father to son since the post of master falconer, or master of the stables, or warden of the forest was just as much subject to inheritance by primogeniture as was the position of the baron himself. Time had solidified (or, perhaps, encrusted) the role of these subordinates, and if the role of one was threatened, so was the role of all. Consequently there was a sort of instinctive trade unionism within the fief, and the imprudent baron who broke tradition where one subordinate was concerned would find his whole cadre of subordinates grown sullen and intractible. The medieval baron would probably be bewildered if he were to encounter the problems of a modern head of state, but it is quite as probable that he would understand the problems of the manager of a modern factory. He would know that if one is to elicit bravery and loyalty from subordinates, one must employ generosity and courtesy in turn.

What about the last and almost least of God's creatures in the fief, those who wrestled with the wooden plow as the ox strained and jerked, who pushed through briar and thicket in the forest after the errant hogs, who plunged arms blue with cold and hands so numb they could only grapple and not hold into brine vats and brought up icy flanks of corned meat for the waiting cooks? They worked hard, aged soon, died young. Were they the hapless victims of the good life of the more fortunate? This is the point at which sentimentality and the romantic impulse must be most sternly curbed. The social theory of the Middle Ages did not make their lives hard, and a change in social theory did not make the lives of their descendants easier. In the Renaissance and the Enlightenment the average man worked hard, aged soon, and died young. So did colonists in colonial America, and citizens of the United States amidst the blessings of democracy in the eighteenth and nineteenth centuries. Steam, oil, and electricity, not social or political theory, have made life physically easier.

Another curb to sentimentality and the romantic impulse is provided by the political theory of the Middle Ages. In the last analysis the fief came into being and always rested upon the need for mutual defense. The theory of feudalism did not start with the feudal lord; it started with the common man. As the *Coutume de Bayonne* (about 1273) puts it, "The people come before the lords; it is the lesser folk, more numerous than the others, who, wishing to live in peace, create lords to restrain and defeat the strong and to maintain each man in his rights, so that each may live according to his condition, the poor with their poverty and the rich with their wealth. And to assure this in perpetuity, the populace has submitted itself to a lord, has given him what he holds, and has kept what the people hold for themselves. It is in witness of this that the lord should take the oath to his people before the people take it to their lord; and this oath taken by the people to their lord is only binding so long as the lord keeps his oath." This is the true foundation on which all feudalism rested.

The life of the worker in the fief was hard; all life was physically hard until modern science made it easier. But the lot of the workers in the fief was not necessarily hard; where the baron exercised the virtues and insured that those between him and the workers exercised the virtues appropriate to the roles they played, the lot of the worker was not hard. The lot of the swineherd in *Ivanhoe* was harder than the lot of his creator Sir Walter Scott, a wealthy man, but not harder than the lot of the impoverished young Charles Dickens as he pasted labels on the bottles of stove blacking. The medieval worker expected his life to be hard, and indeed knew no other form of life. But he did not expect his lot to be hard; that was why he was a worker in a fief, ready, willing, and able to render military and economic service to the liege lord but expecting protection in return and his modest share of the good life as the unlettered worker of the Middle Ages understood it.

January was for rest and feasting, as Rigaut the typical villein of *Garin le Lorrain* understood it, nor was February good for much else. From March through June he worked hard in the vineyard and the fields, but enjoyed April as the best month of the French year and May as the second best. There was a breathing respite in July and August, but then came the vintage and the harvest months of September and October, the hog-fattening and wood-cutting month of November, and December which is a holy month, for then Christ was born and work is tempered as in January with rest and feasting. It was the worker's year, but it was the year as God designed it for the working man, and if the liege lord was a virtuous man and those above the worker virtuous after their proper pattern, for Rigaud of the broad chest and rippling muscles, the black beard and unwashed body, the simple wants, simple lusts, simple satisfactions, it was the good life. And for the true last and least of the fief, the crippled, the aged, the sick, halt, and blind whose life and lot alike were hard and the good life a vision of eternity, there were in the baron, his wife and children, his vassals, his supervisors, and the clergy whose lives paralleled life in the fief, if they were good men and women, the civilized and kindly virtues: generosity, courtesy, and chivalry. The lot and life of the poor were hard, as are the lot and life of God's poor in every age. Their lot in the Middle Ages was not necessarily worse than it has been in other ages, and in some respects it was very much better. The good in high position in the Middle Ages took very seriously the admonition, "And the greatest of these is charity," and they understood the word in a simple, theologically uncluttered sense.

In short, each medieval fief was a little world unto itself, a good world or an evil world as those who lived in it made it good or evil. The liege lord and his lady did not set the pattern of life in it, but they set the quality of the pattern. In the microcosm of the fief every dweller had his appointed place. The fief existed to give security, external security but internal security as well. It existed, as the already quoted *Coutume de Bayonne* has it, that each may live according to his condition, the poor with their poverty and the rich with their wealth. That there were class distinctions in the fief and great divergence in worldly goods was just as much part of the ordained order as the primacy of the liege lord. An acceptance of this fact and loyalty to the established order was fundamental in feudal life, but if feudal life limited opportunity for self-advancement, it provided the attainable maximum of social security.

Security went down the line until one reached the aged cripple whose little hut was on the edge of the acorn forest, by the old thorn hedge. His kettle hung on the pothook and there were a few faggots by his blackened fireplace. His cupboard contained a crock, a basket, and some wooden dishes, and a few half despairing vegetables limped beside his door. Everyone was in debt to him: the liege lord and his young retainers owed him their bravery, for him the stout young men of the fief loyally did their annual forty days of military service, he was the constant object of generosity, and the good of heart of every rank treated him with that consideration and kindness which are the heart of courtesy and chivalry. The picture is idealized, of course, but the Middle Ages did take charity very seriously, and medieval charity was direct and unorganized. The well-ordered fief considered poverty part of the will of God, but it also considered the relief of poverty part of the will of God.

There was, then, in medieval feudal society an interdependence greater than existed in the ancient world and greater than is to be found anywhere in the modern world except in the old-fashioned and isolated village. Yet paradoxically at the very heart of that interdependence lay an individualism quite unknown in antiquity and destined to be gradually obscured in the Renaissance until it emerged again in a secular form during the Enlightenment. Beyond the virtues which the Middle Ages extolled lay the object of those virtues, eternal salvation. Each dweller in the fief should make his contribution to its welfare loyally and honestly, but the object of his final concern was not the fief but his own soul. One did the duties of one's station in life, whether one was liege lord, falconer, plowman, or aged cripple by the thorn hedge, in the immediate sense for the welfare of the fief but in the final sense for one's eternal welfare. Liege lord and falconer, plowman and cripple are born alone, merit salvation alone, and die alone. Everyone in the fief knew that and believed its every implication. Hence in the austerely regimented society of the fief, where opportunity for material advancement was minimized but social security exalted to a prime objective, where each person had his appointed place and each place its appointed duties, there was an individualism that surpassed any freedom of which the Greek or Roman citizen dreamed. Beyond the love of one's fellow man which cemented the fief was the love of God. The good life of the fief was led in the love of God and the contempt of self, and the heavenly city and not the city of man was its objective. The medieval fief had much of the unity and integration of parts that marked the ancient city, but its unity rested on an individualism of purpose that made it profoundly different. When we come to the town, however, we find along with the individualism of spiritual purpose an individualism of secular purpose with implications pregnant for the future. Let us leave the castle high on the rock crag and go down to the town at its base. The castle will protect the town until the day dawns when the town will conquer the castle.

4.

The Town

A YOUNG man stirs uneasily on his pallet and gropes mentally for a way out of the depths of sleep. Consciousness slowly filters in, spurred by a dim awareness of something very important but not yet identified. Then consciousness bursts open, and a surge of exultation fills the young man. He knows what it is, and why this is no ordinary awakening on an ordinary day. This is the day when, he hopes, he will cease to be a journeyman in his craft and become a master. For his seven years of late boyhood he had been an apprentice, living with his master, serving his needs and often his whims, and the needs and whims of his not always serene and placid spouse, but learning his craft as well and as thoroughly as a fundamentally honest master could teach it. Presumably his manners and his morals had been similarly moulded by the master and his spouse, as the contract required. He had worked five years as a journeyman, still living with the master, still serving needs and whims, but pocketing his day's wages and putting as much of them away as he conceivably could for the glorious day when he would be his own master, have his own shop, and operate his own business within the framework of his guild. This was the day of his examination by the guild, the day when he was to present that masterpiece (as he hopefully deemed it) on which he had lavished hours before dawn and after dark, the day when, if all went well, he would take the solemn oath to live by the regulations of the guild and meet his obligations as a guild member, and so emerge into this great, bright, burgeoning, challenging, but in all candor frightening world of the new towns. There was in that world something new, unplumbed, certainly unproven, and immensely alluring. Later generations which knew its nature better would call it personal freedom.

It was this that the young man's father had sought when he left the fief under circumstances into which it was not considered prudent to probe. In any case, the older man had made his way from the fief to the new town that had taken root at the foot of the monastery hill and he had managed to stay there for the year and the day which meant that henceforth he was a free man absolved from serfdom. He was somewhat too old for his freedom to mean opportunity, but the two sons who were born to him by the marriage he contracted in the town might enjoy them both. His older son was doing so already. He had become a clerk, received confirmation and the tonsure after demonstrating his ability to read and write, and suddenly a wide world had opened before him. He chose the priesthood and already held a modest benefice and, more important, the benign approval of the bishop. In theory he might become Pope; in practice he might match Suger, that son of a peasant who became a clerk and school fellow of the future Louis VI of France and later Abbot of St. Denis and confidant of two kings. On the other hand, he might have chosen the secular path. The universities were open to him and beyond them, the learned professions. He might have become a notary, a physician, a doctor of canon law; or, if his vein of talent proved thin, he might at least have been a schoolmaster and a writer of deeds and letters for the unlettered laity. Men went from the fief to the town in the Middle Ages as men went from the Old World to the New in the nineteenth century. Often the opportunity was not for themselves but for their children, but the move made opportunity possible.

The younger son, however, set his mind on trade, did his apprenticeship, worked his years as a journeyman, and this morning stood on the threshold of achievement. He was thoroughly aware of the rigid framework within which achievement would be circumscribed. As a guildsman he would have to accept a guild control which made his freedom something relative only to the position of his ancestors on the fief, not to the position of his descendants in the trades. He would have to obey guild regulations as they pertained to working hours and wages, size of working staff, prices charged, and rate of profit. He would have to accept something analogous to the "most favored nation" concept of later ages; he would have to share with all his fellow guildsmen any purchase more advantageous than the ordinary he might make. He could improve his manufacturing methods and indeed was urged to do so, but in the ointment was a large and sticky fly. He must share all such improvements with his fellow guildsmen. He must accept a system that rigidly controlled every step in production and distribution and do so on the thesis that all guildsmen must share in equal ratio in the prosperity of the guild. He was part of an iron monopoly, a sharer in the benefits of monopoly but subject to the controls of monopoly. He could have opportunity and prosperity, subject to the condition that opportunity and prosperity be alike for all brethren in the craft. And yet, toward the journeymen who would live with him in the years to come when his position as a master and his success in the craft were assured, toward the apprentices who would learn from him and serve his needs and whims, toward the workmen to whom he would pay the designated wage for the appointed hours of work, he would be like a liege lord in that little fief of his which occupied the first floor of the house in which he lived, a liege lord in Lilliput but remotely the ancestor of the capitalist to come. But he, emphatically, was not a capitalist himself.

He could look back, of course, and see from what he had arisen. Had he lived the life of his fathers he too would be subject to the immemorial sequence of the seasons, living close to the rich earth and doing the hard labor the rich earth demands before it looses its riches. Instead he had his substantial and respected share in the active, vibrant life in the new town at the base of the monastery hill, a town so growing that in a gradual and subtle way it was ceasing to be the town of the monastery and the edifice high above was becoming the monastery of the town. It was an active, vibrant life in the town, and one of rich variety. In the center was the public square, in the center of the public square was the public fountain, and that stream which flowed decorously, since it was still the Middle Ages and the Renaissance had not yet let its pagan sense of humor loose on public fountains, might be deemed symbolically the life blood of the town. The square was jammed with people; shop keepers screamed their wares through opened shutters; street hawkers braced themselves before the shutters and screamed in competition. Beggars flicked their cups beneath the defensively glazed eyes of passers-by, and with a mad unawareness of man and beast frenzied football players booted balls from one end of the town to the other, bowling over pedestrians and carts in their careening course. The politicians of the town erupted oratorical lava at the angular corners where narrow, irregular, unpaved streets that lifted and dipped with the contour of the ground came together momentarily and parted. A medieval town was as crowded as the castle itself, as well it might be considering what went into its making. First, the burghers had to dig a moat around their town site. It might be dry or it might be wet, but it had to be deep. Then they built a wall within the moat, with towers perhaps as close together as three hundred feet. These were for protection against attack, of course, but they did double duty as granaries and stables. There was the inevitable street-within-the-wall, which ran around the town just inside the wall and gave quick access to any part of it. At intervals there were drawbridges across the moat and gates in the wall. The town streets were seldom more than ten feet wide and were laid out on the principle of contour plowing; houses were end-jammed the length of the street and had projecting upper storeys, which gave the street the suggestion of a tunnel and most of its darkness. All refuse went into the street, with municipal sanitary services provided by pigs, dogs, and rain. Water came from rivers and wells, both contaminated. One boarded windows and bolted doors at night, and hoped for the best. Since almost all building was of wood, fires were extremely common and there was no fire protection except agility in escape. There was no escaping plagues. And yet it was a full life that was lived in the towns, far more varied than the supervisory rounds and the repetitious field sports of the liege lord of the castle, and infinitely more varied than the earth-rooted life of the serf who had security of a sort at a price which made the townsman shudder.

There was security of a substantial sort, however, for members of the guilds and their families against those ills for which medieval society was able to provide a cushion. It could not protect the townsfolk against plague and fire, the twin perils that always were on hand to remind man of his mortality. But it could and did take care of those bereft of father and husband by the plague, or bereft of house and home by fire. The guild took care of the sick and aged of its company and often assumed the debts of a member whose indebtedness was due to misfortune. The more responsible guilds had an awareness that there was also a public to be protected and elected guild wardens for the purpose. In this regard human frailty showed itself, with millers, bakers, and brewers notorious for the vigorous nature of their human frailty. But at least in theory, and to a substantial degree in practice, the responsible guilds looked out for the public as well. Always operating within a framework vulnerable to disease, warfare, and natural disaster, the guilds did much to keep production under control, employment on a steady keel, speculation at a minimum, and individual aggrandizement under check. Nor did the guilds ever lose sight of the fact that from the viewpoint of the Middle Ages, every human association is an association in the name of the Lord. The members of the guilds prayed together, celebrated feast days together, and in a way possible at no time in human history but the Middle Ages fused religion and frivolity in the miracle and mystery plays that were carted from corner to corner about the town. Our young journeyman turned master was entering a company very much more varied in its composition and more comprehensive in its purpose, and vastly more philosophic in its justification for existence than a modern chamber of commerce or labor union.

And yet, that morning as he awaited his impending elevation to the exalted state of master, there were also in his mind speculations that were destined ultimately to destroy the thing on which he had set his heart. Why should a master be limited in the exercise of his initiative and enterprise by the need for carrying on his economic back his fellow guildsman of limited initiative and enterprise? Why should the ideal be a dead level of achievement, and not the limit that the individual could achieve? Why should a master not be allowed to hire as many workers as his business might require, and pay them the wages for which he could get them to work? Why isn't justice as high an ideal as charity, and isn't it justice that a man reap the full crop that he has sowed? What is wrong with borrowing money to expand a business and paying interest for the hiring of the money? Isn't there a risk involved for the money lender, and isn't a risk worthy of its reward? Even as he aspired to be a master he vaguely dreamed of something beyond the status of a master, a state for which no name had yet been coined, for the state itself hardly existed. We call it capitalism.

The great weakness of the feudal system was its failure to provide a workable relationship among equals. The vertical pattern of the fief was exemplary, once one accepts the axioms on which medieval life rested, but there was no horizontal pattern among fiefs. The result was endemic private wars, and nations that were not yet nations and hardly peoples were endlessly harried by marauding bands. Inevitably the idea of contract and mutual relationship on which feudalism depended had to give way to monarchical supremacy. In a fashion not entirely different the guild system inevitably collapsed once it attempted interregional and international trade. The very limitation the guild system imposed on the economic growth of the individual made impossible his venturing into broader trade relationships than those of his town. No individual guildsman was economically strong enough for such ventures. Hence partnerships and stock companies began to appear. In theory their role was foreign trade, but in effect they tended to dominate all manufacture and trade. The older concept of mutuality in the guilds withered away, and guildsmen of lesser initiative and enterprise slipped back into the ranks of the wage earners. The guildsman slowly passed into history, and the industrialist and capitalist gradually emerged into history. The guild became the corporation, and the aristocracy of the castle was rivalled by the aristocracy of the city. The old sense of guild responsibility for the aged and the sick, the victims of tragic misfortune in whatever form, the old concept that every association is in the name of the Lord and ultimately is dedicated to His work, slowly faded and was forgotten. The new aristocrats were not without the spirit of charity: they built churches and endowed hospitals, they erected architectual jewels like the city hall at Bruges and they made the great factory town of northern Italy, Florence, the world's greatest treasure house of the arts. But they cut wages, extended working hours, widened the gap between the merchant prince and man, and stood their ground against the ground surge of the Lollards and the Fratricelli, against John Ball, Wat Tyler, and the rest. Industrial Florence seethed with discontent, Paris with radicalism, and even the stolid burghers of the Low Countries muttered darkly and peasants sharpened scythes, but they held their ground. That morning, as he awaited his elevation to the state of master, that young son of a runaway serf who took the secular road which his older brother chose not to tread, dreamed the dreams that would end the Middle Ages. Once the town surpassed the castle in importance, once the monastery and the cathedral became landmarks of the town, the Middle Ages were over.

And yet, in many ways the towns of the Middle Ages were dedicated to the good life as the Middle Ages understood it. Some towns had survived from Roman days; more towns were new towns, settlements that formed naturally at the base of monastery hill or under the shadow of the castle, or perhaps by the ford or the bridge, if there was a bridge. The people worked in workshops and not on farms, and their relationship to the liege lord of the castle, the abbot of the monastery, or the vassal on whose fief was the ford or bridge could not be the relationship of the field worker. The fundamental difference was that the townsfolk comprised a community and therefore had a communal relationship with the lord or the abbot. A corollary to this relationship was the need for self-government both for the proper management of their communal affairs and for proper representation in communal dealings with the liege lord. The townsman was as truly an individual as the serf, but collectively the serfs were a mob whereas the townsmen were a town. The medieval town and its sub-divisions the medieval guilds, just as long as they were truly medieval, continued to be confraternities. The interrelationships among the town dwellers were not nearly so close as the interrelationships among the dwellers in the monastery, or indeed in the castle or on the fief, but it was far closer than it has been at any subsequent stage in human history. The dwellers in the towns still worked and prayed as communities, and each man was indeed his brother's keeper and knew it as a solemn obligation. Self-sacrifice and service to one's fellow man lay at the heart of the good life, in the town as truly as in the monastery or the castle, and always for the glory of God and the salvation of one's soul. No matter how far medieval man strayed from the ideal, be it as renegade priest, tyrannical lord, false vassal, or thieving guildsman, he always knew what the ideal was from which he strayed. The medieval ideal, and therefore the foundation of that profound individualism which lies beneath all the corporate organization and activity of the Middle Ages, was not an ideal of this world. The ideal was not the flaming rebel against authority, the all-conquering hero, the born leader of men, or the merchant prince of incalculable wealth, as it is in periods both more secular and more romantic. The ideal was that ultimate individualist whose entire set of values is of another world and in whose eyes the ultimate reality is hereafter and not here. The ultimate model of the good life to the Middle Ages was the saint. Unless it is understood that a man's position in the heavenly hierarchy was the objective of his life on earth, very little in the earthly hierarchy of the Middle Ages makes sense. It was not one's position here on earth, in the Church Militant, that mattered. It was one's position ultimately, in heaven, in the Church Triumphant.

5.

The Saint

THE key that really unlocks the medieval concept of the good life is itself one of the most profound and comprehensive concepts in the history of human thought, the concept of the great chain of being. The great chain of being holds together all life, from the throne of God and Father to the last and least of God's worms that wriggle in the dust. All of the celestial hierarchy have their proper places in it, and all the hierarchy of earthly states as well. The least saint in the most modest place in heaven is higher on the great chain of being than the mightiest king on earth. A saint may have been a serf in his earthly state, a slave in the galleys, a beggar in the dust, but in heaven Lazarus is exalted and Dives is cast down. Every man, woman, and child was created to be a saint; to win immortal salvation is his appointed destiny, which he must gloriously fulfill or fail in a tragedy that surpasses understanding. But the saint who now sees the beatific vision of Omnipotence, yesterday was a human being, perhaps a king, perhaps a serf, perhaps a beggar, perhaps a bishop. There are two totally different hierarchies, one temporal and earthly, one eternal and heavenly. Now, when we see things darkly as in a glass, our position in the earthly hierarchy may seem important. If we become too preoccupied with it, we become denizens of the earthly city,

68

led blindly through love of self into the contempt of God. It is our position in the heavenly hierarchy that matters, and it depends totally on the lives we live on earth and is absolutely without relationship to the positions we occupy on earth. If we concentrate on that vision, we are led through contempt of self into the love of God.

That is what men believed in the Age of Faith. Some acted fully upon their beliefs and upon their passing were canonized as saints. Most acted upon their beliefs by the wavering and uncertain measure of human frailty. Many were satisfied with the earthly city and the temporal delights that it offered. Very few indeed denied the reality of the two hierarchies. It was the Age of Faith not only for those who acted upon their faith but also for those who failed to do so. By and large people in the Middle Ages sinned with gusto, but repented with fervor; there were very few medieval modernists to consider sin a lack of courtesy, or something to be explained away by philosophy. Very few denied the three essential differences between the two hierarchies: that one is earthly and the other heavenly, that one is temporal and the other eternal, that a man is born to his position in one but that he earns his position in the other. The eternal rank of the king is in precise relationship to the earthly life the king has led, and the same is true of the serf, the beggar, and the bishop. The king is born alone, works out his eternal destiny alone, dies alone, and enters eternity alone. So do the serf, the beggar, and the bishop. Beyond this no further individualism is possible.

There is, then, nothing inconsistent in the caste system of the Middle Ages and the individualism which was its secure foundation. In the Middle Ages one was born to a role in life. The Almighty might call a man to Monte Cassino or to the Portiuncula, or with less historic distinction to any abbey, convent, cathedral, or village church in Christendom. He had those above him and as time went on, perhaps those beneath him. He had a set of duties toward both, and a treasury of rights that both should respect. He might move to a post of greater responsibility in his community, or he might not. He accepted as part of the divinely created order the duties and the rights

appropriate to whatever position in life he occupied. The hierarchy of those little microcosms, the monastery and the convent, had that strange sort of security that only transiency
gives: tomorrow it would pass away, and each monk, each
friar, each nun would have the rank in Heaven that his life in
his earthly rank had earned him. The Pope, perhaps, would
look up for eternity in wonder, love, and awe at the little
novice who died just before she took her vows. That same
acceptance of the earthly rank to which one was born, an
acceptance made easy by a steady awareness of its transiency,
prevailed in the castle and throughout the fief. There was no
reason that philosophy could justify for which one would not
accept the position in life which birth had given him, however
much flesh and blood might rebel against philosophy. No conqueror of the earth had a more towering ambition than that of
the serf in the Age of Faith, since his ambition was to storm
the ramparts of Heaven. It is then only an apparent paradox
that the period in the history of western civilization in which
people seem to have been most thoroughly disciplined by the
codes of society into working together in integrated harmony
really rested upon a spiritual individualism. Beyond the spiritual democracy of the Middle Ages no further democracy is
possible.

The entire message of medieval art concerns the great chain
of being and man's eternal destiny. Every Gothic church was
a great book in which the unlettered could read of the great
chain of being, of God, His angels and saints, of man and
man's destiny in eternity after his trial on earth. The final
symbol of the Christian faith is the cross. The Gothic church
is a great cross laid flat upon the earth, the sanctuary where
the head of Christ drooped in agony, the choir where His
lacerated arms and dripping hands were stretched, the nave
where His tortured body tensed and strained. Under all its
glory, the magnificence of its architecture, the splendor of its
sculpture, the "frozen music" of the Gothic cathedral is that
final Christian fact, the cross. Every picture, statue, segment
of stained glass, every last detail of the uncounted myriads of
details that make a great cathedral—there are said to be over

6000 painted and sculptured figures in the cathedral at Chartres—tells its own part of the story of time and eternity, of sin, redemption, and salvation. They all rest, as the cathedral itself rests, upon the cross.

Between man on earth, however, and Christ on the cross are links that no man can number in the great chain of being. Medieval man sought by instinct, as man always seeks by instinct, for someone above him and yet not entirely beyond his reach who would act for him as intercessor. The saint in Heaven once was as he now is, although doubtless stronger in the faith and vastly more confirmed in virtue. The saint has achieved the destiny for which he was created; with all allowance for the span between time and eternity, the saint is just above him in the great chain of being. He turns by instinct to the saint as intercessor, and one can observe time and eternity fusing as medieval art progresses. The saints cease to be angular ikons and become ordinary Frenchmen and Germans, English ladies, Flemish matrons, and Spanish duennas. Even the background becomes the familiar background of the painter's own country. Behind St. Anne's garden are the towers of Tours and the Holy Family travels to Egypt up a familiar French river. Indeed saints and mortals appear side by side in later medieval paintings, patron saint and supplicating mortal to be sure, but the scale is the same.

The entire process of intercession proceeds with proper awareness of the celestial hierarchy and relative positions on the great chain of being. The innkeeper, the problems of whose trade are never light, beseeches St. Julian for his assistance. St. Julian, to whom all innkeepers however errant are wards, beseeches the Virgin Mary. Mary intercedes with her divine Son, Christ pleads with God the Father, and God the Father wills the welfare of the innkeeper and his inn. There was vertical order in the medieval castle and town, and there is vertical order in the heavenly host. It would little beseem an innkeeper, one of a sinful class as all know, to beseech even a major saint, but God with His infinite awareness of the hierarchy of creation has given to the keepers of inns St. Julian, as one properly aware of their needs and a saint accessible to their prayers.

And so the innkeeper prays to St. Julian as the wool comber does to St. Blaise (his attention to sore throats is a different matter entirely), or the shoemaker to St. Crispin. These saints are close enough to ordinary mortals in the great chain of being to be accessible to their prayers. Sometimes those insensitive to matters of relative rank deem the proliferation of local saints superstitious if not idolatrous. One should not confuse ordinary modesty and propriety with superstition and idolatry. But neither should one be oblivious to the fact that the person who obeys the law of God by a life of ordinary modesty and propriety based on the law of God as expounded through the moral teachings of the Church will himself after death be a saint. The medieval innkeeper knew that however tenuous and extended the link between St. Julian and himself, it was a link in the great chain of being and it existed to help him merit eternal life.

6.

The Final Definition

CLEARLY the medieval concept of the good life and the ancient concept had very much in common. In neither case was the good life the prosperous life, although in neither age was the prosperous life held in contempt. The goal of life as man conceived it in the Middle Ages, however, gave to earthly prosperity implications absent from ancient thought. Worldly prosperity is certainly not inconsistent with good citizenship, but it certainly can be a distraction from personal sanctity. The Franciscans renounced worldly prosperity utterly and the Benedictines in large measure, and the other religious orders in varying degrees including totality, but obviously the Church in general did not renounce it, nor did the laity. There was always an uneasy feeling in the Middle Ages, however, that too much worldly prosperity is a bar to sanctity, and the vigorous efforts of the guilds to equalize the prosperity of their members is evidence to the fear that too much prosperity may be bad for the individual spirit as well as for the body politic.

Aristotle placed a much higher premium on family relationships than did Plato, but he did not think of them as comprising the good life. Family relationships were meticulously observed, the duties associated with them painstakingly performed, and the family unit as the foundation of society itself entirely unquestioned by right thinking and right living people

73

in the Middle Ages. The careful performance of every duty implicit in the family relationship was deemed a necessary part of virtue by medieval man, but all that the family implied in the human sense, all its rich rewards and enduring happiness were by-products of what made for the good life and not the good life itself.

To the ancients the good life was not the life of artistic creativity or aesthetic enjoyment of the arts. The unsurpassed achievements of the ancients in the arts in no way nullifies this fact. The same statement can be made with equal truth about the Middle Ages. It is one of the major glories of the Middle Ages that they could keep in perfect perspective the magnificence of their churchly architecture and the fact that it was a means to an end. The cathedral is a cross, Chartres, Rheims, Cologne, and all the rest. The cathedral of Seville is so massive and magnificent that its builders deserved their splendid boast that later generations would deem them mad for having attempted it, but the cathedral of Seville is ultimately reducible to what in the medieval view gave it its importance, two crossed sticks of wood. Medieval man rejoiced in artistic creativity and aesthetic enjoyment, but did not consider them the good life. For the aesthete we must wait until the Renaissance.

The fundamental difference between the ancient and the medieval concept of the good life is the fact that the classical ideal did not rest upon religious convictions and the medieval ideal did. The goal of the classical ideal of the good life is in this world, the goal of the medieval ideal is in the next. Hence we can echo until its last phrase the ancient ideal of the good life and hold it valid for the medieval ideal, but the last phrase must be profoundly different: the good life is the life of virtue in which the mind directs the body, values are accepted in their proper scale, the lower self is sacrificed for the sake of the higher self, and man fulfills himself in the highest degree when he gives what is finest in himself to the service—not of his city but of his God. The ideal of medieval man is not the citizen but the saint.

Beneath all the corporate organization of medieval life was the fundamental individualism which arose from that fact. One was born into a position in the worldly hierarchy, but one achieved his own position in the heavenly hierarchy. The serf humbly tending the hogs as they rooted in the acorn forest, humbly accepting his lot in life since that was the lot the Almighty ordained for him, totally without what later ages conceived of as ambition and the urge for self-advancement, might consciously and energetically entertain an ambition to dwarf the ambition of Alexander. Alexander might have sighed over the lands beyond the Ganges as yet unconquered, but the serf had a vision of the lands beyond the four rivers of Paradise. Self-sacrifice, devotion to duty, proper regard for the welfare of one's fellow man, the concept that the higher one's status in life the more peremptory the call to service, the belief that there is a divinely created moral order and one has an inescapable duty to obey it, all these convictions about the good life the Middle Ages shared with the classical antiquity from which they had drawn so much of their intellectual sustenance. But the goal was different. Once the goal ceased to be the city of man and became the city of God, the ideal of the good life ceased to be a corporate one and became individual. The classical ideal was secular, the medieval ideal religious. The destiny of the citizen is achieved in society, but the destiny of the saint is achieved in solitude. Medieval man, rooted in the soil of the fief, fixed to his station in the castle, pledged to the limitations of his guild, really walked toward his destiny alone.

PART THREE

THE PRINCE

The first Renaissance form of the good life we are to examine is that of the gentleman, the courtier, the governor. The term changes with the viewpoint from which one examines the pattern of living, and one might add whether the pattern be English, Italian, French, or something else. One is a gentleman in attendance on the prince, a courtier in his service, a governor of a portion of his realm. Hence arises the necessity of understanding at the outset the Renaissance concept of the prince and the basis for the absolutism which he assumed or which society accorded to him.

To aid us to this understanding the Englishman Sir Thomas Elyot is much better than either of the far more justly celebrated Italians, sardonic Machiavelli or graceful Castiglione. Elyot is better than they, partly because he is less subtle and therefore more direct, but also because when we reach the Renaissance we reach a parting of the geographic ways. No doubt in the philosophic and therefore inevitably abstract sense, the good life was the same in the Renaissance throughout Europe and the newly opened lands across the Atlantic. If one's approach were philosophic and abstract, one could perhaps write about it in terms generally valid for western man. But at the Renaissance the fortifying unity of life which marked the Middle Ages was fragmented and increasingly diversified, and the concrete and descriptive approach must either be limited geographically, became encyclopedic, or—and this is most likely—became bewilderingly complex. Therefore we shall increasingly limit our consideration of the good life to the ways in which people lived it in the English-speaking world, with full awareness that people lived it at least as well elsewhere, with the proviso that we may turn to foreign patterns when the situation warrants, and with the consolation that in the philosophic and abstract sense one can really "see all the world in Concord."

Among the grave and learned men who made that transition from the old to the new at which the young and inexperienced are so dangerously facile and the grave and learned so wary, Sir Thomas Elyot is always named with high respect. He was born into the old order in its last days, born to the west country gentlefolk of Wiltshire in 1490. He learned the new humanism at the "school" of St. Thomas More, where he certainly met Linacre and Colet, probably Erasmus, and not impossibly Holbein. For fifteen years he was Clerk to the Justices of Assize for the Western Circuit, became Chief Clerk of the King's Council shortly after Cardinal Wolsey rose, and then fell when Cardinal Wolsey fell. It is a fate the grave and learned not infrequently suffer, and he rose above it as Milton was to rise above it or, for that matter, as Magnus Aurelius Cassiodorus had risen above it. He retired to obscurity and immortality, a modest immortality perhaps but a secure one. He went to his manor house at Carlton, near Cambridge, and wrote The Book Named the Governor. *This book, more clearly than any other in English literature, lays down the rules for the good life in the upper classes of the Renaissance.*

What marked Elyot apart from the other humanists and made him rather than they the man of the immediate future was the way in which he emphasized the absolute nature of the prince's

78

power. Aristotle might hold that the worst form government can take is that corruption of monarchy called tyranny. With his usual violence of expression Erasmus spoke for his generation of humanists when he called a tyrant "a frightful, loathsome beast, formed of a dragon, wolf, lion, viper, bear, and like creatures, with six hundred eyes all over it." St. Thomas More died rather than affirm that the prince is absolute in every realm of human life and action. But Elyot was not of their mind. His polity has the simple directness of Edmund Spenser, who assured us in his Faerie Queene *that absolutism is natural and part of the will of God:*

> The hils doe not the lowly dales disdaine;
> The dales doe not the lofty hils envy.
> He maketh Kings to sit in soverainty;
> He maketh subjects to their powre obay.

It is that simple, and that inescapable.

But why? Why did Elyot in his generation, like Spenser and the rest in generations to come, turn his back on Aristotle and the Greeks, on St. Thomas Aquinas and the Middle Ages, on humanism and the fathers of the Renaissance, and conceive of society as a hierarchical pyramid with the king alone at its apex? The best way to grasp their pattern of thinking is by the analogy of the Catholic and therefore the medieval concept of the Pope. The Pope is at once the visible head of the Church, and as such entirely human in his attributes and powers, and the earthly vicar of Christ. But in the second capacity he is not to the believer entirely human in his attributes and powers, since he is vicar for One supernatural and eternal. He may make mistake after catastrophic mistake in the first capacity, but he is infallible in the second. The obvious necessity is to define and limit the two capacities and to indicate how the Pope must function in the second. This task we may leave to the theologians, but the analogy is available to us. The prince also fills a double role. He is an earthly ruler, and as such entirely human and fallible, but he is also the embodiment of the nation. Just as the Pope speaking in Council on matters of faith and morals speaks as Christ's vicar, so the king of England in council with the lords and com-

79

mons speaks as the highest authority in the realm, from whom there is no appeal. Just as the Church headed by Christ's vicar is the mystical body of Christ, so is the king in conjunction with Parliament the mystical body of England. Just as it is ultimately the Pope who speaks for the mystical body of Christ with the voice of Christ's infallibility, since infallibility can have but a single voice, so ultimately it is the King who speaks with infallibility for the mystical body of England. The power is one the Pope rarely uses, and then in conjunction with the Council to confirm the faith and purify the morals of the people. So in the plea of Elyot and all who accepted the rationale of Tudor absolutism must the power be one that the King would rarely use, and then in conjunction with Parliament for the welfare of the people. Such an absolute sovereign, who in theory is no more a tyrant than is the Pope, would need lesser governors or magistrates to aid him, and their training and their lives are Elyot's concern. But once the role of the nobleman has changed from ruler of the fief to assistant to the prince, he has ceased to be a knight and has become a gentleman, a courtier, a governor. The Middle Ages have ended and the medieval concepts of the good life have passed away. To the Renaissance concept of the good life for the ruling class we may now address ourselves.

1.

The Great House

SIR EDMUND LATIMER was not of the older nobility. Behind
him was a long and honorable line of country gentry, but
nothing higher. For reasons that one can determine most pleasantly and profitably by reading Shakespeare's history plays,
Henry VII, the first of the Tudors, had a vigorous and firmly
grounded suspicion of the older nobility. He found his natural
support in the lower landed aristocracy, and favored the country gentry for appointment to high office. Sir Edmund's grandfather had been so favored.

England was now in the complete sense a kingdom and
therefore the protection of the realm was the responsibility of
the Tudor on the throne and not the baron in the fief. Therefore the castle of the medieval knight became the palace of the
Renaissance governor, and the great house came into being.
Its ancestry showed itself. The turrets and battlements were
still there, now to add beauty to the building and not strength.
The moat and the drawbridge had disappeared, but the stately
wall remained and within it the formal gardens and the terrace.
The windows now were larger, to let in light and air, a prosaic
and obvious comment were it not that in the days of the fief
they were slits through which one shot arrows. The great
chamber still remained and was used on occasions of high

81

ceremony, but it was no longer the general living room that it had been in medieval days. The casual sleeping arrangements of the Middle Ages, with beds for the baron and his family, some cots or pallets for the maids, and whatever chance might offer in the great hall for the grooms, had given way to separate sleeping quarters for the family and the servants on opposite sides of the great hall. From this arrangement there gradually developed the H and E-shaped structures characteristic of the great houses built under Henry VIII and Elizabeth. The patriotic impulse behind an H-shaped house or an E-shaped house speaks for itself and for the gratitude of the new nobility, and gives a clue to the period of erection.

Sir Edmund had a great pride in his great house, and a modest comfort. There was, for example, the matter of the great hall. In the days of the baron and the fief, the family were all who lived within the castle walls and the family gathered for the evening hours of relaxation in this massive and cavernous family room. But by Sir Edmund's time the family was much more nearly what it is today and the great house had built into it the paradox that people would huddle together for companionship, and indeed for warmth, in one of its quiet and obscure corners. The great hall remained in the form of a massive vestibule and gallery, where people might gather in great numbers on occasions of high ceremony to dance or hear the music, and then break into smaller groups to admire the paintings and the tapestries. The great house was partly a home and partly a museum, but it was no longer a fort. It was the wonder and bewildered admiration of continentals who now found in England something to rival Florence and, to the more censorious, to suggest Babylon. The royal palace existed to symbolize the glorious realm of England, the glorious person of England's sovereign, the glorious pomp and circumstance that invested her office. Out of this cult of glorious sovereignty grew the great houses of England, houses worthy of their sovereign Queen whose entertainment was their highest reason for existence. It was glorious, and a bit naïve. The age of Shakespeare was simultaneously rich and *nouveau riche*.

Between the pattern of Sir Edmund's daily life and the pattern of the medieval baron whom Sir Edmund thought of with biological inaccuracy as his ancestor the differences were not profound. The statement that life in the Renaissance was very different from life in the Middle Ages has the misleading sort of truth present in statements made with insufficiently defined terms. The philosophy of life in the Renaissance was in important respects very different from the philosophy of life in the Middle Ages, but upper class life itself was not very different. It was to a limited degree more comfortable, to a great degree more luxurious, to a very great degree more ostentatious. Sir Edmund slept with his lady on a lattice work of criss-crossed ropes, but they slept between fine linen sheets and had woolen blankets above them. They also bathed in a wooden tub before the fireplace in the chamber, but their soap was scented and rose leaves were crushed in the water. They breakfasted on beef, bread, and beer, but their table linen was of fine quality and the cook carefully edged the bread into soft, neat squares before serving it. Their dinner had an even more amazingly wide and varied range of dishes than the baron's, but it still was served between ten and twelve in the morning and guests brought their own knives. The wide and varied range of dishes set before Sir Edmund and his guests no more implied in them gluttony or the capacity of Gargantua than the comparable range does in a modern restaurant. The family and guests ate what they chose, and what was left descended in adequate amounts but diminishing variety through the several strata of servants. The eternal corned beef of the Middle Ages, varied with an occasional blessed haunch of venison, by no means passed away with the castle and the fief, but it was more often varied with game and more venison. Dessert for Sir Edmund and his lady was what it still is in England: fruit pie, a tart, in season strawberries and cream.

The dress of Sir Edmund and his lady was amazingly elaborate, as the most bedraggled modern production of Shakespeare in period costume at least sugests. For Sir Edmund, stuffed doublets and great breeches in the most vivid of primary colors with two and even three piled ruffs were the rule, while his lady floated along in the majestic Elizabethan hoopskirt, the farthingale. The elegance was literally skin-deep; beneath was no underwear, although milord did have on his shirt and milady her linen smock. In cold weather he put a jerkin over his doublet and she put a long gown over her dress. Sir Edmund's father had reached a grave and revered age, and so he put a long gown over his doublet and then was like "the dawn in russet mantle clad." As for cleanliness, Sir Edmund and his lady bathed regularly. The nature of their garments posed obvious and grave cleaning problems, but strong perfumes were abundant. In general the great houses of merrie England varied from very clean to very dirty, much as houses do today.

What is very noteworthy about Sir Edmund and his life is a simple fact that in other ages would be a puzzling paradox, the bland combination of virility and luxury. Shakespeare's *The Taming of the Shrew* opens with a practical joke being played on a very drunken tinker named Christopher Sly. He is borne in a comatose state to a great house where the lords will treat him as if he were a nobleman recovering his sanity after years of madness. The instructions to the servants are illuminating. He is to be carried to the lord's finest chamber which is to be hung with the lord's "wanton pictures," scenes from mythology's more titillating pages done in the new Italian manner. Incense is to be burned to make the chamber sweet. He is to be awakened by music, his face washed with scented water, and a basin of rose water with flowers floating on it brought that he may wash his hands. A choice of fine apparel will be offered him, and there will be talk of his horse, his hounds, and his lady, as "twenty caged nightingales do sing." There is ample evidence that the picture is not over-painted. Elizabethan noblemen who sailed the Spanish Main, fought in the muck and mire of the Low Countries, took their stern and fearsome turn on fog-swathed nights in Ireland, and had hot rapiers by their sides at home, lived in ways that recall Suetonius, the more lurid days of imperial Rome, and matters hardly hinted at in the older sort of ancient history textbook. Probably again the best explanation is the *nouveau riche* atmosphere of upper class life in an England that suddenly had become an empire, an opulence with innocence as its saving heart, an attempt at Italian *grazia* that would have brought quickly rolling eyeballs and a fleeting smile to a meticulously disciplined Italian face.

There was a difference between the good life of the Italian courtier and the good life of the English governor, but the basis of the difference was only in part the difference between Italy and England. It was basically the difference between a land of cities like Italy and a unified kingdom like England. Sir Edmund was not part of a city political machine, like Philo or like the typical Italian courtier. He was an independent administrator in his own right. His father had been a Justice of the Peace; with a greater sacrifice of his own peace and comfort, he was a High Sheriff. Sir Edmund and men like him in similar positions were the civil governing class of England, but they were not bureaucrats since no bureaus governed their actions. Sir Edmund assumed as the natural burden of his station in life the administrative and judicial responsibility for his section of the realm implicit in his title of High Sheriff. He was a wealthy man and he enjoyed every comfort and every pomp that an age sparse in comfort by modern standards but lavish in ostentation could afford. He was a showy figure, but there was solid substance beneath the show, just as there was solid substance beneath the aesthetic display of an Italian courtier.

Sir Edmund was born to rule, and he had been meticulously trained to meet his destiny. Many who traveled from the continent to England from the sixteenth into the nineteenth century marveled at what they thought the cruelty of the upper-class English to their children. Sir Edmund had been removed from the family circle when very young, and reared by a Spartan regimen among strangers. As a boy he had been held to a standard of scholarly diligence and personal conduct hardly paralleled across the Channel. Patrician parents of ancient Rome would have understood and approved. He was born to rule, and he was meticulously trained to meet his destiny. He had to be trained in youth to accept responsibility, to curb his emotions by reason, to act with courage but not foolhardiness,

85

to understand what it means to bear responsibility. With due allowance for the moderating effect of the moist air and leaden skies of the British Isles upon the British temperament, Sir Edmund had his social graces but they were no more the final test of the English governor than they were of the Italian courtier. Manners were not the final test, nor was learning, artistic accomplishments, nor certainly fiscal acumen. Sir Edmund was tested by what he contributed to the public weal. The good life of the great house was the life of service. The good life of the nobility and the gentry in the Renaissance was less explicitly founded on religious principles than the good life of the medieval aristocracy, and reliance on human wisdom loomed larger in it than reliance on divine guidance, but it was no less founded on moral principle and no less directed at the public welfare.

The instinct of Sir Edmund Latimer to find in Sir Philip Sidney the great exemplar of the Renaissance ideal was just as sound as the similar American instinct to find the exemplar of the American ideal in Abraham Lincoln. Sidney came from the recently elevated gentry. He had that fine, unabashed love of physical magnificence that betokened the Elizabethan governor and betrayed the *nouveau riche*. His armor was blue and gold and his crest engraved upon it, even his four spare horses were caparisoned with cloth of gold embroidered with pearls and ridden by pages wearing cloth of silver with gold lace, thirty gentlemen and yeomen accompanied him and four trumpeters announced his coming as he approached the ceremonies at which marriage between the Virgin Queen and the Duke of Anjou was to be arranged. He lived far beyond his means, so far that his prospective father-in-law Walsingham had to put up the money that made it possible for him to marry and then to pay his debts after he was killed. But even as he paid the debts he proclaimed them nothing "in respect of the loss of the gentleman who was my chief worldly comfort."

Sidney was one of those rarely gifted persons who somehow epitomize the ideals of the ages in which they live and therefore Sidney was the model of the Sir Edmund Latimers of Renaissance England. No courtier excelled him in grace in

Elizabeth's fiercely competitive court, but no statesman was more disinterested, sincere, and thoughtful in the counsel that he offered. Sidney was the embodiment of what the great houses stood for at their finest, the embodiment of whole-hearted, disinterested service to the land, its Queen, and its people. "His chief ends," said his contemporary biographer Sir Fulke Greville, "were not friends, wife, children, or himself, but above all things the honour of his Maker, and service of his Prince, or country." And so as Sidney lay dying on the battlefield of Zutphen and reached out for the bottle of water being handed to him, and then saw the wounded common soldier yearn for it with parched and anguished eye, he gave the bottle to him with the words, "Thy necessity is yet greater than mine."

That was how those who lived in great houses were supposed to die. That was the price they had to be ready to pay for their good life. Sir Edmund Latimer lived every day of his life with a total awareness of that fact.

2.

The Lady of the House

SIR Edmund had in his manner, and in the reality behind his manner, a touch of the ancient Roman. He was aware of his powers and his pre-eminence, and aware of the authority that birth and breeding gave him, but he was aware as well of the solemn responsibilities and the peremptory duties that birth, breeding, power, and authority carry in their consequence. Edmund Spenser, who certainly expended as much thought on the gentleman of the Renaissance as anyone else and devoted to the subject in his *Faerie Queene* a much richer poetic gift, capped the several virtues of the gentleman with the comprehensive virtue he calls Magnificence. It is the old Aristotelian Magnanimity, with an infusion of Christianity. Sir Edmund had a certain magnificence in his bearing, a magnanimity in his better self, and a sort of uncluttered, muscular Christianity in his way of thinking and acting.

Lady Latimer his wife, on the other hand, was a Christian in a more nearly direct tradition. Chastity, as one might well imagine, was her crowing virtue but other pearls in her diadem were, at least in intent, her piety, patience, long suffering, and self-effacement. Woman is the gentle sex, and women's virtues are the gentle virtues. Her admirers, who were not entirely flatterers in their judgment of her, would add to the pearls already counted her humility, obedience, simplicity, kindness, and benignity. Whether or not she was the total compendium of the virtues which the Renaissance considered indispensible in women and quite dispensible in men, at least she was a serene and placid soul who made straight the path of her lord. In the great house he was the prince, but she was the real governor.

To the Italians who wrote in the tradition of Castiglione's *Courtier,* a pleasantly free and informal relationship between the sexes was considered possible, with the intellectual give and take permitted that sounds so portentous when called Platonic love. It was considered appropriate to spice it with a dash of coquetry. There has always been a bit of jaundice in the English eye as it observes the Italian or the Frenchman about this tricky business of Platonic love, and this was quite true in the Renaissance. "If that thy bent of love be honourable, Thy purpose marriage," says Juliet to Romeo, "send me word tomorrow, By one that I'll procure to come to thee, Where and what time thou wilt perform the rite." That was the way ladies of the Renaissance were supposed to speak, or at least to think, in the English view. The ideal of the English courtesy books is wedded happiness, and a wife is an embellishment to a husband's dignity. Hence, as governor in the home of her prince, she required the embellishing virtues, not the aggressive ones.

As a girl Lady Latimer had an education as painstakingly vocational where her future was concerned as the education of her future husband. For once, the most respected guide to such an education was not an Italian but a Spaniard. Juan Luis Vives, whom Henry VIII chose to be tutor to the Princess Mary, gave Europe in *The Instruction of a Christian Woman* (1523) the guidebook that by and large seemed valid wherever western ideals prevailed. The education of the future Lady Latimer, like that of her husband, was founded on the classics, but scrupulous care was taken in their selection. Plato, with a few obvious excisions, was suitable for her, as was Cicero. The moral epistles of Seneca were exemplary. Poetry was very suspect; poetry was apt to mean Ovid or worse, and her wayward fancy was for Catullus who is worst of all. History, on the other hand, is full of moral lessons and good educational material for both sexes. Oratory also casts a moral light, not so brilliant, perhaps, as that of history but reliable and steady. Therefore the young lady was allowed to read Plato, Cicero, Seneca, Plutarch, and Livy. Since these were all pagans, she was given salutary readings in the Church Fathers to temper their lack of orthodoxy. The education of the future Lady Latimer was handled with great care, and indeed the whole subject of a girl's education when she was destined by birth to be the lady of a great house was one for gingerly treatment. The radical doctrine was already abroad that a woman was a complete human being, especially if she was of the gentry or higher. It was not a convenient doctrine to refute with women holding the throne in England and Scotland. The real danger, of course, was that a woman's mind might be of such quality that a man's education would let her compete on intellectually equal terms with men. There were perils in Platonic love quite different from those of sex, and coquetry itself could be a saving grace.

When Vives turned to the non-academic, the sailing became much smoother. The future Lady Latimer was taught how to handle wool and flax. The commodities to be handled are significant: not woolen yarn and linen thread, but wool and flax. The entire process of preparing cloth for garments and all other purposes went on in the house just as it had in the Middle Ages, and was still woman's province. It was Lady Latimer's province, for all her recollection of Seneca's saws and secret forays into Catullus. She had to know how to sew clothes and care for them, how to prepare foods for future use and how to store them properly, how to manage a productive vegetable garden and poultry yard. None of her responsibilities, however, was quite so great as that of handling people. She had to be the gracious hostess for the high and mighty of the land, and she had to be the competent, vigilant, kindly, yet just and strict employer of the servants. She had a vital role to fill as physician to the household, guardian of a properly stocked medicine chest, and be adept at bandaging wounds, healing cuts, applying simples, and curing those ills not grave enough to warrant the services of a professional physician nor desperate enough for the chaplain. All this must seem to the reader familiar and repetitious, as indeed it is. The Lady of the Renaissance had the same responsibilities as the lady of the Middle Ages, and just about the same resources with which to meet them. One cannot over-emphasize the fact that it is not philosophy but machinery which changes the way in which people live, just as one must at least make some allowance for the possibility that it is not machinery but philosophy which changes their attitude toward life. When one examines the nature of Lady Latimer's responsibility and attempts to enumerate all the details of daily living that comprised it, somehow the lady of the Renaissance, like the lady of the Middle Ages, tends to fuse with the woman of the Renaissance. The theory of the lady is really the theory of the woman, and the theory of the woman is the theory of the wife. It follows that in many respects the good life of country dwellers of the Renaissance is more easily examined in terms of women than of men.

Let us move from the great house to a less pretentious dwelling, but still one that is substantial and commodious, and attests to the prosperity of those who live in it. It is the home of a franklin, a freeholder who owns a substantial tract of land much of which he rents to tenants. He is free born but not of the gentry, and certainly not of the nobility. He can read, since he must read his prayerbook; he can write, since he must write bills of sale and execute bonds. He favors formal education for those who need it: the clergy, the gentry, the schoolmasters. In the quoted words of one franklin of Shakespeare's day, "We can learn to plough and harrow, sow and reap, plant and prune, thrash and fan, brew and bale, and all without book; and these are our chief business in the country." The moral imperatives of the franklin are fully met when he obeys the king and the law, says his prayers, and goes to church on Sunday. He has in his life and his philosophy of life not a scintilla of *noblesse oblige* as Sir Edmund understood the term. Yet the franklin and his wife shared in perfect harmony of spirit a sort of *noblesse oblige* very much like that of Lady Latimer, an obligation of position that arose from the simple, fundamental fact that the Lord had been good to them indeed where worldly possessions were concerned and in the enjoyment of His bounty rested a solemn obligation.

His wife was just as truly the governor of his house as the wife of Sir Edmund was governor of the great house. To enumerate her obligations would be to repeat what was said about the obligations of the lady in the great house, and before her of the lady in the medieval castle. The franklin's wife had fewer servants to manage and to do the physical work at her bidding than did the ladies of the Middle Ages and the Renaissance, but she had an ample retinue. The domain of her lord and master was less extensive than that of the knight or governor, but she was just as truly governor of that domain in her lord's absence as her titled sisters. Like them, she was married to a prosperous man and therefore had the moral obligation to care for the needs, not only of the servants and dependents of her own establishment but for all the needy of the neighborhood as well. As the wife of a prosperous man it followed by the logic of the age that she was a competent physician, and those of lower degree came to her for medical advice and service. Her husband had substantial land holdings, and so it followed by the same logic that she was especially adept at helping neighbors in child birth. In short, there was a consistent framework to the lives of women in the Middle Ages and Renaissance, and the framework was basically the same if one was the wife of a knight and lived in a castle, the lady of a courtier and managed a great house, or the franklin's wife and lived modestly as judged by their standards, luxuriously as judged by the standards of those of lower degree.

The situation did not change if one were the wife of a yeoman. The yeoman himself, especially in England, was a small-scale capitalist intent on increasing his wealth partly by prudent investment and partly by diligent saving. He might have his moments of vision and aspire to the rank of the gentry, and many yeomen made the grade. It was more likely that he was content with the degree which he had by birth, and so added to his lands as opportunity offered, added to their productivity by hard and intelligent cultivation, saw to it that his sons got their start and his daughters were properly married, and earned his worldly rest in the village graveyard and his crown hereafter. His wife, on the other hand, had exactly the same responsibilities within her degree that her more exalted sisters faced. The difference was that they faced their responsibilities with an abundance of domestic help, and thus responsibility was largely that of management, the yeoman's wife might well have a slavey or two to help, but in large measure hers was the responsibility of execution. Beyond the responsibility for the comfortable if modest home which she governed, there was that particular kind of *noblesse oblige* which every right-thinking woman of the Renaissance village felt toward her neighbors. The village is an entity bound together by the firmest ties society ever knows, the ties of mutual dependency and reciprocal need. In a world in which disease struck with sudden and catastrophic force and people had virtually no means of combating it other than the loving care which comforts the afflicted and tries to assuage the symptoms, and no one knew who next would need that comfort and loving care, the yeoman's wife had to be a tower of fortitude. She had her good life in the comfort of her home, and in the comfort she brought to others' homes.

The same was true of the wife of the husbandman, the lowest perhaps in honorable, self-supporting degree in Renaissance society. Her responsibility was totally that of execution. She winnowed and sheared the corn beside her husband, and leveled the hay in the rick as he tossed it up. She spun, wove, dyed, cut, and sewed until clothing resulted, and she sewed with needles made from nettles that she plucked in the waste area beyond the farm. Her husband tanned the leather for the oxen yoke and for his own jerkin, a man's contribution to the tailor's art. She gathered the eggs, milked the cows, and brought the dairy produce to market, then gripped her tongue firmly in her teeth and buckled down to the truly hard part of the job, the putting down on paper of a true and accurate account of the transaction. She was the country milkmaid or shepherdess of idyllic tradition, or at least she was before she married, but her reality was much more like Shakespeare's greasy Joan who keels the pot, or Marian with the red, raw nose, or Jane Smile of the chapped hands whom Touchstone loved before he met Audrey, than like that of the dainty miss who tripped with shepherd's crook or milkmaid's pail across the musical comedy stage in earlier, more innocent days than our own. But come the hour when tragedy struck, when the plague scythed down a father and a mother and there were children left, and the wife of the husbandman who accepted the code of the good life as countryfolk conceived it, opened heart and home and took them in. There was *noblesse oblige* under the thatched roof quite as truly as in the great house.

The picture must not grow somber. The sound and ancient tradition was that one shared the good things of life. Landlords of the right sort were on the best of good terms with their tenants, and gifts flowed back and forth between Renaissance homes as they did between medieval castles. People worked long hours and hard in Shakespeare's day, with the milkmaid off to the dairy and the plowman to the stable by three in the morning on a summer's day. By six the last and laziest of the Lord's creatures would be up, and the day's work that might carry on until seven or eight o'clock at night in the summer would be well launched. The intermissions for dining, however, were leisurely and there was a firm tradition for the afternoon nap in summer. Then no Elizabethan ever overlooked a holiday or missed an excuse for a neighborhood party. The more violent outdoor sports were, the better. Frenzied wrestling matches and what Stubbes called "the bloody and murdering practice" of football were held in the highest esteem by a generation that expected and rather preferred ribs to be cracked and heads to be broken. The franklin or comfortable yeoman would see to it that if ribs were cracked and heads were broken, at least stomachs were comfortably filled. There was even a fine, boisterous quality to the raising of church funds, as church ales were held (which included dancing and bowling on the green) and the proceeds from the sale of ale went to the work of the Lord, which no doubt was substantially increased in volume and complexity by the very raising of funds for it.

Everything but merriment stopped for two weeks at Christmas, rising to a mad crescendo on Twelfth Night. In rural England of the Renaissance and in other lands as well the good life was the hard life, the robust life, crammed with work but also crammed with play. It was no life for weaklings, but weaklings did not live to maturity in the Renaissance. But whether it be work or merriment, joy or sorrow, there was ever the peremptory obligation incumbent on every villager but particularly on every woman to "be full of good neighborhood." What was true in the medieval fief was true in the Renaissance village, as women played their fixed and unchanging role. The foundation of the good life in the rural society of these earlier periods is better observed in the lives of women than of men.

The heart of that good life was service in every relationship that Renaissance life provided. The typical Renaissance woman was not the cloistered nun but the busy housewife; the Renaissance was an age of action, not of contemplation. Industry held first place among the pragmatic virtues, with thrift its closest rival. The woman of the Renaissance set the model of industry to the entire household and made effective through good management the virtue of thrift. The woman of the Renaissance, be her husband lord or franklin, yeoman or husbandman, had full responsibility for everything falling into the category of household tasks, either the responsibility of supervision or the responsibility of execution. She was governor of the establishment of which her husband was the prince, and she governed in a day when the prince brought the prime product from the outer world to the home, whether it be a slaughtered animal, a bag of wool, or a cart of wood, and every other stage in its preparation until it became food on the table, clothes on the back, or heat in the house was the woman's responsibility.

Service lay at the heart of her existence: service to her husband, her children, all those who made up her household. Beyond the immediate circle of her home was the larger circle of her village. Neighborliness was like an eleventh commandment, or perhaps more exactly was that other commandment

95

which ordains love for one's fellow man. Everyone in the Elizabethan village had a duty to everyone else, but in practice it was the woman who most frequently performed it. She did so, knowing that it was her duty and knowing as well that it was by the performance of her duty of neighborliness that she would be judged. She believed that this was true in this world, and that it was true as well in the next. One may speak of degree where the men of the Renaissance are concerned, and do so with clarity, but somehow degree becomes blurred where the women are concerned. The same basic duty of service was a moral imperative to Lady Latimer and to Jane Smile. Both knew that no possession on earth is nearly so precious as the good opinion of the village, and both treasured it at its full worth. The doors of their homes and the doors of their hearts were opened if they were women who understood the good life as the Renaissance understood it, and then lived it. Many did not, but many did and they fortified the concept of the good life in England. Fuller had good reason to say in *The Holy State,* "When hospitality died in England, she gave her last groan amongst the yeomen of Kent."

3.

The Incompleat Puritan

LONDON is studded with names that were picturesque mementos of a vanished past on the day that Shakespeare staged *Henry V* on the wooden O of the Globe Theater, names like Aldgate and Aldersgate, Moorgate and Newgate. They commemorated the gate houses in walls that the city had long outgrown and now had no significance except as fillips to the pride of Londoners who had so outgrown their city's modest medieval limits. There was now no logical northern limit to London, but for all its growth in size the city was as crowded as it was the day our medieval journeyman became a master, and at least as unsanitary. The great highway of the city was still the Thames, swarming with boats, resounding with the cries of boatmen, as swans soundlessly glided on its surface with their effortless oblivion toward time and change. Fine, crowded bridges stepped across the river, and the gardens that are England's reward for all its rain lined its banks punctuated by great houses from which courtiers and their ladies stepped into gaily decorated barges for the pleasant ride into The City. "A place both for the beauty of building, infinite riches, variety of all things, that excelleth all the cities in the world, insomuch that it may be called the storehouse and mart of all Europe," as John Lyly put it. High above it all, soaring above the other hundred and twenty churches of London, with spires lost in the mist or piercing the blue vault on the rare London days when the vault is blue, was the largest and most splendid church in England, the magnificent St. Paul's that was to be the most tragic single loss of the Great Fire of 1666. It was England's tribute to the Lord of hosts, built by the Elizabethan English who were His newly chosen people.

London was the magnet for all England and like all great cities there were in it those to whom the good life meant the bubbles at the brim of life's cup, or the pomp and circumstance of life's stately dignity, as well as those to whom it meant in city terms the solid, simple virtues that it meant to the country dwellers who knew and practiced it. But the final tone of London was not set by the courtiers and certainly not set by the gallants, nor indeed by the simple people of the simple virtues. It was set by the merchants of London, a sober and serious company who knew that the final reality which made London one of the world's supreme cities was not Hampton Court nor Covent Garden, nor even the Globe Theater which indeed they detested, but the warehouses that lined the river banks in The City, the boats that came and went from them, and the great wains that lumbered over the bridges through Southwalk to the farmlands, or up the north roads to the rich and fertile midlands and the north country beyond. Trade had its proper dignity which they respected and maintained, and there was true virtue and solid worth in tradesmen. They also had their concept of the good life and it was grounded in their sort of Protestantism which was partly a religious creed, partly a form of patriotism, but mainly a way of life. From the social crucible of the English Renaissance emerged two dominant upper class types, the gentleman whom we have already met and the industrialist whose ancestor at the moment is in a warehouse by the Thames.

A sedate and dignified figure emerged from the warehouse, looked quickly at the vessel tied up beside it, and speculatively at a wain loading in the yard. There was a sobriety to Amos Parkins's dress that blended with the sedateness and dignity of his person, and the three qualities suggested a man of substance and importance, but of a substance and importance very different from that of a courtier or a governor. He watched some young men tugging at long and loosely tied bundles of that new and curious plant that was being brought in from the Virginia colony. He had taken a little flyer in this tobacco as they called it, in the sort of spirit that might lead a courtier to lay a wager on a cock fight. To every successful man his business or profession is also his game, and every now and then the spirit of ordinary economic enterprise slips into the spirit of athletics. Amos Parkins occasionally did a bit of business for the fun of it; he had bought some hands of tobacco in that spirit. It seemed incredible that there could be a profit in this exotic plant, but somehow the idea of agriculture producing a product to go up in smoke for the sake of the smoke itself intrigued him. He had in sacrosanct privacy drunk several pipes of the stuff, as the current phrase had it, and found it acrid and unpleasant. The whole business would be ungodly were there not a profit in it.

Amos Parkins was actuated by the profit motive, to be sure, but he was also actuated by godliness. He would be honestly puzzled by the viewpoint of those who saw an inconsistency in his motives. He was close enough to the money market to know something about upper-class finances, and no one could calculate more shrewdly than he the depths of indebtedness in which the aristocracy would wallow that the king might be entertained to the king's taste. Extravagance was the curse of the elite and indebtedness their appropriate punishment. Parkins was also close enough to the streets and lanes of London to see how the lower classes lived today at the expense of tomorrow. Improvidence was the curse of the lowly, and misery their appropriate punishment. To him thrift and industry comprised the virtuous mean that lies between extravagance and improvidence. The virtuous mean is godly, and so are its component parts.

There was in his attitude toward life much of the old and much of the new. His private life was marked by a vigorous affirmation of attitudes and acts well established in the thirteenth century. He believed that marriage was divinely insti-

99

tuted for sinful man, but he did not consider it the highest state since some men have the special grace to resist sin and yet stay celibate. He believed that marriage was instituted for procreation and he applied to the frequency of the marital act the same principle of the virtuous mean that he struck between extravagance and improvidence in his economic views. He looked with an intense theoretical disfavor on second marriages, although the intensity could be modified in practice.

He was lord and master of his wife, by a principle that is eternal, unchangeable, and so totally grounded in the very nature of God's universe that any deviation from it would be unnatural and blasphemous. That gave him no privilege whatever to abuse her. She was the wife of his bosom, chosen for him by his wise and prudent parents, the soundness of whose wisdom of choice the fourth commandment forbade him to question. As her lord and master he could instruct her, counsel her, advise and admonish her, and when he had done his best by peaceable means, he could accept what was good in her and bear what was bad in the spirit of a godly man who knows that every man has his cross and must bear it in this vale of tears. His parents had tested his prospective bride by the five tests: "the report, the looks, the speech, the apparel, and the companions," as the authoritative Puritan divine Henry Smith compiled them, and had found her good, and so did he. He loved his wife and they lived the good life together with just about the same degree of harmony as Sir Edmund and his lady, the franklin and his wife, and the husbandman and his helpmeet. By and large that ancient institution the arranged marriage worked well with the Puritans of England.

When Amos Parkins married there was no nonsense in his mind or in the mind of his young wife about the size of their family. That was totally a matter of dispensation by Providence, but he took it for granted that the number of his offspring would be substantial, although he also took it for granted that a substantial proportion of them would be stillborn or die in infancy. He selected Biblical names for most of them, abstract nouns for others, and since his whimsy ran that way, hortatory phrases for still others. Puritan nomenclature is still with us in such names as Samuel and Sarah; Faith, Hope, Prudence, and Constance; but time has run out on the hortatory phrases. For some reason doubtless within the ken of those skilled in Semitic linguistics, Scriptural names for men tend to a rugged, jaw-breaking pattern but Scriptural names for women to a pleasant simplicity. He had a daughter Ruth and a son Abimelech; two other daughters Mercy and Charity; and he had applied as names without overtones indicative of sex such pious exhortations as Faint Not and More Trials. One thing is certain: little Ruth, Mercy, Abimelech, Faint Not and the rest were brought up with a transparently clear and meticulously detailed understanding of parental discipline, its objectives and methodology. Everything they learned, be it from books or from life, was directed at their moral uplift. The Puritans did have a zeal for learning, but learning was never anything but a means to a moral end.

There is, perhaps, something characteristic and important about Amos Parkins and his kind in this fact. There has been an enormous volume of controversial writing about Puritan education and the subject lends itself to controversy since diametrically opposite conclusions can be reached about it by impeccably logical routes. One can prove the presence in the Puritan movement of Renaissance humanism by the fact that Puritan education used as its tools the Latin classics. One can also prove by the same fact the presence of inertia. One can prove by the many schools and colleges opened by the Puritans their dedication to learning but one cannot do so as a triumphant secularist unless one disregards the fact that all the Puritan schools and colleges were seedbeds for the Puritan clergy. The truth is that Amos and his brethren had a simple and pragmatic attitude toward learning. It existed as a handmaid to religion, and unless learning was in that service it had no value. Hence the classics were taught, but the classics were not liberal studies. Human reason was respected, but only when it remained obedient to the checkrein of Scriptural authority.

Our London tradesman had a simple and pragmatic attitude toward life itself. He had entered into a covenant with

God whereby he undertook to obey the law of God and God promised him as his recompense eternal salvation. He had to know the law of God and understand it to fulfill his part of the covenant, and therefore he required education. By and large he felt more at home battling the clearcut and obvious temptations; the subtle ones he tended to overlook or not to consider temptations at all. Ostentatious dress of the sort affected by courtiers was clearly a yielding to the sin of pride; therefore he wore somber and old-fashioned dress and cut short his hair, avoiding the sin of pride possibly at the cost of the sin of righteousness. Drunkenness and profligate living were clearly sins of excess and immorality; add swearing, and indeed one has the three deadly sins he recognized. Virtue was sobriety, fidelity to the home, and decent speech. Virtue was also shutting down ale houses and brothels, and imposing fines for profanity. But if Amos Parkins's attitude was simple and pragmatic, it is well to remember what gave it substance and enduring worth. He lived to sanctify himself and to sanctify society, as he viewed the matter in the deep and undisturbed privacy of his conscience. In his way, he had as simple and clear-cut an idea of sanctification as did any medieval knight.

His code started with duty. His duty was to obey the law of God, and therefore a corollary to that duty was to know the law of God. Everything in his education was the fulfillment of that corollary. God's law was not a subtle and complex law, but rather one codified in ten simple and direct commandments. In his youth it was his duty to obey his parents and other superiors; in his adult years, to exact proper obedience from those under him and to do so with a full awareness that the exacting of obedience involves at least as solemn a responsibility as the observance of it. Thus he was the lord and master of his house, his wife and children, his men servants and maid servants; but he was an understanding and compassionate lord, a wise, prudent, and benevolent master. His wife was viceroy in these matters, as wives were in every stratum of medieval and Renaissance society.

It was his duty to cultivate the virtues, but the virtues were simple and direct: sobriety, industry, honesty, thrift, decency.

Work was prayer, and the fruits of one's labor were testimonials that prayer was answered. Industry, honesty, and thrift do pay, as the Almighty intended they should, and prosperity was proof that a man was obeying the law of God. It is one of the ironies of scholarship that the Puritan tradesman is so frequently praised for virtues that he did not have and would not have recognized as virtues had they been paraded before him. He was not dedicated to learning. He was dedicated to the Christian way of life, in the attaining of which learning is a tool. He was not dedicated to the democratic way of life, which indeed he would have denounced as the work of Satan had he encountered it. He was dedicated to the principle of personal responsibility, a principle integral to the democratic way of life. The truth is that he really was dedicated to a set of medieval values which he reinterpreted in the light of his own religious convictions. To him the good life was the life of duty led in obedience to the ten commandments, marked by sobriety and honesty, industry and thrift. However, by a process of ideological change that would be incomprehensible to him, Amos Parkins the "incompleat Puritan" was the father of the nineteenth-century industrialist. The future did not belong to Sir Edmund Latimer but to Amos Parkins. To understand how this came about, with its profound implications where later concepts of the good life are concerned, requires not only an analysis of the Puritan ethic but a review of the medieval ethic from which it evolved.

No one in the Middle Ages ever doubted that business must justify itself by the principles of religion. What later would be called the acquisitive instinct, or more pleasantly the competitive instinct, was then quite clearly the deadly sin of greed which in turn is a product of the supreme sin, pride. Trade is obviously necessary and therefore craftsmen and merchants are necessary, but the purpose of trade is to make a living, not to make a profit. From this principle developed all the specific economic attitudes of the Middle Ages: price fixing, wage ceilings, a ban on interest unless risk was involved in the lending, and the multitude of limitations on freedom of activity that the guilds imposed upon their members. The entire economics of the Middle Ages depended on the thesis that industry is merely a means of subsistence that permits one to concentrate on his true function in life, which is to merit salvation. Work is prayer, but making money isn't prayer.

None of this changed with the Reformation. If anything, the reformers held to medieval economics more tenaciously than did the Catholics. Luther denounced with equal fire the plundering of the Church by the Papacy and the plundering of the peasant by the money lender, and no writer of pastoral verse ever idealized the life of the simple country dweller more thoroughly than Melanchthon. Yet the Protestant ethic, which the Lord in His infinite compassion would have shielded Luther from recognizing as an outcome of his thought, was at least to a degree a logical outcome, as it was more clearly the outcome of the thought of John Calvin. Why this is true comprises one of the most fascinating chapters in the history of thought.

Luther held that God speaks directly to the human soul, which thus lives in direct spiritual communion with its Maker. Salvation is God's grace working in the human heart and therefore the machinery of organized religion is at the best peripheral to the purpose of religion. To Luther, even more than to the moralists and theologians of the Middle Ages, there was a deep and perilous gulf between the spirit and the flesh, a clear and peremptory division between good and evil. Man had two beacons to guide his pilgrim's progress, the outer light of Scripture and the inner light of conscience. Both lights, however, shone to the individual heart. Luther intended, of course, to purify human conduct in economic matters as in matters vastly more important, but by concentrating on the inner life of the spirit, he made the outer life of the body and the regulations by which it is governed seem incidental and even irrelevant to man's fundamental purpose. Luther never intended that there be one good life for the spirit and another good life for the body, but by limiting religion in the full sense to the inner life of the spirit he opened the door to those who would draw that lamentable distinction.

Luther lived, worked, thought, and acted in a world of peasants and craftsmen where the main economic threat came

from the village money lender and the principle of neighborhood was imperative and sacrosanct. In such a world the danger of uncurbed economic individualism is very slight indeed,
but the world of Martin Luther was not the world that even in
his day was taking shape in Europe. John Calvin, on the other
hand, lived in the new world of growing economic enterprise
and complex city life. In his world economic matters were
neither simple nor self-governing. Luther lived in a natural
economy, Calvin in a money economy. In the world of Luther
the accumulation of money was an evil. In the world of Calvin
the misuse of accumulated money was an evil. In the world of
Luther the hiring of money by the payment of interest was
deemed an all but natural evil. In the world of Calvin one
could at least understand the aphorism attributed to Christopher Columbus: "Gold constitutes treasure, and he who pos-
sesses it has all he needs in this world, as also the means of
rescuing souls from Purgatory, and restoring them to the enjoyment of Paradise." The Calvinist might take the most ani-
mated exception to the theological foundation of the aphorism,
but he would agree that it is the use to which money is put
that counts. No true Calvinist ever lost sight of the principle
that it is not money which is the root of all evil, but the love of
money.

It was no more the intent of John Calvin to bring into being
a state of unrestrained economic individualism than it was the
intent of Martin Luther to exempt economics from the principles of Christian morality. Actually to Calvin the duty of the
church to bring into being the disciplined Christian community
was every bit as paramount as the duty of the individual to discipline his personality. Where Calvinism was dominant as in
Boston and the Massachusetts Bay Colony, society was thoroughly regimented, but it was a society in which industry and
thrift were deemed cardinal virtues and prosperity a mark of
God's favor. Where Calvinism was present but not dominant
as in London and England in general, industry and thrift were
still honored and prosperity and virtue still equated, but the
fundamental division between the good life of the spirit and
the good life of the body came to be an accepted principle
and with it a foothold gained for that other principle which

105

exempted industry, thrift, and prosperity from the control of Christian morality. No more than Luther did Calvin intend that there be two independent good lives, that of the spirit and that of the body, but the Calvinistic concentration on the life of the spirit opened even wider than did the Lutheran concentration the door to those who would draw that distinction.

There is a difference between work for one's fellow man and work for oneself. "Work is prayer" meant one thing when the monks from Monte Cassino repaired the road to Subiaco, something else again when Amos Parkins took inventory at his warehouse on the Thames. Amos Parkins, whose Calvinism was more than adequately diluted with the thrill of aggrandizement, would say that work is prayer, the harder one works the more devout his prayer, and the greater his wealth on earth the greater his invisible treasure in heaven. Such is neither Lutheranism nor Calvinism, but it is an understandable end result of the individualism and the distinction between spirit and body which are cornerstones of Lutheranism and Calvinism. Protestantism can no more disown Amos Parkins than Catholicism can absolve itself of the Medicis.

The difficulty is a fairly obvious one. The mind of Amos Parkins was not capable of applying the old standards of economic justice based on religious principles to the expansion of commerce, the development of capitalism, and the emergence of joint stock enterprise in mining, textiles, and foreign trade which made up the actual business structure and practices of his age. Gradually Amos Parkins ceased to believe in a divinely instituted law of nature which underlay the standards of economic justice and was a manifestation of the will of God. He came to consider the law of nature something integral to the economic process itself which was then to be codified in statute law. Gradually in his mind the concepts of right and law drew apart, the world of nature separated from the world of grace, and a new concept of right came into being whereby he considered right to be the creation of man and law its explicit formulation. The result was his at least silent denial that business transactions were based on moral principles, his tacit assumption of the thesis that the domain of morality was his private life, and his bland assumption that economic success revealed conformity to the law of nature which in turn revealed the benign approval of the Almighty. The apotheosis of the type of Amos Parkins was to be found in Holland, the Dutch Calvinists whom an admiring Englishman of the ilk called "thinking, sober, and patient men, and such as believe that labor and industry is their duty toward God." It followed logically that the richest were the most God-fearing and righteous, the poorest those most lacking in virtue, that wealth was a virtue and poverty a crime.

Amos Parkins was a self-reliant man who both formulated his ethical judgments and tested them himself. His moral self-sufficiency drew him apart from his fellows and reinforced his individualism. If he was self-justified and succeeded, that was proof that he was right. If he was ethically right, and his success proved that he was, then his methods were their own justification. Hence came his deduction which was never part of the Puritan creed but rather one of its unintended corollaries, that the sober, hard working, successful businessman was the anointed of the Lord and any attempt by State or Church to curb his undertakings was an attempt to curb the will of God. Work, not good works, was the test of virtue. To ask what it profiteth a man to win the whole world and suffer the loss of his soul was a stupid question. If he had won the whole world, what better proof could there be that he had saved his soul? It was individual character that mattered and the individual achievement that resulted from it, and not one's attitude toward his fellow man or his contributions to the welfare of society. Only the individual could save his own soul. The good life was the life of hard work, unflagging industry, unremitting thrift, uninterrupted financial success, with a crown of twenty-four-carat gold assured in the heavenly kingdom to which one was translated from a warehouse by the Thames up to the serried ranks of the saints marshalled before the enthroned Almighty One, who read in the Golden Ledger and smiled with the smile that carried with it the promise of unimaginable, unalterable bliss as the centuries of eternity solemnly tick off one by one.

4.

The Final Definition

IT is no longer fashionable and it never was accurate to consider the Renaissance antithetical to the Middle Ages and a wholehearted return in spirit to classical antiquity. The danger now is that the change in fashion may itself produce a fashion whereby the return in the Renaissance to the spirit of antiquity will be obliterated by emphasis on its continuity with the Middle Ages. There was indeed continuity with the Middle Ages, and there was indeed change from them in both the pattern of life and in its spirit. Both continuity and change, as well as indebtedness to antiquity, are important to the Renaissance concept of the good life. At least as important is the third factor, the new viewpoints that emerged in the Renaissance itself and distinguish it from both the ancient and the medieval periods.

In neither antiquity nor the Middle Ages was the good life the prosperous life, although in neither age was the prosperous life held in contempt. The first part of the statement is not quite true of the Renaissance, although a man crass enough to equate entirely prosperity with virtue would not be philosophic enough to have abstract ideas of virtue. Prosperity was an important factor in the good life of both Sir Edmund Latimer and Amos Parkins. The governor needed wealth for the life he led, the prosperous Puritan acquired wealth by the life he led. In the one case wealth was a means to an end, in the other wealth was reassurance that one was destined for a joyous end. For those who were neither governors nor upper-class Calvinists one may reasonably surmise that wealth comprised about that part of the good life that it has comprised for average man in all climes and ages. The difference is that in the Renaissance, unlike antiquity and the Middle Ages, the possession of wealth was an integral part of the good life as it was understood by the two most important viewpoints in contemporary thought.

In neither antiquity nor the Middle Ages was the good life the life of artistic creativity or the aesthetic enjoyment of the arts. This statement stands as well for the Renaissance, but on a less solid foundation. A philosophy of sheer aestheticism was no more held by a substantial body of people in the Renaissance than it has been at any other period of history, but Renaissance thought was more kindly disposed to aestheticism than ancient or medieval thought. One of the major mysteries of classical thought is its innocent unawareness of the greatness of classical art; the Greeks took Phidias and Praxiteles for granted as dwellers in the vale of Kashmir take the Himalayas for granted. In similar fashion, as the medieval craftsman achieved his artistic triumph the cathedral, he kept in sight the perspective from which it must be viewed. The cathedral towered to the greater glory of God, not of architect or workman. The Renaissance courtier, on the other hand, consciously entertained the ideal of the complete man living the complete life, and the arts are part of the complete life. A Renaissance madonna might be for the greater glory of God, but a Renaissance Jupiter and Europa was not, and the trend was to Jupiter and Europa, not to the madonna. If Renaissance Italy was the land of art, Renaissance England was the land of music and the theatre and Renaissance France the land of poetry. The enjoyment of painting, music, poetry, and the theatre for their own sake was far more widespread than it had been in the Middle Ages, and with some reservations and hesitation the same can be said of classical antiquity. Perhaps the very vitriol from which Puritan denunciations of painting, music, theatricals,

109

and similar lewd and lascivious shows were brewed is evidence of the extent to which the arts were part of the good life of those who did not share the convictions of Amos Parkins. Yet the esthete pure and simple was not a common Renaissance figure, nor did his concept of the good life hold much appeal to the Renaissance mind. The exaltation and exaggeration of Renaissance aesthetics was an achievement of belated romantics like Walter Pater.

The significance of the family in the Renaissance concept of the good life is a different matter. Aristotle treats family life more seriously than Plato, but neither philosopher nor anyone else in classical philosophy or literature ever thought of the good life in terms of family relations. The truth is that the classical family is better understood in Oriental than in Occidental terms. Neither were sound family relations thought of as the essence of the good life in the Middle Ages, when family life followed a pattern much more familiar to the modern world than the ancient family pattern which made the husband so much a public figure and the wife so thoroughly a private one. However, as the division between the city of God and the city of Man's pilgrimage became less a chasm and man's concentration on the former less intent, as was true in the Renaissance, the simple and natural human relationships loomed larger as possible bases for serious thought. The Renaissance was an age of magnificence, but also an age of neighborliness; it was an age of Calvinistic rectitude, but simple duties are vital components of rectitude. It is not that husbands and wives were more in love than in other and earlier ages, or parents more devoted to their children. It is simply that in an age with a literature less given to cold abstractions of thought than antiquity knew or to eternal verities than the literature of the Middle Ages, there is more room in the literary record for simple human relations among the categories of the virtues. The ancient thought of the good life in terms of his city, the medieval monk in terms of his God. The father and mother of the Renaissance, be they gentry, yeomen, husbandmen, or city dwellers, thought of the good life at least in part in terms of their families. It is hardly an exaggeration to say that the first family to appear in English history is the family of Thomas More, in whose home it has been said the English Renaissance began.

In the relatively greater importance that the family had in the Renaissance concept of the good life than in the concepts entertained before is something at least symbolic of the Renaissance attitude in its entirety. The Renaissance was neither so secular a period as classical antiquity nor so religious minded a period as the Middle Ages. Because it was more secular minded than the Middle Ages, secular loyalties loomed larger in the Renaissance that they had before. The Renaissance courtier and governor knew that in his final convictions, final loyalty was due to God and not to the prince, but he was less given to thinking in terms of final convictions than was the medieval baron. Hence the men of the Renaissance thought less in terms of Christ and Christ's spiritual vicar, and more in terms of Christ's secular vicar. The result was a tendency to think of society less in terms of the chain of being and more in terms of the hierarchical pyramid, with the prince at its apex.

There is a paradox present in this that recurs so frequently in history as to make it not a paradox but a principle. Renaissance man freed himself from that intense preoccupation with the other world that marked medieval man. Hence he freed himself from the more cramping fetters of religion, as the older school of Renaissance apologists used to put it, and became a free man, a self-expressive and self-assertive man, an individual triumphant in his individualism. To what end? A new chain of being was created, fastened not to the throne of God but to the throne of the prince. A new pyramid was created, not with God the Father at the apex but with the king at its uppermost point. The final result of an individualism freed from the cramping fetters of religion (to beg the question implicit in a pejorative adjective and noun) was a different sort of human corporation, and one actually less hospitable to the spirit of individualism than the medieval corporation it succeeded. Absolutism came with the Renaissance, not with the Middle Ages.

There is a sense in which the Reformation was an attempt

111

to shift the vision of Renaissance man back from time to eternity. Once more Renaissance individualism produced its paradoxical result. The real tungsten steel of the Reformation was in the Calvinists; only among them was the concept of the good life really rooted in the concept of the saint and not the concept of the prince. By the logic of Calvinism, there are two churches, the invisible church comprising the elect and the visible church comprising the church-goers. Only God knows the roster of the former, and therefore the visible church is an institution of this world comprising both the elect and the non-elect. Since the visible church and the invisible church are not identical, it follows that hierarchical degree is necessary in the visible church and only those are to be elevated to such degree as give convincing evidence of presumptive election. The result, achieved perhaps through semi-conscious processes of thought more susceptible to psychological analysis than to logical, was to make the saints a body of men on earth, headed at Geneva and the various New World Genevas by the council of pastors and the consistory, standing in righteous array at the apex of a hierarchical pyramid loftier even than the pyramid the prince crowned.

The Renaissance concept of the good life, then, whether one seeks it in the courts of the mighty, the homes of the lordly, the dwellings of the comfortable, the hovels of the uncomfortable, or indeed in the abodes of the elected saints and those who harbored a hope of being saints that eternity would frustrate, had a certain uniformity of pattern for which the pyramid is a better symbol than the chain of being. The good life is founded upon the principle of duty. That means the duty of a child to his parents, a wife to her husband, a communicant to his pastor, a subject to his governor, a governor to his prince. Conversely, it means the far more difficult and solemn duties of the prince, the governor, the pastor, the husband, and the parent. The good life of the Renaissance had secular aspects reminiscent of the classical and religious aspects inherited from the medieval, but their fusion with the Renaissance concept of society as a pyramid made it something distinctive from them both. It was lived partly in accordance with that covenant between God and man, as the Calvinists conceived it, which is the moral law, but it was also led by what Governor John Winthrop of the Massachusetts Bay Colony called "the politic covenants and constitutions amongst men themselves." But beyond all this, the good life of the Renaissance was lived within the four walls of the home. It always is and always has been, but neither antiquity nor the Middle Ages were explicit on the point. The Renaissance was.

PART FOUR

THE PHILOSOPHER

George Saintsbury called his benignly pleasant survey of eigh-teenth-century literature The Peace of the Augustans. There was a peace that descended over Europe in the early eighteenth century, and especially over England. A new kind of certitude suffused the period like the balm of Gilead, different indeed from the peace of mind that religious certitude gave the Middle Ages and yet in unexpected and confusing ways rather suggestive of the peace of religious certitude. It was the peace of philosophy buttressed by science, the peace of mind that comes with the calm conviction that now the questions are answered, the doubts allayed, the truth revealed, and the way ahead clear and direct. Enlightenment had come. For a moment society was in equilib-rium, with the rich secure in their riches and the poor quiescent in their poverty. The serpent of uncertainty still lay stunned in the wreckage of that far more profound and far more disturbed century, the seventeenth. To make the peace more placid and secure there appeared beside formal religion, which was never *quite so formal or so little religious as in the eighteenth century, an embodiment called Nature.*

Nature was sometimes an ally of formal religion, sometimes an alternative to it, sometimes its implacable enemy. In the earlier part of the century, the peaceful part when society was in equilibrium and reason reigned, Nature was identified with the status quo. Although the aphorism of Alexander Pope, "Whatever is, is right," had deeper philosophic roots than its surface smugness suggests, when voiced by those in a position to enjoy the fleshpots of the century it meant that Nature was on their side, whether their side was fat, rolling acres in the pleasant south of England or bulging warehouses by the Thames. Later in the century philosophers, first French, then American and British, would give to Nature and to natural man a meaning that would shake the century to its roots and impose upon society new and unanticipated patterns, including new patterns of the good life.

So far our emerging pattern of the good life has tended to polarize around two figures and two ideals. The first living figure has been the autocrat of the rolling acres whom we met first as the medieval knight and then as the Renaissance governor. His ideal of the good life was embodied in such words as authority, responsibility, and charity, but with pride and prestige of position and their material embellishments an unquestioned part of the ideal. The other living figure has been the tradesman whom we first met as an emerging master in a medieval guild and then as a wealthy merchant in prosperous, mercantile London. His ideal of the good life was embodied in such words as opportunity, initiative, and independence, and one may be certain in his case also the material embellishments besides. Both figures, however, have been drawn in varying degree to a magnetic pole, religion, which in turn embodied its good life in the lives of the Benedictine monk and prioress, the Franciscan friar and the man whose solid claim to worth has been implicit rather than personalized, the "compleat Puritan." The medieval fief was contained within a definite framework of rivers, mountain ridges, and seacoast, but it was also contained within a framework of mutual faith, hope, and charity, and the same was true of the lordly acres of

116

the Renaissance governor and the typical domain of the compleat Puritan, the Massachusetts Bay Colony. The knight, governor, or Puritan may have been inconsistent to his ideal in living practice, but he never denied it in theory. Similarly the guildsman and the merchant may have been unaware of the substantial motes in their eyes, but each saw himself as a God-fearing man practicing his craft or conducting his business by the highest ethical principles as expounded in Rome or Geneva.

In the Middle Ages and Renaissance the country pattern of the good life had been set by the knight or governor after the model of the saint or the prince. It was accepted as valid by the gentry, franklins, yeomen, husbandmen, journeyman farm hands, by the indigent, aged, and crippled, by the lame, blind, halt, and the unabashedly idle of the countryside. Within the shrinking framework of their respective status in life, they either lived the good life by the country pattern or set it at defiance. Similarly the town pattern was set by the wealthy tradesman and accepted as valid by the lesser masters, the journeymen, the apprentices, the day laborers, the corrigible poor and the incorrigible of the town. They too, within their ample or their restricted scope of life, either lived the good life by the town pattern or failed to do so.

It was a very different matter, however, when Nature became the norm, and Nature was beginning to be the norm even in the seventeenth century. When Nature became the norm, the saint ceased to be the inspiration and so did the prince. The ideal embodied in such words as authority, responsibility, and charity began to fade and the ideal embodied in such words as opportunity, initiative, and independence began to dominate. For a brief moment as the surge of history counts time, life was in equilibrium and the peace of the Augustus soothed the earth. The moment was brief and it passed away. As the eighteenth century progressed, common man in country and town alike stirred and became restive. His good life ceased to be modelled on the good life of his superiors and indeed was often antithetical to it. The Methodist, for example, looked to neither the squire nor the merchant as his model of probity, but to something very ancient in the Christian tradition, and the Republican

117

looked to something very fundamental in the human heart. Once the polarization of the good life disappeared, the modern world was born. It was born when philosophy bore its eighteenth-century offspring, Nature during the earlier part of the century and Revolution in the later. Let us turn first to the hour of equilibrium, the hour when the nature of life was peace.

1.

Augustans at Peace

HUGH GILBERT looked out into the freshness of the morning and found it good. A three-foot haze hung above the meadow, blending into the clear air above it that slowly turned back into a haze again made saffron by a sun not yet about its work of the day. Hugh Gilbert sighed with contentment. Today would be a replica of yesterday, and held fair promise for tomorrow. There was a blessed peace and a thrice-blessed monotony to the prospect that gladdened his heart. He wanted peace and he relished monotony. They came from an order that was stable and good, an order that was natural.

Squire Hugh stood on a lawn so lush that as one walked, there was a moment of hesitation until the yielding grass rested on the solid ground. The lawn had a gentle concave roll that hastened at the end to meet the brook which emerged from the elders and sank away into the ferns. Massive elms held sentry post about the estate, and at its heart rested the broad, symmetrical house of weathered brick with its clean, rectangular lines, the crown jewel in a setting worthy of it. The last suggestion of a medieval fortress was gone, and some-thing faintly suggestive of the Greek spirit had taken its place. There were order, balance, symmetry, and proportion in this eighteenth-century gentleman's home which so admirably retained simplicity and dignity in the presence of opulence and mass.

Windows were larger than they had been in the home of Sir Edmund and since they were sash windows, they let in more light and air. As there was a window tax on dwellings with more than seven windows, the thriftier gentry boarded up windows but Hugh Gilbert was above petty thrift. The windows in his home all opened into rooms that were bright, their walls decorated with tastefully printed wallpaper, classical motifs framed in a delicate blue, or shimmering with the sheen of satin wall covering. The panelled walls of Sir Edmund's house were gone, not to reappear until the Elizabethan manner would become an interior decorator's vogue. The furniture was light, delicate, and airy; chairs and sofas had spindle legs; cabinets were made of satin wood; the hallmark of Hepplewhite and Sheraton rested lightly on the dwelling. The great and cavernous hearth with the great darkened kettles hanging in its dim recesses had shrunk in size and now rooms had fireplaces equipped with nicely wrought and carefully polished iron grates. The squire and his wife had their bedroom and so did each of their five children. The house was capacious and Hugh Gilbert could afford it; that the boys of the family sleep in one room and the girls in another had ceased to be a matter of universal practice and had sunk to the social level at which it was a matter of economics. There was a distinction, however, between the high poster bed in which Hugh and Mrs. Gilbert slept behind elaborate curtains and the low beds without posters, curtains, or elegance of any other sort in which the children slept. Such distinctions were natural in the mind of Hugh Gilbert, as was the other distinction that his children each slept in his own bed and not two or even three to the bed as did the servants. There was order and proportion asleep as well as awake in the home of Squire Gilbert.

Like the baroness in the thirteenth century and Lady Latimer in the sixteenth, Mrs. Gilbert ran the house, enjoying in the eighteenth-century domestic conveniences and aids slightly superior if at all to those enjoyed by the baroness and the Lady. She had, of course, the usual bevy of domestic help, which

brought to its multitude of tasks about the same aptitude and
enthusiasm as its predecessors. She did have an aide de camp
of a sort less common in the centuries past, a young gentlewoman to help her in her supervisory responsibilities. Catherine was the eldest daughter of a cousin of Mrs. Gilbert's who
had died of a fever subsequent to her eleventh accouchement.
The arrangement was helpful for Mrs. Gilbert and very good
indeed for Catherine. The lot of girls in her position was far
from enviable. They were the social equals of their mistresses
and the economic inferiors, and the latter fact revealed itself
in both their wages and their treatment. Catherine ate with the
family and had a room of her own. In many establishments
she would eat with the housekeeper and share her bed with
the governess. Catherine looked forward to marriage in a
wholesome and normal fashion, not with the corrosive longing
of girls for whom it was the only means of escape. There was
little indeed of the good life for eighteenth-century girls of
breeding who were unmarried and lacked protection. There was
little to choose in degree of drabness among the lives of the
school mistress, the governess, and the dependent gentlewoman,
the three lives open to them.

The entire position of women in the eighteenth century
showed signs of the hard and brittle thinking so characteristic of
the age. A woman should liken herself to a fortress and think
of every man as a potential invader, the Marquess of Halifax wrote cheerfully in his "Advice to a Daughter." A gracious
smile from an unmarried woman is an invitation to a man to
do his worst. A clever woman can wheedle what she wants
from a weak husband, but a wife should grit her teeth and
take the worst if a husband is not weak; any fate is better than
ridicule. Halifax wrote just before the century dawned, and
his voice was prophetic for much of it. "Children of a larger
growth," Lord Chesterfield characterized women for that far
from sparkling pupil his son. "A man of sense only trifles with
them, plays with them, humours and flatters them." That a
child of larger growth should manage a complex estate seemed
no paradox to Chesterfield, nor had it seemed a paradox five
hundred years before that the baroness, who had successfully

defended the fief in her husband's absence when it was invaded from across the ridge, was a minor until she died at seventy-three. Squire Gilbert was too shrewd a man, fortunately for Mrs. Gilbert and even for his daughters and for Catherine, to think in terms of theory. Furthermore, he loved his wife and daughters, was very fond of Catherine, and subscribed to Mr. Addison's periodical, *The Spectator,* which was not hard and brittle in its thought. All this helped him enjoy the good life at home.

The truth is that Squire Gilbert owed more of his thinking to Mr. Addison than he might have willingly admitted. He lived a spacious and comfortable life in his lordly home and gracious park. He had a town house as well, but it was in the shire town and not in London. He collected books and did it quite successfully, since he had a good eye for bindings and an artistic taste in leather. He was somewhat more cautious where pictures were concerned, but gradually came to trust his instinct for what was conventional. His natural bent really was for those functions which were his by nature of his position. When the town vestry met at Easter he accepted easily and naturally the position of primacy accorded him by the parson, farmers, and tradesmen in attendance. The vestry elected as he indicated the appropriate persons to be constable, overseers of the poor, and surveyors of the highways. He served as justice of the peace and did so to the entire satisfaction of the village. Otherwise, he inclosed and drained land in a fashion more beneficial to the villagers than is always conceded, improved breeds of sheep and cattle, rode to hounds and preferred it to attendance at the balls in the shire town, a decided preference of Mrs. Gilbert's. At heart he was merely first among his equals, nor did he ever think of himself as cut of finer cloth than the respectable men and women of the village whose deference he accepted easily and repaid in friendship and kindliness. There was a simple and wholesome unity to the eighteenth-century village at its best, and Squire Gilbert was a villager and not a man of the larger world. Since he needed a window into the larger world, he sought and found one in Mr. Addison's *Spectator.*

Joseph Addison was Squire Gilbert's philosopher and philosopher for those like him. The squire sensed a kinship with Addison, whose common-sense view of life and simple, practical morality he approved and understood. The squire was uneasy in the presence of witty and irreverent men who scoffed at religion, mocked marriage, and turned morality inside out. Not that he met many such, but the breed was in the shire town and not entirely to be avoided. He knew that they were wrong, but he lacked the mental dexterity and verbal deftness to show them why. But Mr. Addison had both and to the queen's taste, and Squire Gilbert thrilled adventitiously as Mr. Addison demolished them and their hollow shams. On the other hand, the squire had no stomach for those skinflint killjoys who somehow had survived the seventeenth century and soured the eighteenth. Mr. Addison put them also in their place. Of course the good man is the cheerful man and of course man is made for happiness. Virtue is not only right, it is natural, and the virtuous man is in harmony with the Almighty and His creation. Squire Gilbert sighed with contentment and approval when he read in Mr. Addison's *Spectator,* "Such an habitual Disposition of Mind consecrates every Field and Wood, turns an ordinary Walk into a morning or evening Sacrifice, and will improve those transient Gleams of Joy, which naturally brighten and refresh the Soul on such Occasions, into an inviolable and perpetual State of Bliss and Happiness." That was exactly how Squire Gilbert felt when he walked around the estate and down into the village. The squire loved Nature, but Nature included far more in the eighteenth century than it ever has before or since.

Nature is the consummate chameleon of words, taking its coloration and shade of meaning not only from its context but also from the time and circumstances under which it is used. To the squire the rising sun, the dew on the grass, the haze in the air were part of Nature, but in no particularly important sense. It was a far more significant part of Nature that he was squire, that these gently billowing fields were his, that he owned a fine home and the farm buildings beyond, the plowed acres and the fallow, the salmon stream and the woods across it, and all the animals that roamed these acres and the plants that grew upon them. Nature was the sum of what existed, the order in which creation was arranged, the reason which inspired the whole, the immutable and infallible laws by which the universe operated. It was part of Nature that the salmon spawned at a certain season in the salmon stream, and it was part of Nature that he owned both the stream and the salmon.

God was subordinated to Nature in his thinking, and the devil really had no place in it at all. While the squire had only the haziest of notions about the work of Galileo and Newton, confused the Royal Society with society at the court of the Queen, and had never heard the names of Harvey and Boyle, he did not know that science had established the uniformity and reliability of Nature. He did know that design and order were universal principles, manifestations of the first law of God. Just as the medieval knight believed in the Father and the Son but felt closer to the Son, and as the Renaissance governor believed in God and His prince but felt closer to the prince, so Hugh Gilbert believed in God and Nature but felt closer to Nature. Nature in a sense was God as made manifest to man, an incarnation eternally visible and tangible. Since design, order, and right were its undeviating and eternal principles, there was no evil in it except as introduced by man and the perversity of his ways. The Prince of Darkness was left in exterior darkness, somewhere beyond the realms of light of which this world is a central part.

Therefore the code of conduct by which Squire Gilbert created for himself the ethical pattern of the good life was a simple one, suffused with optimism. Nature is the external manifestation of God. Since the principles of Nature are design and order, reason is its guiding norm. Since it is the hallmark of man that he is rational, man has within himself the guiding light by which he may lead the good life and merit salvation. Put more simply, and the squire liked things put simply, if a person is reasonable, leads a life of dignity and propriety, does what the established conventions of his class ordain that he do, he is leading the good life. To attend church on Sunday would be an estimable embellishment of his conduct, but hardly an integral part, nor should he entertain qualms of conscience about disregarding church dogma. The simple and direct teaching of Jesus was obviously natural, and hence as part of Nature could be comprehended by reason.

As he looked out into the freshness of the morning and found it good, he felt a sense of liberation which he had come to identify as an important part of the good life. The truth is that he did enjoy a freedom very much greater than enjoyed by either of his predecessors the knight or the governor. The knight had all but final responsibility for the fief and everything appertaining to it, and the responsibility of the governor while less was analogous. In principle at least the knight knew that he must lead the good life that leads to holiness and the governor the good life founded on loyal service, but the squire was called to neither sanctification nor loyalty. His was the good life that leads to happiness, and reason told him that the life of virtue which made him happy made its contribution to the universal happiness.

> *Thus God and Nature fixed the general frame,*
> *And bade self-love and social be the same.*

The word *Nature* in the sense understood by the squire would have been entirely incomprehensible to the knight and very nearly so to the governor, but each would have an understanding of what it represented. The knight knew his place in the state of things, and knew the duties he must perform in that place. So did the governor. They obeyed the laws of Nature, but the squire enjoyed the rights of Nature.

The squire enjoyed what is the rarest of earthly blessings, to be born at precisely the right time for the complete enjoyment of the rights of Nature as they appertain to one's personal state in life. He was born at a time when the centralization of government through the parliamentary system had brought into being a bureaucracy of professional administrators to rule the land. Like the knight and the governor he owned a spacious dwelling and an extensive estate, but unlike them he was responsible to no higher authority for their administration. They were his to manage and enjoy, and although like his

125

predecessors he had a retinue beneath him, he had no moral qualms about his duties toward them. He had reason to guide him in the ways of Nature, and that was the way God revealed His will to man. Science had proved that the world is orderly, systematic, and good; let him be the same, and he leads the good life. The forces of darkness, spiritual and physical alike, had been exorcised. The natural life was the good life, and to the squire the natural life was the life he led as master of the manor house, the farm, the woods, and the stream; husband of his dutiful wife and father of his obedient children; benign employer of many of lower rank who, like their medieval and Renaissance ancestors, accepted their degree as part of the immutable order and sought no other. He enjoyed stability, the rarest of social conditions, and peace, the most fleeting of worldly blessings. The social hurricane, like the physical, has a quiet eye. The hurricane of the seventeenth century had blown itself out, and the counterblast of revolution which would harry the end of the eighteenth century had not begun to blow. The squire lived his serene, comfortable, unperturbed, spiritually thin and philosophically shallow life in the eye of the hurricane. In many physical respects he lived the good life of the medieval baron and the Renaissance governor but there was a fundamental moral respect in which his life differed profoundly from theirs. Authority, responsibility, and the peremptory duty of charity were the very essence of the baron's life; the physically good things of life were perquisites that followed. The same was true but to a lessening degree of the Renaissance governor, since his authority and responsibility were subordinated to that of the prince, but they remained substantial and his duty of charity peremptory. But for the eighteenth-century squire authority had largely dwindled into the eliciting of deference, responsibility into the show of compassion, and the duty of charity into the instinct of kindliness. There were those like Squire Gilbert who were good men and lived good lives, but the iron was largely gone from them. Something gentle, pliant, soothing, even somnolent called Nature had replaced the saint and the prince as guide to action and challenge to achievement. For all too many the good life had ceased to be the life of service to others and become the life of indulgence to oneself.

Church-going was part of the life of Hugh Gilbert and his wife and served them, and the intent of the remark is not cynical, as an entirely adequate substitute for religion. Their two-dimensional lives provided an appropriate place for church-going, but did not have the depth where religion roots. After reading Addison's *Spectator 112* and noting the benefactions of Sir Roger de Coverley, Squire Hugh spruced up the village church, putting a railing around the communion table and having refinished by a London craftsman the fine old three-decker pulpit and scallop-shell sounding board. He also intimated, with an unaccustomed nuance of which he was rather proud, that the pinhole in the sandglass by which the parson timed his hour-long sermon had somehow become enlarged. The parson took the hint and padded the following Sunday sermon accordingly.

It was understood, of course, that the parson should preach the gospel according to Squire Gilbert. The parson was the son of a farmer who had profited by enclosure and had provided for his son as much education as a hungry servitor with a good many tasks to perform could bring from the university. The parson was fortunate to be located under Squire Gilbert, and reacted accordingly. He read the service and preached each Sunday, and even did the more discreet kind of parochial visiting. Unlike many less fortunate clerics who had to hold two livings to make a single living and so engaged some clerical wretch to act as curate in the lesser of the two, he lived in modest comfort on his single holding. He knew, and everyone knew, how deplorable were the living standards of many of the clergy, and how debased their lives. There were drunkards in the cloth and there were gamblers, ready to spur their cocks and set them in the fighting ring. There were not a few whom the Marquess of Halifax could warn a poor man's daughter to shun as she would the smallpox. But the literature of the period produced Parson Adams and the Vicar of Wakefield, and so did life. The parson of Squire Gilbert's village was an honest and honorable man who did his duty as he saw it, celebrating the Sacrament at least three times a year, giving to the deserving poor, and bringing at least a thin gruel of consolation to the afflicted.

The great lack was in the spirit. Even when medieval man sinned gravely, he believed profoundly and repented with his full heart. Faith was the core of his being and the motive force behind his life. The seventeenth-century Puritan was not by temperament an adventurer, but he left everything known and familiar, loved and desired, to live with grim fortitude between the estranging sea and the beetling forest because his faith in the God of hosts and his hope to fullfil his portion of the covenant bade him do so. One cannot picture the parson of Hugh Gilbert's village leaving everything to join Governor Winthrop at Boston. One cannot picture him leaving Hugh Gilbert's village for anything but a better living. His God was not the God of hosts nor the compassionate Christ of the Franciscans, but a dim abstraction, an essence hardly perceived in His works, the divine principle of the deists as aloof as the gods of Epicurus, Who showed Himself to man only through his vice-regent, Nature.

This was the God the parson preached and the congregation accepted. Sunday was observed, even by the ungodly. One could sell on Sunday in London, by a statute of Charles II, milk and mackerel (mysterious ordainment!) and nothing else. When Parson Woodforde broke his razor on Sunday, he wrote in his diary, "May it be a warning to me not to shave on the Lord's Day, or to do any other work to profane it, *pro futuro*." But it was Sunday that was observed, not the law of charity. The Church had become a junior partner of the State, and the peace of the Augustans rested upon it. But the peace of philosophy is always short-lived. Even as the parson watched with satisfaction the last grains of sand easily slip through the pinhole in the sandglass, John Wesley was mounting a footstool at a street corner in Coventry, and the living word was pouring from his lips to common people who thirsted for something more Christlike than philosophy.

2.
Down in the Village

THE fact is too infrequently observed that the closer we get to
our own day and age, the less important youth really is from
the cold viewpoint of the statistician. In the eighteenth century
just about half the population lived to maturity and consequently just about half the population of the village were ju-
veniles. The problem of educating youth in a society at least
half youth is obviously a sticky one. It was not a serious problem for the squire, who sent his sons to Westminster. The
parson did a bit of moonlighting as a pedagogue, but the relationship between the smattering of Latin he gave the sons of
ambitious tradesmen and the lives they were destined to lead
would tax the social scientist to establish. Indeed something
curiously reminiscent of the education of the young aristocrat
of the Middle Ages was present in eighteenth-century education. A typical school of the period is described in the Verney
letters. The curriculum comprised riding, fencing, dancing,
vaulting, using the pike, firing the musket, geography, and
mathematics. There was an extra charge for Latin. Squire Gilbert's village was fortunate enough to have a grammar school,
but the day when grammar was Latin grammar had passed
away. The farmers' children who attended learned the three
R's and had their morals slightly polished by pious exhortation.

129

Curiously, there was educational opportunity of a modest sort for the children of laboring families. For some years the Society for Promoting Christian Knowledge had been opening rural charity schools and there was one in the village. It was conducted by a local shopkeeper who had failed. It had a faculty of two, the other being the widow of the parson's predecessor, both of whom could read, write, and do simple sums. Their attainments were slight, but this was the century which saw a man appointed Regius Professor of Greek at Oxford on his promise to learn the language. As a practical matter, most of the effective teaching in the village was done at the local Sunday school which necessarily combined secular with religious instruction. A child must be able to read the Bible.

The eighteenth century was the heyday of village trade. The village weaver had his loom in the kitchen and his simple cottage industry provided employment for the family. The village miller plied his vital craft, retaining the name for roguery that was his from the day when Chaucer swung the pendulum in his *Canterbury Tales* from his first and noblest speaker the Knight to his second and most rascally the Miller. Then there were the butcher and the barber, the baker and the tailor, the grocer, the goldsmith, the druggist, and the charcoal burner. All were required to take apprentices, the boys serving until they were twenty-one and the girls until they were married. No generalization is legitimate about the lot of an apprentice. An honest tradesman who wanted to give a boy a good start in life taught him a trade with an efficiency no subsequent form of vocational education has ever matched, but all too many tradesmen set their apprentices to profitless drudgery and taught them nothing. The real weakness of the apprenticeship system arose from a fundamental fact of economic life: the number of businessmen in any age who are willing to train their own competition is austerely limited.

Eighteenth-century farmers worked hard hours and long, but good farmers with good farms prospered. Enclosure of the common lands in the Renaissance had been largely to promote sheepherding, and farmers had suffered. Enclosure in the eighteenth century was largely to make farming more efficient. The normal system in the open fields had been three-field rotation: one field in wheat, one in spring corn, and one fallow. Each farmer had his holdings divided among the three fields, with a long walk from plot to plot. Enclosure meant the elimination of many small farmers, who really had lived on the verge of poverty, but it meant the creation of more compact and more efficient farms, with mixed farming possible and better use of farm lands. The result was greater prosperity for the better farmers, and reduction to the laboring class for those who could not meet the competitive test. The farmer was in the field by five in the morning, but when dressed for church on Sunday he was the figure on Staffordshire pottery often taken for a squire. His wife was milking the cows at the same hour, but in the evening she played the harpsichord at least as deftly as Mrs. Gilbert. The farmer's home was the attractive cottage which is still part of the tourist's England. The laborer lived in a two-room hut to which he returned after his twelve-hour work day, but he had had a substantial dinner at noon and he would earn enough in harvest time to pay his annual rent. The one luxury in his life was tea, the price of which was kept within his reach by the salutary practice of smuggling. On the other hand, men like Squire Gilbert knew that the laborer existed and saw to it that he had coal and bed coverings in the winter, something extra for the celebration of Christmas, and help when he was ill.

All this, however, was little enough and depended on the existence of a Squire Gilbert. The laborer belonged to a class known as the laboring poor and by current economics, he was believed to lessen the wealth of the nation since his living expenses tended to be greater than his earnings. Economics, the dismal science, would not produce for many decades the iconoclast who would ask why a man who works hard and is not paid enough to support his family decreases the national wealth. It was taken for granted, however, that no laboring man could support more than two children. Poor relief was customarily geared to the number of children, and it was considered a valuable and practical charity to find employment for a laborer's wife and children. John Locke, whose status among the enlightened is very respectable, urged that laborers' children over the age of three be trained to earn their living at schools where they would be taught to spin and knit, and Daniel Defoe used as a yardstick for sectional prosperity the percentage of mothers and children gainfully employed.

The picture had another side. Working hours were long and wages were low, but working hours were not always irregular because employers made them such. Many laborers preferred to work long and hard for a few days, and then to enjoy, preferably on gin, the fruits of their labors. In a reverential spirit many of them abstained from work on Saint Monday, and some even observed Saint Tuesday. The belief that laborers would work steadily only when wages were low and food costs high, and hence that high wages were injurious since they simply increased the consumption of gin, does not necessarily brand one who held it as a social troglodyte. It does say much about the eighteenth-century mentality, however, that the notion that working men can be highly skilled, well paid, industrious, dependable, ambitious, and frugal was little entertained by members of the upper classes. The fact, of course, is that such working men speedily joined the economic upper classes themselves, and had toward those they left behind the usual contempt of the newly arrived. What is really striking and fundamental about the laborer's lot is the length of his work hours, the low rate of his pay, the irregular nature of his employment, and the fact that unless he had an unusually fine endowment in health, endurance, determination, and ambition, no matter how long and hard he worked, he would end his days as a laborer by walking out of that two-room hut and slowly trudging down the road to the village poor house. Unless he was very fortunate indeed, he would end his days under the ministrations of some eighteenth-century Mr. Bumble who got the poor house concession as lowest bidder to the vestrymen and made his profit out of the pittance the vestry allowed for its maintenance. The good life down in the eighteenth-century village was indeed what the villager made it, and he got precious little assistance from anyone. Village life was never quite so precarious before, and it has never been quite so precarious since.

3.

Self-Love as a Philosophy

AMONG the characteristic marks of the earlier part of the eighteenth century none is more striking than the sincerity with which its more fortunate figures believed that they had achieved happiness. The belief was by no means limited to Enland. The French *philosophe* Helvetius, intent on poetic immortality, felt it best achieved by a poem on his own happiness and that of all mankind. Gaiety makes gods of us, the Prussian Frederick the Great wrote to Voltaire, and austerity makes us devils. *L'Encyclopedie,* that philosophic compendium in thirty-five volumes of the known and the knowable which was at least in intent the great contribution of French thought and knowledge to the Enlightenment, blended into its religious scepticism and its philosophic materialism a system of ethics grounded on hedonism. Little wonder, then, that when the spirit of the age was sufficiently distilled and diluted to reach Squire Gilbert he saw himself as the happy man that indeed he was, and then was beguiled into the belief that his happiness somehow had developed out of the nature of things.

As an Englishman and a church-goer who had railed in the communion table, he framed his pattern of happiness in admirably moral terms: a clear conscience, contentment with his place in the order of Nature, a kindly spirit and a virtuous life.

133

To the extent that philosophy was at his command, he pressed philosophy into his service. We mortals are created to enjoy eternal happiness in heaven. How inconsistent and illogical it would be for God to intend earthly unhappiness to be a prelude to heavenly happiness! How unreasonable that time should contradict eternity! All mankind is actuated by the desire for happiness. Is it not logical, then, that our rules of conduct and our moral principles should be formulated in terms of felicity? Furthermore, if happiness is our destiny, then happiness is our right and we are right in examining to what degree we enjoy that right. If happiness is both our right and our goal, then happiness is virtue and the happy man is the good man.

It would be crediting Hugh Gilbert with more than he would ever claim for himself to suggest that there was in his mind any such systematic and conscious rationalization of self-love. He would certainly be appalled at the explicit enunciation of the doctrine in that essay by Frederick the Great the title of which bears its own clear message, "Essay on Self-Love Considered as a Moral Principle." Frederick's statement that Christianity and traditional philosophy both have failed to make men virtuous because they have failed to make men happy would stagger him. If Christianity had not made him happy, what had? He would find equally abhorrent the dictum of the Prussian philosopher-conqueror that common man must be given a new set of values, must be trained to cultivate neither the love of God nor the love of wisdom, but the love of self. And yet, underneath what would be his conscious rejection of such damnable doctrines would be an unconscious acceptance of them. Hugh Gilbert had not a vestige of the responsibility and the power of the medieval baron, and hardly the shadow of the responsibility and power of the Renaissance governor, but he had their rolling acres, their lordly dwellings, their staff of servants, their income, their prestige. Authority, responsibility, and duty had been largely removed from the good life that he led, and little of the spirit remained to inspire its material rewards but his natural kindliness, compassion, and good nature. Utilitarianism, the characteristic philosophy of the century with its calculus of pleasure and pain as the foundation of good and evil, is an explicit rationalization of the doctrine of self-love. It is a fair supposition that Hugh Gilbert never read Jeremy Bentham, but he was a follower of Jeremy Bentham just the same.

The unconscious tenor of Squire Gilbert's thought could be found as well down in the village. Enclosure aided farming and aided many farmers, but it heightened the competitive situation in farming and reduced many marginal farmers to the ranks of the laborers. The old fetters that the guild system and Renaissance economic controls had placed on trade had been struck off. The village was a busy place, and the business in its streets helped the farmers in its outskirts. The woolen trade produced great social divergences in the villages where it prospered. A successful clothier had a standard of living not far short of the one Hugh Gilbert enjoyed, but the poor spinners and weavers could earn only their pittance and think of the future that they hoped was remote, prayed might never come, but knew was there in waiting, the village workhouse. And yet visitors from the continent were unanimous in their belief that English villagers lived better lives in more comfortable homes and with less of the grinding poverty and degrading drudgery that marked village life in France, Germany, and Italy. The twin gospels of self-love and self-help lighted the way to self-improvement.

No doubt much of the ancient spirit of good neighborhood remained in the village. Disease still stalked the land, and suffering and bereavement were never far away. The simple comforts of the human heart were still longed for and still given. Charity and compassion were still part of the good life, but somehow a lesser part, it would seem, than once they were. Now the good life of material success and well-being loomed larger than it had before, and the competitive way more attractive than the cooperative. The result is that nearly anything one may say by way of praise or blame about the eighteenth century village is true. It was a more active and alert place than its predecessors had been, people who were getting ahead were getting higher and farther than their cramped and fettered ancestors had. Good farmers were becoming successful farmers, and the most successful were becoming rich farmers. There were new village industries, and at their most prosperous they brought a high living standard to those who most prospered by them. This was the great age of village life, as villagers became craftsmen as well as farmers and led more varied lives than their ancestors, lives that were more energetic and richer in opportunity. There was something like the Augustan peace in the village as there was on the country gentleman's estate. Prosperity, a rising living standard, better homes, better food, better clothes were Nature's reward for initiative and self-help.

On the other hand the laboring man could not be expected to support more than two children; the three-year-old was old enough for the first lessons in spinning and knitting; obviously one did the poor man's family no service by paying any member of it more than the iron minimum of wages since the surplus went for gin; and beyond the village, on the road to the next village which was its replica, was the workhouse which was farmed out to the lowest bidder, who made his own living out of the difference between his bid and what he doled out to those who lessened the national prosperity by existing. There was nothing beyond the workhouse except the graveyard and eternal salvation, the latter assured for the prosperous and available, one might hope, for the souls that entered eternity from the workhouse. To be sure, no one who philosophized explicity about self-love ever confused self-love and selfishness, or failed to stress the theoretically social nature of self-love. But unfortunately, not all villagers were philosophers any more than all who lived in great houses, nor indeed are all philosophers such in practice. The most that can be claimed for enlightened self-love in the eighteenth century is that it aspired to enlightenment, a claim that can often be honestly made for specious and inadequate philosophies. When one speaks of light, one speaks not only of its existence but also of its penetrating power and its reliability.

We have chosen to illustrate the philosophy of self-love in the village. The same philosophy prevailed in the cities, of course, and nowhere more than in that great city, now approaching 675,000 in population, which dominated England in the eighteenth century as it never had before or has since. London streets were crowded, street cries were deafening, street after street glittered with seductive shop windows suggestive of brilliant luxury within. It was a massive industry to feed the city, another to clothe it, a third to transport necessities to it. London was an electromagnet, drawing to its pulsating heart the most virile and original, unconventional and energetic of the English people. Here more than in any other English city, and certainly more than in any English village, the new philosophy of self-love would have its devotees. This was the city of massive opportunity. Tobacco and cotton might be making that sleepy seaport Liverpool a bustling city of great potential; American iron might be forging what would be the Manchester and Birmingham of the nineteenth century; Glasgow, Leeds, and Sheffield might be developing a breed of merchant princes; something like field factories might be emerging to feed the workers of Lancashire. Put them all together, and London towered above them all.

Three men met on Rotten Row, and the past they shared in a quiet Worcestershire village merged with their immediate pasts and their glamorous presents. All had come up to the city from that quiet village. One had been the village squire. He had sold his estate, invested in South Sea securities, and got out in time. The second had been a yeoman farmer. He had sold his farm, gone to St. Kitts, and returned a prosperous planter. The third had been a shopkeeper. He had sold his shop, come to London, and discovered a fortune in Jamaica rum. The old social degrees of the village were forgotten in this new democracy of wealth, and three old villagers shared recipes for the good life.

The quick way to make money, they agreed, was by gambling on the market. The gambler was totally unprotected, but he was also totally uncontrolled. Wits were matched against wits, in a game as totally stripped of luck as chess. Indeed lotteries were the ordinary way to finance the most laudable of enterprises, and many of London's most estimable charities had as their fairy godmother Lady Chance. In the view of the erstwhile village squire a speculative enterprise that should be especially attractive to those who preferred rapid appreciation to security was to purchase a seat in Commons. Brokers sold them on the Stock Exchange, he assured his farmer and shopkeeper friends who had not totally shaken off their pasts and found this revelation a bit heady. Nabobs returning from India, with opulence at their disposal and the sweet wine of authority now familiar to them, were frequent purchasers. A seat for a rotten borough, the squire said, would go for about 1400 pounds. It would be an unenterprising public servant who could not turn that much over in a year, and have prestige as his unearned increment. But the farmer turned St. Kitts planter had his own ideas. To him prestige mattered, and it mattered that it be enjoyed in the right place. He bought the estate that his quondam landlord the squire had vacated and became himself the head of a county family.

Those who talk and write of the monied aristocracy, frequently in a muddled blend of rebuke and envy, might consider on occasion the phenomenon that so often exists within its ranks, the monied democracy. It was particularly in evidence in eighteenth-century London in Hyde Park and St. James's Park. The consecrated promenade period was from noon to two o'clock, after a lady had finished the cup of chocolate that refreshed her following the exhausting morning toilette. The world of true fashion might have grudgingly admitted the erstwhile squire whom we met on Rotten Row, but willy nilly it had to admit as well the farmer turned planter and then himself squire, and even the shopkeeper now expanded into warehouse owner. They walked and their ladies walked beside the true aristocrats, and in the summer they congregated with the *beau monde* at Bath and except to Beau Nash and the few with his powers of perception were indistinguishable from it. That sour Scottish surgeon turned novelist, Tobias Smollett, catalogues them in *Humphrey Clinker:* "Every upstart of fortune, harnessed in the trappings of the mode, presents himself at Bath, as in the very focus of observation. Clerks and factors from the East Indies, loaded with the spoil of plundered provinces; planters, negro-drivers, and hucksters, from our American plantations, enriched they know not how; agents, commissaries, and contractors, who had fattened, in two successive wars, on the blood of the nation; usurers, brokers, and jobbers, have found themselves suddenly translated into a state of affluence, unknown to former ages; and no wonder that their brains should be intoxicated with pride, vanity, and presumption. Knowing no other criterion of greatness but the ostentation of wealth, they discharge their affluence without taste or conduct through every channel of the most absurd extravagance; and all of them hurry to Bath, because here, without any further qualification, they can mingle with the princes and nobles of the land." Since the lesser tradesmen and even the office clerks within their capacities imitated them, this was the monied democracy with which that arbiter of the elegant at Bath, Beau Nash, had to contend. Beau Nash is usually depicted as the ultimate in affected effeminacy of behavior. In truth, by using his prestige to make balls begin and end at reasonable hours, by making people behave at them, dress properly and act properly—he saw nothing about a dance at a watering place that would require a man to use a sword and hence no grounds for his wearing one—Beau Nash was trying to introduce at Bath a set of distinguishing characteristics for the true aristocrats. Artificiality can at least be courteous and graceful, and commoners who would play the game can at least learn the correct rules from the aristocrats.

Perhaps the most rewarding place in which to seek the philosophic foundation of the good life as so much of England in the earlier part of the century understood it is David Hume's *Enquiry Concerning the Principles of Morals* (1752). Hume reduces ethics to approval or disapproval of human conduct, and morality to a calculus of pleasure and pain. An action that causes pleasure merits approval, an action that causes pain deserves disapproval. "Nothing can be more real, or concern us more, than our own sentiments of pleasure or uneasiness," Hume wrote, "and if these be favorable to virtue, and unfavorable to vice, no more can be requisite to the regulation of our conduct and behaviour." Hume allows no place for reason as a determinant of distinctions between right and wrong. Reason deals with what is or is not, and not with what should or should not be. The specific qualities that make for pleasure and hence win moral approval Hume divides into three groups, those pleasing in themselves, those that make for the pleasure of others, and those that please us when present in others. Hume does not fall into the trap of reducing all motives to self-love. If that could be done, self-love could justify actions detrimental to others. Indeed no right thinking Augustan ever confused self-love and selfishness, or failed to stress the necessarily social nature of self-love.

The true weakness which made the peace of the Augustans so short-lived must be sought elsewhere. The new morality of the eighteenth century, as expounded most clearly by David Hume, disregarded what have been the two foundations of enduring moral systems, the sense of objectivity and the sense of duty. Does self-interest cast a light penetrating enough to illuminate the heart of society's needs? Is the light of self-interest reliable enough to flood the dark corners and hidden recesses of the human heart? These are the questions the Augustans never asked, and never would have thought to ask. Hume and those who agreed with him made the foundation of their morality empirical and not ethical. To them the good life is the life of which men of common sense approve. Nowhere in the concept is there a place for responsibility and consequently morality is by nature attractive rather than imperative. The good life is the attractive life, the one that is good because it promises us the greatest happiness as the world understands happiness.

Much of what is termed with disparagement and contempt "the nineteenth-century attitude" really was a continuation into the nineteenth-century of the eighteenth-century attitude. Much of what is really characteristic of the nineteenth-century attitude is the attempt to combat that individualism, often so heartless and self-centered, which was part of an unhappy legacy from its predecessor. As Nature replaced God in man's thinking, success became its own excuse for being. The moral aspect of the good life subsided into a feeling of quiet satisfaction and approval of one's own conduct. The satisfaction and approval might have solid grounds; charity, benevolence, kindliness are not the exclusive prerogatives of any time and place. There was many a benevolent country squire in England, many a kindly and charitable villager, many a city dweller who sacrificed himself for those near and dear to him, and whose benefactions extended to his neighbors. The difficulty with the thinking of the age was that it encouraged the sort of self-love which leads to spiritual pride and discouraged the subordination of self-love to the sense of responsibility and duty to the laws of God and man.

Consequently the good life became increasingly materialist, increasingly something measured in acres and pounds sterling, in houses, dress, horses, equipages; something lived where fashion dictated and as fashion dictated, and the arbiter, useful and well intentioned though he might be, was an arbiter of manners like Beau Nash and not an arbiter of morals. Those in possession of it lived the good life of material prosperity and deemed it theirs by Nature. Those ambitious for it worked hard and, in an atmosphere of free enterprise less sullied than it ever was before or has been since, achieved it and deemed achievement proper to their personal Nature. Those not born to either prosperity or ambition tended to slide backward and downward in the economic scale, to have more and more of the hard and bitter life, and to find such alternative recompense as their spirits dictated. To some it was gin, to others the hope of eternity, for still others there was no alternative recompense at all. In the thirteenth century the cripple in the hut was the responsibility of everyone in the fief; in the eighteenth century the cripple in the workhouse was the responsibility of the warden who got the concession by making the lowest bid to the vestrymen. For a time, as we have said, society was in equilibrium, with the rich secure in their riches, the poor quiescent in their poverty, and the peace of the Augustans over the land. The philosophy of the deists and the sceptics, of Bolingbroke, Shaftesbury, and Hume was triumphant. But John Wesley was preaching on a street corner in Leeds, and some very obscure men in London were puzzling with their inadequate French over this new philosophy of human rights that was being penned across the Channel.

4.

The Inner Church

SARAH FINCH was far from certain that she was doing the right thing, and farther still from certainty that she was doing the safe thing. Nothing but the trust and confidence she had in the other woman who had been her neighbor for so short a time and yet in kindliness and neighborly service seemed to have been her neighbor forever gave her the confidence to climb the rickety and dingy steps to the upper story of that old and weather-beaten house. Her neighbor had prepared her for what in her mind she thought of as the ordeal but in her neighbor's reassurance was the opportunity to grasp and to cherish what she had sought in a dim and fumbling way since she came to Leeds after the farm was sold. Her neighbor assured her that in that old and weather-beaten house she could hear the simple gospel preached that could no longer be heard in the cathedrals of England, and she could meet other women who lived by it. Therefore she entered the room.

Her neighbor presented her to the five women inside, and each greeted her in a spirit somehow compounded of friendliness, sympathy, and understanding. Then she was questioned about her life, about what was covert as well as what was open, about what was in her mind and heart as well as what was on her lips. This was the ordeal, but somehow it seemed less an ordeal than a baptism out of an old life into a new. Later, when she went down the rickety and dingy steps into the drab street that already was taking on that look of grime in the grain that marks industrial England, she had a new confidence that she could walk through dirt and grime unsoiled. She had been invited to return again to that little room, to join her newly made friends. She knew that return would require confession as well as bring consolation, but she also sensed that somehow the price paid for the consolation was part of the reward. Truth crushed to earth will rise again, and so will the true spirit of religion. Sara Finch had been introduced to a Methodist band and before long would be a member.

There were two worlds of the English eighteenth century, the world of the Augustans and their emulators, and the world of poverty, disease, and the oblivion of gin into which Sara Finch had sunk but to which she did not belong. Sara had attended the village church in the days when her father owned the farm, and the contented worldliness of the parson's preaching seemed to her worlds apart from the message of the gospels. She had attended several chapels in Leeds, and found dissent no improvement on establishment: services were dull and dreary, and dullness in the preaching was hardly relieved by the sort of futile bitterness that at times pervaded it. The village church had belonged to the world of the Augustans but was open, of course, to their retainers. The city chapel belonged to the world of poverty and the Augustans were unaware of its existence. Sara Finch felt vaguely that the spirit of the gospels had died in the village church of spiritual complacency and died in the city chapel of spiritual malnutrition. She was, then, a seeker who gradually came to know that what she sought she had found.

The ideal of John Wesley was one of reformation in a simple and even austere sense. It was to make religion once more a personal experience, a vivification of the soul, a current that flowed through a person's being and formed his thoughts, words, and actions. The pattern of reformation he sought in the primitive church, where Christianity was fresh, young, pure, and fired with enthusiasm for the holy and the righteous life. Hence the thought of reformation in terms of tiny bands of seekers and believers. Sara Finch became a member of such a band and in the course of time had two simple and unforgettable experiences in religion pure and unsullied. One was a love feast, what the early Christians called the *agape*. The men had had theirs, then the women had theirs, and then they held a joint love feast. The food was plain cake and the drink was water, but those present ate in gladness of heart and fraternity of spirit. In the little room there was a warmth, a sense of union, a feeling that however weak a single reed may be, there is a strength in the bundle on which one can rely. It was not the eighteenth century in that little room but the second century, with the light of Christ quietly burning in a dark and pagan world. Sara Finch could not tell what happened there, not because it was unspeakable in the sense that the suspicious and prurient charged of Methodist love feasts but because it was unspeakable in the sense that language is not equipped to tell the surge of faith, the light of hope, and the warmth of charity. The other experience was a watch night. For this several bands joined and from early evening through midnight until nearly three the following morning there was unending prayer. Then, as Wesley himself recorded of a similar watch night, "the power of God came mightily upon us, insomuch that many cried out for exceeding joy, and many fell to the ground. As soon as we were recovered a little from that awe and amazement at the presence of His majesty we broke out with one voice, 'We praise thee, O God; we acknowledge thee to be the Lord.' " Sara Finch was long in recovering from that memorable experience. There had been an exaltation about it, a visionary quality that somehow seemed to her both inspirational and perilous. And yet the experience bothered her. She was not sure that its high emotionalism was any more consistent with the gospel message than was the contented worldliness of the village church or the arid bitterness of the city chapel. Somehow the customary, reassuring, by now familiar band meeting did seem consistent with that message.

The two fundamentals about the organization of early Methodism were that the unit was the little band and the entirety was an inner church within the Church of England. John Wesley had inherited from his clerical father the high church tradition, and he was justified when he claimed in his old age that he had preached for forty years the identical Christian doctrine. He valued the sacraments highly, considered new birth the essence of baptism, urged frequent Holy Communion, conceived of the Church as catholic and apostolic. He opposed predestination and made the cornerstone of his preaching his belief in justification by faith. Justification and personal regeneration promote that growth in holiness which is sanctification: "Christians are called to love God with all their hearts and to serve Him with all their strength, which is precisely what I apprehend to be meant by the scriptural term, perfection." Wesley firmly believed that God wills the salvation of everyone.

Wesley quite obviously posed a problem to the Church of England and to its bishops, and ultimately individual clerics solved the problem by their individual good judgments. Orthodox Anglicans could find nothing heretical in his teaching and many opened their pulpits to him. It is perhaps significant that Bishop Potter of Oxford, who conceived of Establishment in religious terms and not political, was especially cordial to him, whereas the politically oriented Bishop Gibson of London wavered, with an inclination toward hostility. What all the clergy saw was that Methodist preachers invaded their parishes, gathered congregations far beyond the capacity of the local churches to attract, and through their annual conference, which had a set of rules after 1743, constituted something that was really an inner church quite beyond control by the parent body. But the open-minded also saw in the Methodist bands which remained the cornerstone of Methodist organization a sense of community of purpose and dedication no longer present in the Church of England or the dissenting churches, and in the lives of their members a sobriety, wholesomeness, dignity, and something seldom found in church or chapel that certainly approached sanctification and in many cases undeniably achieved it.

Sara Finch never developed an interest in Methodism that transcended her local band in her obscure corner of Leeds. She and her fellow Christians lived the Christian life as the band leader expounded it to them, confessing their faults to one another and strengthened in their penitence by one another's support. That when need arose in the life of one, all the women and the men of the companion band came to her assistance went without saying. But without saying much, it went farther. Sara Finch quietly visited the sick of the street on which she lived, and brought a little something for the stricken family to eat after darkness masked her benefactions. She and another member of the band once went to that section where no right-thinking Methodist would go except in the name of charity and brought back a girl to the street from which she had strayed. Sara was frightened to death every moment of the time, as she freely admitted, but perhaps the Lord is as willing to accept fear as the offering of the fearful as He is to accept courage of the courageous.

Sara Finch had heard of what the saintly Wesley brothers had done at Oxford, of the little society of earnest men they formed who went to the prisons of Oxford, the Castle and the Bocardo, bringing food, clothing, fuel, and the word of God. She knew how as time went on the cells of the Castle and Bocardo became as much a part of John Wesley's life as the common rooms of Lincoln College where he was a tutor, how he started a school for the prisoners, saw to it that they had legal help, and then extended his ministrations to the Oxford workhouses which were down the road beyond the point in Oxford at which learning, tradition, architecture, and security end. She also heard that the methodical pattern of the lives of the little group, and especially their appraisal of the method of study employed at the university and its contents, had won them that nickname, Methodists, which had stuck. She also had heard the most garbled and unintelligible stories of the experiences of the Wesley brothers in Georgia but since she could make no heads nor tails of them, she sensibly dismissed them from her mind. She knew that no one in her century had done what John Wesley did with his quarter-million miles of missionary travels in England and his 40,000 sermons, his preaching in the open air, at markets, on village greens, whenever opportunity permitted, wherever there were those who would listen to the word of God. She had heard of George Whitefield, but had not heard him. She knew that he was a magnificent preacher, a showman of the first order, a Calvinist by background and indeed by instinct but one whose Calvinism was modified by charity. She had heard, however, that he had his doctrinal differences with Wesley and she counted herself in Wesley's flock. She knew, of course, of the emotional displays that once accompanied John Wesley's sermons, the raving and screaming of the hysteric and that later quiet of exhaustion that somehow was considered conversion, and she was glad to learn that that sort of thing was subsiding. She had seen it herself that first watch night and it seemed to her to bear no relationship to the gospel. The formal organization of Methodism never particularly concerned Sara Finch, nor indeed did she live to see it in the full sense. She was dead and buried by 1784 when the Methodist constitution was adopted and her son died in 1791, the year the Methodists broke away from the Church of England and founded the Wesleyan Methodist Church or, as it is known in the United States, the Methodist Episcopal Church.

The brotherhood of man never survives for very long the fatherhood of God. The formal religion of the eighteenth century had surrendered to philosophy. God the Father was reduced to a philosopher's abstraction and Christ to a teacher of ethics. Even when the orthodox opposed deism, they did so in legalistic terms. William Warburton Bishop of Gloucester refuted deism by proving that God acted according to the British constitution; as Leslie Stephen put it, "There is but one God, and Warburton is his Attorney-General." Once belief in a personal Deity had shrunk to belief in deism and the gospels had been replaced by Nature as the norm of man's actions, the good life ceased to be rooted in authority, responsibility, and duty and became the good life of the senses. Once God was dead the brotherhood of man died also, and what we ordinarily think of as the eighteenth century took on shape

147

and spirit. But beside the eighteenth century of the enlightened Augustans who lived in peace, there was the eighteenth century of Sara Finch, who also lived in peace. The salvation of the century started in Oxford, but not in college halls and common rooms. It started in the cells of condemned men and women, humans condemned to the two kinds of prison the century knew, the Bocardo and the workhouse. The spirit of Christ found life again behind their dismal walls, His spirit spread through mean streets and dingy dwellings, His Church had a rebirth as little bands lit once more the candle of faith and handed on the light, and the dead God returned to life.

It is equally easy to ridicule Methodism and to idealize it. Its very informality and intimacy encouraged aberration; fanaticism could glow quite as truly as faith in the seclusion of a band meeting; not only the impassioned oratory of Whitefield but even the prosaic preaching of Wesley himself—and it is repeatedly so described—gave rise to exhibitionism and true hysteria; its confessional element invited the pathological. All this can be said against the movement, as well as everything that can be said against the "we happy few" mentality when it wraps itself in the cloak of sanctimony and is holier than thou. When all that has been said, it can be said in sober seriousness that Methodism was the redemption of the century. The Methodists led austerely rigid lives when dedicated to their principles. Sometimes the rigidity was repellent; Wesley's views on the treatment and education of little children test to the ultimate both one's charity and one's willingness to believe in the essential rightness of his message. And yet in the heart of that austerity rested the jewel of charity. The Methodists visited the sick and attended to their needs; they visited the prison and the workhouse and brought comfort to both and a certain measure of hope; they gave of what they had to each other and to their fellow man. As they grew in numbers and in influence, they extended their benefactions. They worked for the betterment of children where they were exploited; they worked for humane treatment of men in military and naval service; they fought against the press gang and the misuse of the penal colonies. They assumed the fight against human

148

slavery and carried it to victory. By the Treaty of Utrecht (1713) England had gained a monopoly on the slave trade and contracted to supply the Spanish West Indies with 144,000 slaves in thirty years; by the treaties of Vienna and Paris (1814–1815) England renounced the entire slave trade and dedicated itself to its overthrow. The change in national sentiment toward that foulest of human blots was not the work of the Augustans but of the Methodists.

When we speak, then, of the good life of the eighteenth century, it is not entirely the good life of Squire Gilbert and the successful farmers of the village, nor the good life of the returning planter and the successful gambler in securities enjoying the delights of Bath; neither is it entirely the good life as rationalized by the deists and given its final expression in the lucid but limiting scepticism of David Hume. This is the good life as patterned in its most sensible and proper form by Addison; satirized in its shortcomings savagely by Swift, ponderously by Johnson, and urbanely by Goldsmith; justified philosophically by Bolingbroke and Shaftesbury, Hutcheson and Hume. It is the good life one meets in eighteenth-century literature, and implicit in that very fact is a solemn warning: no age in history should ever be judged exclusively by its literature, or indeed by its art. The person who knows the eighteenth century only by the writings of Addison, Johnson, and Hume, or by the paintings of Gainsborough, Reynolds, and Allston, knows as much of eighteenth-century England as the modern tourist knows of twentieth-century England who visits only London, the picturebook counties in the south of England, and the shrines of Stratford and never sees Birmingham and Manchester, Lancashire and Yorkshire.

There was also the eighteenth century of John Wesley and his disciple Sara Finch. Their pattern of the good life was quite literally centuries apart from what we ordinarily think of as the eighteenth-century pattern. Explicitly their pattern was the early Christian centuries. Limitations of their theological vision might make them repudiate the charge with acrimony, but in spirit the eighteenth-century Methodists were much closer to the Benedictine monks and the Franciscan

149

friars than they were to the church of their own day and age. The leader of a Methodist band knew what authority and responsibility meant; the members of a band understood the law of charity. Their good life rested on the ancient values and the primitive Christian principles. There was nothing classical about them at all, nothing to suggest the good citizen of Athens. There was more than a little that was medieval about them, and for all their rejection of Calvinist theology, in their austerity and seriousness there was in them much of the Puritan. Most important of all, there was so very little about them suggestive of what we think of as the eighteenth century. They reached down into the world of the poor and depressed, and gave a purpose to their lives. They brought an elevation of purpose and a vision into mean and sordid streets. As time went on they saw between their charitable aims and brotherly spirit and the aims and purposes of the trade unions a certain similarity, and Methodists became trade unionists and for a time at least a certain moral fervor was instilled in the union movement. Beyond lay the politics of the nineteenth century, and Methodism again demonstrated the possible affinity between religious dedication and political reform. The full growth of Methodism has belonged to the nineteenth and twentieth centuries. In 1801 there were 825 Methodist meeting houses in England, in 1850 there were 11,000; the Methodists numbered 90,000 in 1801 and 358,000 in 1850. There were still Augustans of the spirit to be found in 1801, and indeed in 1850, but by 1850 the world of Pope and Johnson had long been dead and buried, and the world of Gainsborough and Reynolds grown quaint and archaic. It would hardly be accurate to say that the meek Methodists had inherited the earth, but at least they were doing distinctly better than the Augustans. Sara Finch outlived Hugh Gilbert.

5.

The Better Day

ISAAC BATES had an excellent memory, a curse from which he often wished heartily to be freed. One picture burned into his memory would take much explaining before the incredulity of our generation could be removed. The picture could even be thought a pleasant one: a group of young girls, none beyond their teens, being drawn in a large wagon through London streets. It could have been a hay ride. It could have been a day's outing in the country that was getting under way, or the girls could have been on their way to the river for a boat ride up the quiet Thames. But these young girls were not going on a hay ride, or to the country, or up the river. They were going to Tyburn to be hanged. They had been apprehended setting fires during the Gordon riots. Isaac Bates stood and watched them as they passed, and with unmoving lips thought the kind of deep and solemn curse that somehow is a prayer. Samuel Rogers also was in London that day and saw them, and recorded the sight in his *Table Talk*.

Isaac Bates knew how incredibly common such sights were, and how hardened even the good become when the incredible is the common. When the century started there were 160 capital offenses; before the century was over there were 253. The death penalty was imposed for any theft of five shillings or

over, and indeed of one shilling if a pickpocket was apprehended lifting it. The bodies of the hanged swayed and pirou-
etted in the Tyburn dance of death, and good people hoped
that somehow good might come of it as weak souls played
Russian roulette with their lives for the sake of a purloined
shilling or a few stolen handkerchiefs. Some, like Isaac Bates,
were sickened by the vindictiveness of the law, and perhaps
as much and more by the hollowness, futility, and shame of it
all. He knew the phrase the philosophers used, the Enlightenment, and when he spoke the word there was a curl to his lip
that suggested what he dared not speak aloud.

There was a drab and dreary tone to London life as Isaac
Bates knew it, far from Hyde Park and St. James's Park, that
gave way now and then to something sulfuric and obscene.
There was the vicious perversion of sport, with savage dogs
fighting death battles with bulls until the dogs were gored and
the bull lacerated to death. There were the cock fights, battles
of insanely maddened birds with sharpened beaks and steel
spurs two inches long. Blood welled and dripped and formed
black pools, thickening and trapping the flies until freshened
with new blood. The fashionably morbid from that seraglio of
eighteenth-century London, Drury Lane, came down to watch,
and mingled with those from the mean and sordid streets,
their blood brothers pathologically speaking. Something deep
in the heart of Isaac Bates was moved by such sights and
sounds, moved in a way that no passage of time nor healing
other sights would ever reverse.

There was the great balm of souls and opener of magic
casements to which the England of Isaac Bates turned with
such ready instinct when the world was too much with it. The
peak consumption year of gin was 1750, with eleven million
gallons consumed by a population hardly greater than six
million. That year there were 506 gin shops among the 2000
houses of St. Giles, London. At first there was rejoicing among
the greedy theorists in the rude and harsh beginnings of what
would become the respectable science economics. The tremen-
dous surge in the consumption of gin was bringing an increased
prosperity to a country in need of a fiscal fillip; a private vice

is indeed a public benefit, as that shrewd philosopher Bernard de Mandeville had pointed out. The benefit was less clear to Isaac Bates, as he picked his way around those fallen on the dismal street on which the magic casements really opened, and weaved to avoid the lurches of those whose souls were not yet completely embalmed. Neither was it clear to that police court judge and novelist Henry Fielding, who is immortal for *Tom Jones* but whose "Enquiry into the Late Increase of Robbers" (1751) is pertinent to our present point.

Isaac Bates was not a church-goer. He was not, except perhaps in the sense that mattered to Christ, a Christian. He lived around the corner from a gentle Methodist named Ruth and Ruth had attempted to proselytize him but without success. Isaac was gentle with Ruth and made no attempt to overwhelm her with arguments she would not understand and the citing of authorities of whom she had never heard. He knew that in the little band to which she belonged there was a sincerity and spirit of charity that were priceless. He could not give intellectual assent to what they believed, but he gave his entire heart to the spirit in which they believed it. He would concede that there is a light of Christ, but maintained that it is not to be found in religion but in philosophy.

To Isaac Bates, a man with his own limitations which were indeed partly his own and partly those of his age, religion was theology and theology was the churches. As for the Church of England, it was what the cupidity of man made it. There was the Manners family, with its eight English sees and its twelve Irish sees, and the 650,000 pounds a year religion paid the Manners. That had to be divided among the members of a family. The Bishop of Llandaff had for himself his fourteen livings in Huntingdonshire, Leicestershire, and Shropshire. But Isaac Bates knew that when the hour of decision came, the high prelates of the Church earned their recompense. They earned it in the House of Lords, where Walpole had the votes of twenty-four of the twenty-six bishops to start with on any contested issue. Viscount Bolingbroke defined a bishop as "a layman with a crook," and Isaac Bates would give the definition an even unkinder twist. To him the Church was the branch of the State which gave the purple tinge of piety to the black practices of government. The Church was there to make it right that Old Sarum have two members of Parliament although no one lived in the abandoned borough, that Sir Mark Wood who owned the six houses at Gratton be the only voter, and that Glasgow, with its population of 200,000 have thirty-three voters. The Church was also there to make it right that 30,000 children in Lancashire work the fourteen hour day in the mills, with men behind them with whips to keep them awake and in their charity save them from falling into the machinery and becoming maimed (as many perversely did) and therefore economically unprofitable and drains upon the national income. The Church could also make it right that contractors roam the country selling the services of gangs of workhouse children, and explain to the fifteen Englishmen in a hundred who were on parish relief that whatever is, is right, that eternity provides the perfect round and time the broken arc.

The real tragedy of Isaac Bates was that he was not cynical enough to measure the true nature of his own cynicism. He was bitterly cynical about the Church and bitterly cynical about the government, but he was not quite cynical enough to see that the Church was not the Church, and that the government was not government. In her simple way, which was entirely without guile or cynicism, Sara Finch had a clear picture of what the Church was, and possibly in the respect she paid the leader of her band coupled with the sense she had of personal responsibility for her share of the work of the world, she had an instinctive understanding of what government really is. She had her limitations, to be sure, as Isaac had his, but they were not the same limitations. The basic difference was that Sara was the daughter of the layman turned monk who came down from Monte Cassino to repair the road to Subiaco, whereas Isaac Bates was the son of Socrates. She pinned her faith on charity and he on knowledge, she on religion and he on philosophy.

The solemn fact was that as the century progressed, the war between "the two nations" intensified and became inveterate. The Augustans had their peace so long as the lower classes did not rebel at their lot. The peace of the Augustans, however, was an uneasy peace and it was fated to end when the masses no longer believed that whatever is, is right, and there were those among them who murmured, whatever is, is wrong. Americans are conscious of the Tories on their side of the ocean who never accepted the thesis on which the American Revolution rested, never made the mental shift from the viewpoint of British subjects agitating for their rights to the viewpoint of American citizens fighting for their freedom. Americans are less conscious of the fact that for every Tory on the western shore, there were at least five sympathizers with America in the British Isles. They are less conscious of the thousands of Britons who viewed the surrender at Yorktown as a glorious victory for the right, and who later viewed the French Revolution as the dawn in Europe of the glorious reality of human freedom which the American Revolution presaged. Had it been otherwise, when war broke out between England and France in 1793 it would not have seemed necessary to repeal habeas corpus, to prohibit public meetings, to censor the press, to place stern penalties on seditious writings, and to give magistrates the power to impose the death penalty. Let us return to Isaac Bates, as he passes from his not unlucrative toil as a wainwright to his obscure lodgings where he has his books, from his means of livelihood to his life itself.

If Isaac Bates were given to vanity, he probably would choose to be vain about his ability to read French. It would be easy enough, and cruel enough, to joke about Isaac and his French since he had no capacity whatever to speak the language and had he attempted it in the presence of a Frenchman, Gallic politeness would have been unnecessary since no Frenchman would recognize that this curious Englishman was speaking French. Isaac's primal innocence of French pronunciation was of not the slightest consequence, for Isaac had made a discovery that often escapes the linguists. Language is a medium for the communication of ideas, and Isaac grasped the ideas while knowing very little about the medium. In short, he did with French what the scholars of the Renaissance did

155

with ancient Greek. He read a language he could not speak nor even pronounce.

Night after night as he slowly chewed his way through Turgot, Voltaire, Rousseau, Diderot, Chastellux, and the rest, new and yeasty ideas fermented in his head. He met in Fontenelle the theory of inevitable progress; "if Descartes was not born, someone else would have done his work." Progress is more rapid in science than in morals, but progress in morals can be more rapid than it is. The idea drove him back to the old Abbé de Saint-Pierre and such a thundering herd of chimeras that his faith in his own ability to progress was badly shaken. But he emerged with the central thought: given the right form of government and the right laws, moral progress and therefore social progress are inevitable. Not all the cynicism of Voltaire could shake his instinctive acceptance of that resolute optimism. Then he found in Helvetius something to which every fibre of his being was resonant. The intellectual and moral differences among men are not the result of innate differences but of differences in education and social background. Change education and change the social background, and you will change men. Not all the misgivings of Diderot about this doctrine could shake his faith in it, a faith somewhat pathetic since he so ardently wished it to be true. Man can be perfected, if man perfects his government, his institutions, and his laws. Isaac read Rousseau, and was highly selective in accepting what he read. He sensed something limiting and defeatist in the very nature of Rousseau's primitivism, but he responded strongly to Rousseau's faith in equality and democracy. He found in the Chevalier de Chastellux a writer whom he knew to be a lesser man in writing power but one closer to the position which he instinctively assumed. Chastellux assumed inequalities to be inevitable as man progressed toward perfection, but certain to disappear as he approached it. Enlightenment through education made possible that progress to equality which is man's earthly destiny.

As Isaac chewed his way through the French literature of thought in all its complexity and confusion, and saw how men of sincerity and competence could differ on fundamentals and

156

become embattled over means to ends they held in common, there slowly emerged a realization that there are two basic theories about the progress which all right thinking men deemed necessary and many deemed inevitable. One group of writers believed that progress is something managed by government and law, something achieved when the state is supreme and the authority of its benevolent institutions is unquestioned. The other group—and it seemed to him somewhat mystical and vague and yet his instincts told him that he belonged to it —believed that progress was something achieved by man as an individual, that freedom was the atmosphere in which it took place, education the means to the end, opportunity for self-advancement the catalyst, and equality before the law its necessary first condition. To this group government was a negative rather than a positive concept, a force that stepped in to protect individual freedom and opportunity for self-advancement when they were threatened. Without suspecting it, Isaac had marshalled the forces destined to struggle through the century ahead. That Isaac Bates rejoiced when he heard of Lexington and Concord, sensed the peril in what Burgoyne and Gates were to attempt and felt a mighty weight fall off when he learned of Bennington and Saratoga, thrilled to the romance of Trenton and Princeton, and felt that Yorktown opened an era of unparalleled promise follows logically enough. It was equally logical that he take his stand and nearly pay with his life when repression crushed the spirit of democracy in 1793. He lived to see the nineteenth century dawn, and he died never suspecting that it would not be the millennium.

Isaac Bates never lived the good life, never thought of the good life as possible for his generation, and yet his every thought and hope centered about it. He was a man with a sense of ability far greater than his possibility of accomplishment. He sensed that his intelligence was not less than that of the formally educated. He had fought his way through the terrors of the French language and emerged triumphant. He had wrestled with the thought of men like Diderot, Helvetius, Voltaire, and Rousseau and done so on the alien grounds of their own tongue, and he had forced their thought to reveal it-

157

self to him in all its complexity and subtlety. He knew that there were men and women in Hyde Park who could prattle in French with self-confident ease, but he also knew that they could not talk as he could about the ideas of Rousseau and Helvetius. Indeed the difference between him and them was not innate, but the result of education and social background. Give him their education and he would have their fluency, give him their background and he would have their social grace. But they need not give him their brains. He had his own.

He knew that mental progress was possible and that the circumstances of one's life could either expedite or hinder it. He knew that the end of mental progress was not contained within itself but rather was a means to several more exalted ends. Mental progress gave a man greater knowledge and therefore greater wisdom, greater wisdom and therefore greater virtue. Virtue is knowledge of the right: Isaac Bates had not read Plato but the particular kind of optimism which equates knowing the right thing with doing the right thing is instinctive Platonism. Actually, beneath his bitterness and cynicism there was in Isaac Bates a heart warming naivete and an optimism of the sort the Lord must love. Change education, change the social background, give men opportunity and freedom to advance and you will breed a new and finer generation of men. Isaac Bates could walk through all the sordidness, the vice and degeneracy, the vicious brutality and the calloused indifference of the mean and sordid streets of London where his life was lived, be profoundly saddened and sickened by it, flare up in rage against it, and never forget that above the blackest clouds are the eternal stars, that the clouds bewilder man but the stars lead him to his destiny.

Therefore Isaac Bates did not live the good life today, nor would Isaac live it tomorrow. But there would dawn a better day when men would be free, when opportunity would be universal, when education would be open to all, when man would slough off his bestial part and emerge the son of God which God created him to be. That was the religion of Isaac Bates. He was what the eighteenth century called a republican and the twentieth century calls a democrat. He was eternally right about the American Revolution and eternally wrong about the French Revolution. He was not an Edmund Burke, nor could he have been with the finest education and social background because there are differences in men that are innate. Not being an Edmund Burke, he could not sense the difference between a conservative revolution guided by moral principle like the American and a radical revolution inspired by passion like the French. He did have his vision, however, of a society in which all men were free and equal, in which opportunity of every proper sort would be open to all, in which that blank tablet which is the human mind according to John Locke might bear the message of hope, progress, enlightenment, and rich fulfillment. In that democratic society, in which there would be no bondsmen, no inequality, no special privilege, and no artificial rank, mental progress, social progress, and moral progress would be assured. The good life is the life of democratic equality and unfettered opportunity, and in the good life of the democratic society is humanity's salvation. Thus far the gospel according to Isaac Bates.

Isaac Bates finally broke the ancient twofold pattern of the good life which had prevailed from the dawn of the Middle Ages, the country pattern which was set by the knight or governor and the town pattern which was set by the guildsman or merchant. After Isaac Bates the lesser folk of the country would not necessarily look to the great house for guidance, nor would the lesser folk of the town inevitably pattern their lives after the merchant prince. Isaac Bates had his concept of Nature quite as truly as Squire Gilbert or the three entrepreneurs who met on Rotten Row. Nature to him was human nature, just as it had been to the ancient Greeks some of whose ideas had filtered into him through the French. When men are free and equal, education universal and opportunity unfettered, they are living according to Nature; "Man is born free, and everywhere he is in chains." The good life is actually lived in America, where man is close to Nature in each sense of that subtle word. Such was the conviction of Isaac Bates, and it was his inspiration as well. Couple the ideas of progress, freedom, equality, and opportunity and there emerges from the amalgam

159

an idea of the good life that is new and yet has roots that are ancient, that is secular and yet has the flavor of the authentic gospel, that is utopian and yet Utopia is the western shore of the Atlantic. The concept of the good life which Isaac Bates held and which men of good will and strong determination labored for decades to bring to being in the Old World was caused by the confluence of French theory with American example. Let us turn, then, to that American state where the eighteenth century had its richest fulfillment, the state where Squire Gilbert, the merchants of Rotten Row, Sara Finch and Isaac Bates might in their several and conflicting ways find the good life as they understood it, the state of Pennsylvania.

6.

The Holy Experiment

WHEN William Penn arrived in 1682, he brought with him the physical necessities for the founding of a colony and two ideas for its sustenance. One idea was that man shows himself at his best where he is free; the other was that man best preserves his freedom in a varied society. He implemented his second concept by welcoming to his colony men who varied in religion, race, and language. Consequently almost from the start Pennsylvania was not one thing like Massachusetts, nor two things like Virginia, but several varied and contrasting things that blended pleasantly and peacefully into the unity of Pennsylvania. It is half forgotten that the Pennsylvania to which William Penn came consisted, in addition to Indians, of Swedes, Finns, and Dutch. The change to English government was hardly one they could consider without concern. "I hope you will not be troubled with your change," he wrote to them. "You shall be governed by laws of your own making, and live a free and, if you will, a sober and industrious people." Before the year was over he presented them with a Frame of Government and a Great Law that accompanied it. In itself a remarkably democratic document for the late seventeenth century, it was followed by a Charter of Privileges in 1701 which ended proprietary rule and made Pennsylvania self-governing. This

161

Charter in turn was succeeded by a second, third, and fourth Frame. There was in William Penn's Holy Experiment a quality seldom found in experiments, and very seldom indeed when they are considered holy. There was the understanding that experiment is a continuing process, and that success just as truly as failure would require change in its pattern.

Pennsylvania is an endless series of ups and downs, and at times a very beautiful one indeed. Appalachia got squeezed together in geological antiquity and Pennsylvania came out its picturesquely wrinkled self, with the sharpest wrinkle and deepest furrow the Kittatinny Mountain and the wrinkles and furrows to the west progressively gentler. There is something suggestive of the Pennsylvania landscape in the history of Pennsylvania settlement, except that a shift in metaphor becomes necessary. The settlement of Pennsylvania was like the series of concentric rings sent evolving across a still pond when a stone is thrown into the water. Philadelphia was the point of impact, and the circles spread westward from Philadelphia until the motion became vague and formless out near Pittsburgh.

In the beginning were the Indians, but almost in the beginning as American history records such matters were the Swedes, the Finns, and the Dutch. Their domain was the Delaware, from Trenton down to Delaware Bay, and they were a fortifying influence for William Penn. They were sturdy settlers, friendly with the Indians, aware of liberty and willing that others possess it, even in the difficult and unstable form of religious liberty. Then came the Welsh, most of them farmers but some professional men of wealth and education. The first doctors of Pennsylvania were nearly all Welshmen. Their language proved an impractical import but their customs did not, and the pleasant towns west and northwest of Philadelphia mark the first ring, the Welsh ring, of immigration: Merion and Haverford, Bryn Mawr and Bryn Athyn, Cynwyd and Pen Argyl. The next ring was the English ring, as Quakers and Episcopalians poured in through the Philadelphia funnel and then spread out across eastern Pennsylvania, with York County becoming English in a different way as the sons of Englishmen moved up from Maryland. Next came the Germans, probably the most distinctive and picturesque, as well as misunderstood, body of immigrants ever to enter America. The plain people of the black dresses, beards, buggies, and incredibly fine farms are the Pennsylvania Dutch, but the overwhelmingly greater numbers of Lutherans, Baptists, and Moravians who came from Germany to Pennsylvania and merged easily into its social and political structure are also Pennsylvania Dutch. The church people comprised the great majority of the great German ring that expanded westward to Harrisburg and beyond, but made in Lancaster County the garden of the New World that matches and probably surpasses any comparable area that the Old World has treasured and enriched by centuries of meticulous cultivation. Beyond the Germans were the Scotch-Irish, who pushed to the Susquehanna and beyond, up the Juniata valley into Indian country, across the Alleghenies and on to the western country with its tangled hills, clear country streams, its solitude and remoteness which they loved, and its challenge which they answered. This was, and in large measure is, Pennsylvania. By the time the American Revolution was over, its main outlines existed, and Pennsylvania was testing the pattern of the good life that depends on freedom, equality, opportunity, and the idea of progress for its fulfillment. Unlike every other pattern we have considered, it was dynamic and change was of its essence. The Holy Experiment of William Penn, who paid two short visits to Pennsylvania and spent there a total of three years, and now had been dead for some seventy years, was in full development.

At the town of Sunbury is the confluence of the North and West Branches of the Susquehanna. Each branch rolls through its rich valleys and between its cliffs, sometimes broadening into a lake with islands in it, sometimes compressing itself into a silvery line that winds and wavers through a countryside of folds and flats, and sudden upward surges. There are days when the air is clear and golden above the Susquehanna, and the river is beautiful enough to be one of the four rivers of Paradise. The forests march across the folded hills and grow indistinct at a horizon which suggests that beyond is infinity. The forests now are second growth and punctuated by towns

163

and cities, but one can imagine a day before man came, when the forest was first growth and still except for the forest noises of the birds and the wind, the lapping of the water and the quiet rustle of the lower leaves.

This was the Susquehanna that a traveling Englishman named Thomas Cooper saw in 1794 and reported to his father-in-law Joseph Priestley, who needed a place of refuge since his Birmingham home had fallen victim to mob vengeance. The discoverer of oxygen, like our imaginary Isaac Bates, had been guilty of espousing the French Revolution and of preaching primitive Christianity. The answer of Birmingham had been to destroy his home, smash his laboratory, and make a funeral pyre of English ideals out of his thirty thousand books. Come to America, urged his son-in-law: "There is little fault to find with the government of America either in principle or practice; we have very few taxes to pay, and those of acknowledged necessity are moderate in amount; we have no animosities about religion; it is a subject about which no questions are asked; we have few respecting political men or political measures; the present irritation in men's minds in Great Britain, and the discordant state of society on political accounts is not known there. The government is the government *of* the people and *for* the people." Even the italics are there in Cooper's anticipation of Abraham Lincoln.

Priestley came, and found more than an idyllic wilderness. He found a cultivated seaboard to do him honor, with a University of Pennsylvania to offer him a lectureship. He established the first Unitarian Church in Philadelphia, preached against the slave trade, and urged Thomas Jefferson to send the czar of Russia a copy of the American Constitution that the light of freedom might penetrate his benighted land. Priestley and his combative son-in-law carried their Americanism to the point of arousing Federalist ire and being denounced as "wandering vagabonds who had trampled under foot the laws, the government, the sovereignty of the United States," and so as proper targets for the Alien Enemies Act. President John Adams felt that the description was a shade lurid for Priestley, a somewhat cotton-headed and unscientific little scientist who

164

had stumbled into the discovery of oxygen and carbon monoxide, but not really into sedition.

Priestley had been a well-intentioned and soberly dedicated odd stick from his boyhood. He was brought up by an aunt in comfortable circumstances whose home, he wrote, "was the resort of all the Dissenting ministers in the neighborhood without distinction; and those who were most obnoxious on account of their heresy were almost as welcome to her, if she thought them honest and good men—which she was not unwilling to do—as any others." There was a shade of heresy to his own boyhood theology; try as he would he could not find sorrow in his heart for Adam's sin nor could he bring himself to believe he shared the guilt. This was enough to keep him out of the church his aunt attended, but not out of the nonconformist academy at Davantry. His frail constitution made his aunt think of the ministry for him, and others to think of a mercantile career. With the former in mind he taught himself Hebrew, Syriac, and at least dabbled in Arabic; for the other potential string to his bow he learned French, Italian, and German without assistance. A speech defect made him a teacher and not a preacher, and a home beside a brewery aroused his curiosity about "different kinds of air." He moved from a sort of loose Arianism in religion to Socinianism, passed up a chance to accompany Captain Cook to the South Seas, did a laborious *History of the Corruptions of Christianity,* and succeeded in forcing carbonic acid, which he called "fixed air," into water. He believed that all scientific discoveries are made by chance, comparing the investigation of nature to a hound wildly running after game. On this thesis he discovered oxygen and carbon monoxide, and in a sense he may be said to have discovered chemistry, a science which really did not exist before Priestley. He paid with a ruined career for his advocacy of the godless French Revolution, and on his deathbed he made his grandchildren kneel beside him while he heard their prayers.

It was for the likes of Joseph Priestley that Pennsylvania existed, and one would like to think still exists. Priestley was a nonconformist in the technical religious sense and in the all-embracing general sense. There was a consistency to his religious views, but the consistency must be sought in the simple lessons of the gospels and not in the theology of any church. There was a consistency to his political views, but the consistency rested in a dedication to human freedom and human rights and not to governmental forms and operations. There was a submerged consistency in his educational views; his opposition to any governmental interference with education would lie fallow for a generation and then emerge in economics as the doctrine of *laissez faire*. Priestley was a kind-hearted, idealistic, muddled man with an occasional penetrating insight. He lived at the wrong period in England, and he did not come to Pennsylvania soon enough to profit from its atmosphere. But Pennsylvania was the haven for those to whom nonconformity was the breath of life or, as Priestley would put it, the dephlogisticated air. The air above the Susquehanna is the proper air for the Priestleys of this world.

This is precisely the point which made the good life of Pennsylvania, and in varying degrees the good life of the other colonies and the infant states, profoundly different from the good life of England and the continent. The good life of Europe had been led in conformity to certain generally accepted norms, the norms of the castle or the monastery, the barony or the industrial town, the country or the city. The norms varied from time to time and from place to place, and from social rank to social rank. By and large, however, the norms of a particular time, place, and setting were generally accepted and life interpreted in their terms. A Joseph Priestley could never have been at home in a medieval fief or monastery, on an Elizabethan estate or in an eighteenth century industrial community; indeed he suffered mob violence in the last. He could be at home, however, in Pennsylvania because in William Penn's Holy Experiment man shows himself at his best when he is free and he best preserves his freedom in a varied society.

A Dutch burgher might build his baroque little homestead far down the Delaware where river and land are evenly flat and peaceful, while a sinewy Finn, far up the river where the water is white in the spring, could level and notch the pines, fit them together, caulk them in, and make a log house as he

would in distant Finland and so give pioneer America a form
of dwelling whose origins are long forgotten. The vigorous and
enterprising Welsh could revel in a rich black earth of a
fertility unknown in distant Wales and reveal to those who
came after them the unbelievable richness of southeastern
Pennsylvania. The sturdy, dedicated Germans could bring to
the new homeland a firm faith, a firm devotion to duty, a firm
resolution to succeed, and a firm belief in virtues so antique
that they seemed almost to grow out of the rich soil itself that
they tilled with such consummate skill. Welshman, Englishman, or German might have his reward as he watched the
wheat in July flame into deep copper, burnish into brass, and
then quiet down to the mellow gold of maturity, and bless
the good life of this new homeland and the Lord Who gave it
as he readied himself for the harvest. And far to the west,
where the ridges buckle and break into a formless mass of hills,
where the trees grow tall and thick and the water cleaves the
valleys in foaming torrents, where the primeval quiet of creation still rests upon the land and the unknown is a footstep beyond the camp site, the Scotch-Irish pushed through the forests
and across the rivers following man's immemorial urge to seek
the west.

They all knew they were leading the good life. Many of
them solemnly attested to the fact. But was there a common
principle upon which it rested, a common denominator to
which its complexity could be resolved? Quite clearly it was
not to be found in material comfort; a solid competence was
general, but not a showy affluence. It was certainly not to be
found in any jointly shared philosophy of life; the pattern of
Pennsylvania thinking was as varied as the pattern of Pennsylvania living. In this very fact is probably the answer to the
question. Everyone in Pennsylvania was to some extent and in
some personal fashion a Joseph Priestley. All had left their
European homelands to satisfy if possible a "divine discontent." Just as Joseph Priestley was by some strange formula
compounded of scientist and mystic, preacher, teacher, and
political rebel, so in the hearts and minds of all who came to
Pennsylvania there was something that was old and something

new, something that sought freedom for a pattern of living or a school of thought that was stultified in the Old World, but also something that sought adventure and discovery of new patterns of living and of thought.

Pennsylvania gave them opportunity. It gave economic and social opportunity, but even more it gave intellectual and spiritual opportunity. To be an American was to be a new man, one who had created a new concept of the state and of the citizen. America had brought unity out of diversity without impairing diversity, New World harmony out of Old World discord without limiting the wholesome differences which had degenerated into discord. Englishman and German, Scot and Irishman, Finn and Swede were neighbors and friends in Pennsylvania. Lutheran and Anglican, Calvinist and Catholic could till adjacent fields, share equipment, lunch together under the willows by the spring where the cool air lay like a blessed pool on August days when the Pennsylvania sun was merciless. There was a peace of the plebians in those years when the Revolution was finished and Penn's Holy Experiment could continue in a land at peace, a peace quite as placid as the peace of the Augustans and far more solidly founded. The good life of common man in the Old World had always been at best an imperfect and very partial replica of the good life of the lord of the manor or the master of the counting house. In Pennsylvania, and in all the new-born states in their varying degrees, the good life of common man had a pattern of its own, created, perfected, loved, and trusted by common man. A discovery was made in America not completely overshadowed by the discovery of America itself: there is a good life of the common man in which the differences that habitually have set men apart grow blurred and indistinct, and quite unimportant. Man does show his best side when he is free and equal, and man does best preserve that freedom and equality in a mixed society. William Penn's Holy Experiment in the good life was one of the most successful in history, and America has been happiest when that experiment has been carried closest to its entire fulfillment.

7.

The Final Definition

PHILOSOPHY gave birth to two children in the eighteenth century, Nature and Revolution, and one cannot talk realistically about the century unless one talks about both. The eighteenth century is the country squire surveying his mellow acres with the satisfied peace of the man whose heart and mind are at rest in the calm awareness that his well-being is a part of Nature. The eighteenth century is also the Jacobin growing feverish over French precept and American example, and plotting the downfall of everything the country squire represents. The century is stability and change, contentment and challenge, the reward of yesterday and the promise of tomorrow, the benediction of Nature and the firebrand of Revolution.

Is there a common denominator that lies between the thought and aspirations of such disparate figures as Squire Gilbert and the merchants of Rotten Row, Sara Finch and Isaac Bates, and our one figure from literal history who somehow embodied all four and therefore could not have been convincing if fictional, Joseph Priestley? Three of them entertained concepts of the good life that were of ancient lineage. Behind Squire Gilbert was the baron of the medieval fief and the lord of the Elizabethan manor, the oldest and most solid upper-class tradition in England. Behind the merchants of Rotten

169

Row were the newly created guildsman of the medieval village and the trader of the Renaissance, the most dynamic and challenging tradition of England. Behind the modest and self-effacing Sara Finch was a lineage which would have made Sara gasp in incredulous bewilderment had she seen it in a vision: all the saints and sages who had been led through contempt of self into the love of God. On the other hand behind Isaac Bates, who watched today for the promise of tomorrow as he ground away at the books which soon would blow the massive gates off the Bastille and drench in blood that tomorrow which Isaac thought would be lambent with heavenly glories, there really was no lineage at all unless in some obscure and distant fashion it was the lineage of Philo and ancient Athens. Isaac Bates was an apocalyptic nightmare to Squire Gilbert and the merchants of Rotten Row, but to Ruth the gentle Methodist who lived around the corner and knew him as a man and not a menace he was a kindly and idealistic soul in whose heart was room for nothing but the charity with which it overflowed. Finally, and strangest of all, was Joseph Priestley who had an instinct for the expansive life of Squire Gilbert as the beautiful Georgian Colonial mansion he erected in Northumberland, Pennsylvania, attested, an instinct for the new and venturesome which made him kin to the merchants of Rotten Row, a simple and childlike piety of the sort that brought Sara Finch to the Methodist band, and that mystic sense of brotherhood which gave a spiritual benediction to the rebel soul of Isaac Bates. Is there a common denominator among them, and is there a sense in which it is embodied in Joseph Priestley?

It is not to be sought in material prosperity. Only the merchants of Rotten Row sought material prosperity. Squire Gilbert had it, in the legal sense by right of birth but as he well knew, in the true sense by Nature. He enjoyed it and was expansively generous with it, but it was never other than the obvious and inevitable means to the end which Nature had designed, that he be lord of the manor and that he have a kindly regard for those whose natures did not require material prosperity. Sara Finch never dreamed of it and this was wise, for her dreams concerned treasure that does not perish. Isaac

Bates thought much of material prosperity, and he thought nothing of it. In one sense his entire philosophy of the rights of man concerned the rights of man to material well-being, but that was not the higher sense of his philosophy and he never applied the aspiration to himself. But the merchants of Rotten Row sought prosperity, and so did the merchants of the little village which basked in the sun of Squire Gilbert's benignity but also made hay while the sun shone. The merchants great and small had not the least vestigial remain of the medieval belief that too much worldly prosperity is a bar to sanctity, but they were quite willing to accept without really understanding it the Calvinistic thesis that worldly prosperity is a sign of God's abiding favor and a pledge of eternal salvation. Perhaps one may say that material prosperity was the good life to those of the eighteenth century incapable of understanding a better one: the merchants of Rotten Row, the idlers of St. James's Park, the dealers in rotten boroughs, in general Smollett's usurers, brokers, and jobbers who had been suddenly translated into the state of affluence and knew no other badge of the good life but ostentation. No doubt every age of human history has known them as they have squirmed, wriggled, and twisted to the fore through all the bolts and bars society raises against them, but time blows the dust of oblivion across them and they pass into forgetfulness. The eighteenth century is known for Squire Gilbert, Sara Finch, and Isaac Bates, but the merchants are forgotten and nothing remains to ponder but the circumstances which made it so much easier for them to prosper than for their medieval and Renaissance forebears.

We may pass by quickly the possibility that the eighteenth century saw in artistic creativity the good life. The eighteenth century had its distinctive art. The most superficial knowledge of painting lets one murmur "eighteenth century" as he moves down the corridor and sees ahead the gallery where the Gainsboroughs and Reynolds hang. The painters of the eighteenth century were embellishments of the good life as lived by Squire Gilbert and his fellows, and borrowed by the merchants of Rotten Row. They recorded upon canvas for the wealthy who engaged them the porcelain perfection of their wives' complex-

171

ions, those models in miniature of their own adult elegance their children, and naturally their self-assured and happy selves. It is all there in eighteenth-century painting, the perfection of the surface and the absence of a third dimension; there is no Rembrandt with his haunting depths, no Titian with his proud magnificence, no Raphael with his "intimations of immortality." The eighteenth century also had its distinctive music and perhaps it is unfair to disparage it because mechanical ingenuity with instruments had yet to make possible the musical genius of Beethoven and his successors, but eighteenth-century music was made by fiddlers and fiddlers were servants of no especially high status. Rather the eighteenth century was at its best in the smaller arts, in Chippendale chairs, delicate wainscoting, beautifully proportioned stairways and graceful balustrades, and at its very best in houses that translated into eighteenth-century terms the eternal values of symmetry and proportion. The home of Squire Gilbert, or for that matter the beautiful Georgian Colonial house in Northumberland where Joseph Priestley lived, was as much part of Nature as the life itself of Squire Gilbert and one of the facets of the life of Joseph Priestley. Yet somehow there is missing a warmth from the eighteenth-century home despite its graceful beauty, and there is missing a warmth from the pictures of family life in the upper classes that have drifted down from that classically modulated era. No doubt the latter is an illusion. Probably the very simplicity and crudeness of the child's trundle bed or the little girl's doll of the Elizabethan age and colonial America touch the nerve of parenthood in every grownup in a way that the artfully designed child's bed and the beautifully gowned china doll of the eighteenth century do not. Behind the artful, or artistic, there may be just as much true love as there is behind the simple and the crude, but it is not so poignant. The fair thing to say is that family life was just as vital a part of the good life in the eighteenth century as in any other, but until the century rolled toward its somewhat sentimental close the arts do not reveal the fact. The good life of the family is transparent in Burns's "The Cotter's Saturday Night," but where does one find it among the Augustans?

The record of the eighteenth century in religion is notorious. As the fires of the seventeenth century died down, Deity faded to a vague abstraction, religion to a pallid reverence, and Nature took the place once occupied by the tablets and the cross. The Church of England became an arm of government, and Dissenter enthusiasm died away into the dreary chop logic of interminable sermons seasoned with the vinegar of acrimony. Religion ceased to offer more than the vaguest of formulas for the good life, formulas somehow closer to ancient Stoicism when Dissenter and to ancient Epicureanism when Anglican than to the living inspiration that it offered in the Middle Ages and Reformation. There was, of course, the exception. Sara Finch and her tiny Methodist band did lead the good life by the immemorial principles of faith, hope, and love, but such bands were tiny and their eighteenth-century numbers few. Methodism would not inherit its substantial share of the English-speaking earth until the eighteenth century was over.

There was much that was ancient and classical in the art and architecture of the eighteenth century, but little in its thought where the good life was concerned. Squire Gilbert had a sense of compassion toward the poor folk of the village, but no sense of civic obligation. The ruthless competition in which they had survived and then succeeded had squeezed the compassion from the merchants of Rotten Row, and from the traders of the village who were their replicas in miniature. The sense of duty toward the less fortunate and of service to the state whose laws and institutions had made possible their prosperity was as foreign to their dispositions as would be the charity of St. Francis or the civic sense of Socrates. Sara Finch and Isaac Bates in their several ways had a profound sense of duty toward the less fortunate and their hearts were wellsprings of charity, but her well of charity was filled with the waters of religion and the country of his loyalty and devotion was not a country in which he lived or could live. The principle of duty, so strong in the best minds and hearts of antiquity, so peremptory in the Middle Ages and still so potent in the Renaissance, had surrendered to the principle of rights and the lack of principle of pleasure, and service to the state dwindled and disap-

173

peared before service to self. And yet, at this point history raises the finger of caution against the peril of the generalization. The principle of duty and of service to the state has never found a finer, more intelligent, more dedicated expression than found in the American Founding Fathers, and the United States has never since been quite so mature as it was the hour it was born. It may be soberly questioned if any nation in history has ever had at one time the dedicated and unselfish service the incipient United States was given by Washington, Franklin, Adams, Jefferson, Madison, Jay, Hamilton, and the rest. They were indeed antique Romans, and antiquity never saw exemplified in finer fashion the principle that the good life is the life of service to one's fellow man through the medium of the state than the New World saw late in the eighteenth century. They are one of history's miracles, the American Founding Fathers, and a miracle appreciated although not necessarily understood only when one has a comprehensive knowledge of what history usually has recorded. They are no less a miracle and a mystery because they appeared in the eighteenth century. They were in the century and they embodied its best thought, but they certainly were not characteristic of the century as a whole.

The good life of the eighteenth century, then, did not ultimately rest upon material prosperity, artistic creativity, family life, religious fervor, or civic dedication. The question returns upon us: is there a common denominator that underlies the lives of Squire Gilbert, the merchants of Rotten Row, Sara Finch, Isaac Bates, and Joseph Priestley? Is it possible, somehow, to find that common denominator also in the work of the Founding Fathers?

The common denominator does exist, and it may be discovered in the Founding Fathers quite as truly as in our hypothetical Englishmen and our actual American immigrant. Just as the cornerstone of the good life in classical antiquity was service to the state, as the cornerstone in the Middle Ages was imitation of the saint and in the Renaissance observance of the principle of duty, so in the eighteenth century the good life rested as on a cornerstone on the principle of personal freedom. What personal freedom meant, what implications it carried, how it was to be reconciled with other principles with which it might conflict, varied so greatly from person to person and from social setting to social setting that the structure raised upon it easily obscures the foundation on which it rests.

The foundation is by no means obscure in the life of Squire Gilbert. He retained the prerogatives and privileges of his burly and self-reliant ancestors, the medieval baron and the Renaissance governor, but he was totally freed from their duties. The fief was not his to have and to hold, nor did he have to muster armed forces and lead them into battle when the king was in need. With obligation to those above him gone, the sense of obligation to those below him went as well. The baron had a potent sense of obligation to every last dweller on the fief, and the sense of obligation was still strong when the Renaissance governor assumed the imperatives of responsibility along with its perquisites. But with obligation gone and religion faded to a vague reverence due a vague and distant Eternal Principle, Squire Gilbert really had only his inner moral resources on which to rely. They were not inadequate. The spirit of charity was strong in him and responsibility was for Squire Gilbert an adequate substitute for obligation. He did lead the good life, and charity and responsibility were important components in it. The trouble was that Squire Gilbert was not characteristic of his time and his social class, whereas the medieval baron and the Renaissance governor were. Personal freedom of the sort he enjoyed was not compatible with the duty which they faced, and in very many country squires the sense of responsibility was a weak substitute for the fact of duty.

The foundation is starkly naked in the case of the three merchants who met on Rotten Row. An economic freedom was theirs compared to which nineteenth-century *laissez faire* was bolts and shackles. The economic game they played had no rules, the players had no compunction, and the stakes were high. A very few had the physical energy, the mental agility, and the moral license to play for the highest stakes and win. Triumph was its own excuse for being, and the game was as free from morals as chess and as free from rules as total warfare. It is by no means difficult to wrap oneself in the cloak of righteousness and proclaim that the good life of the merchants of Rotten Row was merely the good life of those incapable of understanding a better. Let it be added that the merchants of the village in their small way played for their small stakes with the same lack of rules, and prospered in their degree in much the same fashion. Indeed one may add that much of the undoubted economic progress of the English-speaking people of the eighteenth century came about because men of the eighteenth century practiced self-help and individualism without bothering to write books about it. Yet their achievement would impress Socrates and the medieval baron not at all, and the Renaissance governor very little. The ancient tradition did not make economic prosperity identical with the good life. The point is that the good life as the merchants of Rotten Row understood it and as their little siblings of the villages understood it was made possible by personal freedom translated into economic freedom.

But what of those we mention with far greater respect, what of Sara Finch and Isaac Bates? The case of Isaac Bates is entirely clear. Isaac believed in the rights of man and did so for all the right reasons. He believed that liberty and equality are the prime requisites for the betterment of man, and that when men were free and equal they would lead the good life. There was nothing selfish or self-seeking in his creed, and never for a moment did he hope that he would achieve it himself. He pinned his faith and hope on the future, and pledged his charity to it. But in the very simplicity and honesty of Isaac Bates's creed lay its fallacy, as the French Revolution demonstrated. Isaac accepted just as completely as Squire Gilbert the thesis that this is an orderly universe, as explained in its constitution by Galileo and in its operating principle by Newton. The rule of Nature is the rule of order, because it is natural for man to be orderly in his thoughts and in his deeds. It is the fetters that can bind the minds of men just as truly as their hands which frustrate the rule of Nature and right reason. Strike off the fetters, make men free and equal, and guided by sovereign reason man will achieve redemption. It was indeed sad that Squire Gilbert considered Isaac Bates a lurid portent and Isaac Bates was vowed to the destruction of what Squire Gilbert stood for. Both were good men and both believed in the good life according to the same gospel, the old, simple, comforting gospel of Deism. The cornerstone of the good life is personal freedom.

And Sara Finch. Sara gave no thought to Nature, and if she knew of Nature no doubt she would be shocked by it and find it impious. It was certainly not natural for her to have authority or to be prosperous or to entertain hard, high thoughts about man and his destiny. It was natural for her to obey the two commandments, to show her love for God in the Methodist band and her love for her neighbor by caring for the children when her neighbor had smallpox. Sara did not have the kind of courage that could stand the roar of musketry. Her courage was the kind that let her care for a child taken from the arms of a mother with those deep-seated pustules the meaning of which she all too clearly knew. The good life of Sara Finch was in the noblest of all traditions, and yet it rested as truly on the foundation of individualism as that of the last and meanest merchant who haggled and cheated his way to wealth. Man's communion with the Almighty is immediate and direct, and membership in a Methodist band merely fortified one's resolution to achieve communion and facilitated the endeavor. Man's service to his fellow man is equally immediate and direct: care for the child taken from the arms of the mother with smallpox. Whenever one aspires to lead the good life in the city of God and not the city of man, his ideal of the good life is individual and rests on individual freedom. Like the medieval serf who aspired to sanctity, Sara Finch walked toward her destiny alone.

There remains Joseph Priestley, that strange composite of the squire and the merchant, the saint, the scientist, and the rebel. For such a man there cannot be a niche, nor can he breathe any air but that of freedom. The Holy Experiment of William Penn was designed for many different people, and he was one of them. Pennsylvania had the rich, rolling acres teem-

177

ing with fertility and waiting for the plow. It was land for the country squire. It had the busiest port in the newly created states, the most active and diversified commerce. Philadelphia was the city for the enterprising merchant. It had the best of the new nation's active, probing intelligence, alert to the new idea, poised for the new discovery. Benjamin Franklin gravitated to Pennsylvania as to his natural home, and so did Joseph Priestley. But Pennsylvania had as well its places of withdrawal from the active life, its cloisters at Ephrata, its little settlements of the plain people, and beyond for those to whom Nature is a cathedral, it had the Allegheny country. There was a place in Pennsylvania for the recluse, the hermit, the visionary, as well for the man whose horizons are bounded by wooded hills and mountain clefts as for the man whose horizon is the infinite. Pennsylvania had all this because it had the precious ingredient which made it possible, freedom for the individual man. Thus the good life of Pennsylvania could be the good life of the country squire or the city merchant, the scientist, the quietist, the explorer, the recluse, and the saint because the Holy Experiment of William Penn was founded on the principle that man is at his best when he is free and in a varied society. Our Joseph Priestley was merely Pennsylvania in miniature, Pennsylvania was Joseph Priestley writ large.

When everything else has been said about the American Constitution, the final fact is that it rests on a philosophic foundation entirely consistent with the Holy Experiment of William Penn. It is not without significance that Thomas Jefferson always believed that a Bill of Rights should precede a Constitution, and that in point of historic fact the writing of the Bill of Rights virtually accompanied the writing of the Constitution. It is equally significant that just as William Penn believed in a divinely created moral order and held that his Holy Experiment must be conducted within its framework, so the Founding Fathers believed in a divinely created moral order and held that human rights must be exercised within it. This is the precise point at which Sara Finch and Isaac Bates parted intellectual company, a fact which would have puzzled both could either have known that he kept intellectual company with the other. Sara Finch had a freedom as nearly total as a human being can achieve, a freedom like that of St. Francis, but its encompassing control was exercised by moral law. Isaac Bates, grinding away at his Diderot, Voltaire, and Rousseau, conceived of freedom entirely in terms of right and took his moral guidance from his own good, sound, reliable sense of right and wrong. But one had to be an Isaac Bates to trust guidance of that sort. His road led to the Terror, hers to the ecstasy.

Thus the eighteenth century worked out, in the slow, cumbersome, faltering, groping, and instinctive way that centuries work out their spiritual destinies, its formulation of the good life. Probably in the final terms, which are always very simple terms, the actual living of it did not differ much from living in the centuries that went before. The difference was in the philosophy upon which it rested. There were those like the American Founding Fathers who so largely conceived of the good life in antique terms of service to the state, and they were prodigiously important, but their viewpoint was not the fundamental one of their century. There were those like Sara Finch who thought of time in terms of eternity, as medieval man did when he lived the good life, and the little Methodist band to which she belonged was destined to outlive much that was magnificent in the century, but the good life that she conceived was not fundamental to the century. There were those like Isaac Bates and Squire Gilbert in their several ways who had a strong sense of duty to their fellow man and tried to live their duty and make of it the good life as the best men had done in the Renaissance, but neither pattern set the underlying tone of the century. Rather the fundamental spirit of the century was that freedom which let Squire Gilbert live on his acres as Nature had ordained, let Sara Finch obey the two commandments as her conscience dictated, let Isaac Bates devote himself to human progress, let the merchants of Rotten Row put money in their purse, let Joseph Priestley be scientist and saint, squire and rebel, let William Penn's experiment in freedom and diversity grow and develop into a "new nation conceived in liberty and dedicated to the proposition that all men are created equal." The eighteenth century conceived the new nation in liberty, and the eighteenth century was mother to the nineteenth century. Furthermore, the eighteenth century was grandmother to the twentieth century. It remains to be seen how the good life fared under freedom and equality, and what freedom and equality have done to the good life.

PART FIVE

THE INDIVIDUAL

Each age in human history has its own particular certainties. The ancient world was certain that the state was central in the order of being, the Middle Ages were certain about the pattern of eternity. Certitude for the Renaissance concerned the nature and encompassing quality of royal power, for the Enlightenment the serene and unquestioned lordship of Nature over all man's being and works. Thus in the ancient world the best pattern of the good life was service to the state, in the Middle Ages service to God, in the Renaissance service to the prince, in the Enlightenment service to oneself.

The modern world is the child of the Enlightenment and so its parents are Nature and Revolution. Revolution is not of necessity bloody and even when it is, the day comes when blood ceases to flow and revolution quiets into peace. Revolution becomes evolution, and the slogans by which men have died quietly change into the slogans by which men live. The slogan of the nineteenth century was Progress, and the certainty of the nine-

181

teenth century was grounded on the certainty of progress. Yet sometime and somewhere in the twentieth century the certainty of progress died away. Perhaps it was at Verdun and Ypres. Perhaps it was on bleak city streets where the wind probed with icy fingers into the thin, torn clothing of men and women with nowhere to go and nothing to do, in the depression years. Perhaps Progress died when the world knew that Stalin and Hitler were possible. Centuries seldom heed the calendar and when the certainty of progress passed away, the nineteenth century passed away with it and the somber twentieth century was upon us.

The reconciliation of Nature and Revolution is not easy, but it is possible. The link between the two is furnished by the concept of evolution which in turn underlies the doctrine of progress. The nature of life is not static but dynamic; the one abiding certainty is change; change in its characteristic form is systematic and evolutionary; therefore progress is natural, even revolutionary progress. It follows that the good life is not static but dynamic, that change is in its warp and woof, that it is founded on the evolutionary principle, and that progress is the hallmark by which it is recognized. The modern age will still produce the disinterested servant of the people who finds the good life in service to his city. In the ancient world he was an amateur politician; in the modern world he may still be that, but he is more likely to be a physician or a teacher. The modern world still knows that man and woman who find the good life in service to the Lord. In the Middle Ages he was a priest or a nun; in the modern world he may still be either, but he is often a layman who works in the name of charity, and sometimes in surprising capacities. There are sons of Portiuncula who wear the uniforms of policemen. Service to the prince is not unknown today, although the panoply of the Renaissance governor and the perquisites of his office are no more. The good life of service today is lived in the most tawdry of city halls and the most corrupt of state houses by quiet people whom nobody knows but who keep the government going. The government of France has been known to fall with the regularity of Old Faithful, but France does not fall. The bureaus will not let it.

When all has been said, however, about the abiding good life of service to the people which in divergent ways was character-istic of the ancient world, the Middle Ages, and the Renaissance, the fact remains that the characteristic good life of the modern world is rather an extension of the good life of the Enlighten-ment, the good life of the individual which may be sought at any key on the gamut from the highest note of self-sacrifice to the crassest note of self-aggrandizement. But it is an extension that is founded, not on contentment with things as they are as was the life of Squire Gilbert or on the hope of things as they might become as was the life of Isaac Bates, but on the conviction that the good life is not lived in a state of being but in a state of becoming, that it is dynamic, evolutionary, progressive. It was the expectation of Squire Gilbert that Life tomorrow would be as life today, and it was the dream of Isaac Bates that life tomorrow would be infinitely finer than life today. Modern man has looked for more. It has been not merely the expectation of modern man that life tomorrow will be better, richer, finer than it is today, but indeed his conviction that unless it is so it is not the good life. And, then, the expectation weakens, falters, grows uneasy, gives way to formless fears and vague uncertainties. Is the modern age finished? There is no more vital question one can ask about the modern age than that.

1.

In the Footsteps of the Pioneer

It was the summer of 1816 that finally convinced Eben Gardner that the step must be taken. The British raid on New London had cost his father dearly, with the fine frame house he had erected with his own hands and what help young Eben, then a boy, could give him left to smolder in its ruins and the smoke to drift across his ravaged acres. The work of one man's life had gone that day and although his father's life had survived, what had made it vigorous and resourceful had drained away from it. Yet that was an act of war. It was that ominous and fearsome summer which made godly men turn to the Old Testament and bethink themselves of the wrath of Jehovah. Eben thought of flight from the sinful cities of the plain, and wrestled with the new and terrifying thought that Jehovah might still be God and His wrath still unappeased.

The year 1816 is still unique in New England annals as the year without a summer. It was still winter in May and June, there was ice on the ponds in July, the potato crop was destroyed by the August frosts, and it was full winter again when it should have been the mellow days of autumn. God had visited His people first with the violence of war and now with the far more terrifying death of nature. That year famine stalked the land, and a fear as least as devastating to the spirit as famine. Yet escape was possible. There was the other Connecticut far to the west, the Connecticut Western Reserve where winters were mild and open, where livestock could winter outdoors, where the benediction of spring came early to a land of bountiful soil, easy for the plow to turn, incredibly easy to cultivate, plant, and harvest when one was schooled in the rocky, thin, and grimly barren slopes of eastern Connecticut. The year 1817 had a normal summer in New England, but it saw Connecticut on the move as family after family decided to attempt the new life on the Western Reserve.

The good life on the Western Reserve. The phrase indeed would have had a sardonic and a bitter ring had people talked in such terms in 1817 and the thirty years or more that followed. Whatever 1816 might have been, Nature was no more obviously a kindly deity in eastern Ohio than she had been on the coast of Connecticut. There was no place for Nature as Squire Gilbert understood the word in that wedge of northern Ohio bounded by Lake Erie west to Sandusky and then back east again on the forty-first parallel to the Pennsylvania line at a point just south of Youngstown. But nature was abundant in the other sense, in dense forests where a few steps could bring confusion and then tragedy, in animals that might not kill a man but could claw, lacerate, and disfigure him, in isolation, eerie quiet, loneliness, and the agonizing sense of separation from everything that was known, familiar, and secure. The rich earth was there, but over it nature's protective cover that was back-breaking to penetrate and then remove. The Western Reserve had its seasons quite as truly as Connecticut, with snows at least as early and as deep and with summers far more hot and parching. There was something else that can be overlooked when economics is a matter for academic speculation and not a matter of root, hog, or die. When everyone keeps some poultry, has some hogs that can dig in the forest, and manages to get a few hills of corn in the ground, there is no local market for eggs, pork, or corn, or even for

186

corn whiskey. One understands why Dr. Zerah Hawley who practiced medicine in the Reserve from the fall of 1820 to the summer of 1821 published his Journal in New Haven in 1822 "to undeceive the community, respecting a portion of the Western Country, which has been represented as an *earthly Paradise.*"

The melancholy truth is that we wax romantic over the pioneers, and seldom consider what it meant to follow in the footsteps of the pioneers. The French have and deserve a full share of the romantic acclaim for opening North America, but when we say the French we really mean the French explorers who traversed an unknown land with enormous courage and perseverance and in that sense opened it, but nothing more. In the same sense but severely limited in scope the Scotch-Irish of western Pennsylvania opened eastern Ohio, but they lived, so to speak, off the surface of the land and not off the land itself. They fished and hunted, and left nature essentially undisturbed. It was those who followed in the footsteps of the pioneers—and they could be French in Quebec and Scotch-Irish in western Virginia just as truly as men of Connecticut in the Western Reserve—who cut the trees, dug the compacted ground, cultivated the stubborn soil, raised the log cabins, fed, clothed, and protected the very young and the often prematurely old, the ones who followed in the footsteps of the pioneers but have about them far less of the halo of romance who really opened the land. Specifically, Eben Gardner opened a piece of land not far from what is now Warren, Ohio.

Eben and his bride had about the usual experiences with about the usual results. They lived in the ordinary one-room cabin, although Eben did achieve a chimney before many in the area. They had the ordinary times of tribulation when one of them was sick or the children were sick, and the ordinary agony when the oldest boy died. Perhaps there was nothing harder to bear than the visible evidence of the tooth of time in a land where one had to live so much on what one had brought there from the past: the dishes from Connecticut that got cracked and then broken and useless, the furniture that was patched and repaired and then without much hope repaired again, the clothes that became worn and frayed and even when trimmed down in size for smaller fry so obviously belonged to yesterday, and what always brought a lump to Eben's throat, his wife's one good and treasured dress that somehow caught on the nail and ripped. And there were things of the spirit that had to be treasured and preserved from yesterday. Schools were few and casual, and the school year was a few weeks in the summer. Children learned mainly what their parents taught them, and the attrition of learning was severe in the Reserve. There were grandchildren of Yale graduates in the Western Reserve who could not read and write.

And yet, Eben Gardner and his family did achieve the good life on the Western Reserve and in achieving it, created both a pattern and a tradition peculiarly American, the tradition perpetuating itself long after the literal pattern had disappeared. They fought the good fight against nature, and they won. The one-room cabin phase passed, and with it the farming phase itself. The simple truth was that Eben Gardner was not intended to live by his hands but by his shrewd and practical intelligence, not to produce goods but to handle them, not to follow in the footsteps of the pioneers but to be the forerunner of the industrialists.

His first choice of home site had been accidentally a sound one. It was quite clear by 1825 that Warren, Ohio, was one of the most promising settlements in the Reserve. It had been the seat of Trumbull County for a generation, and both its bank and its newspaper were now nearly fifteen years old. There was already talk of incorporating the village. The land in the vicinity was beginning to prove unusually well adapted to the growing of flax, although this development belonged to a still distant future. There were several small carding mills along the river and some rather primitive blast furnaces were in operation that turned out iron parts for carriages. Eben Gardner had a sense that there was something fundamentally solid about a village with an economy that looked in two directions, out to the farm and in toward the town itself. Eben operated a blast furnace of sorts.

On Sunday after church services, and sometimes during

them, Eben Gardner dreamed. There was coal in Trumbull County, and Eben Gardner dreamed of coal. There were so very many uses to which coal could be put and serve them better than wood or charcoal. The great problem was inertia coupled with tradition; everyone knew that the forests of the Reserve were endless, that wood was free for the hauling, and that charcoal is not too hard to process. Eben knew that coal can do things that wood cannot do and charcoal does not do especially well, even if he did not know that the forests of the Reserve were not endless. He dreamed of machines run by coal, of boats powered by coal, of homes heated by coal, and he experimented with coal at his furnace. He knew that there were shrewd and enterprising men far down the Ohio at Pomeroy who were shipping coal in substantial quantities down the Ohio and the Mississippi, and so far as he knew had a monopoly on the trade. Already Warren was looking forward to its own tortuous and remote water route to the Atlantic Ocean and the world beyond. The canal from Cleveland to Akron along the Cuyahoga River had been in operation since 1827 and work was already under way on the Cross-Cut Canal which would link that canal with the Ohio near Pittsburgh, passing through Warren in the process. Eben Gardner never confused a dream with reality nor graded a dream by the standard appropriate to reality. It was well enough to dream of coal from the Mahoning Valley being shipped by barge over the Cross-Cut Canal to the Ohio and Erie Canal and so to Cleveland and beyond. The thing to do was to get the coal mined, the barge loaded, the voyage made, and the consignment sold. This Eben Gardner did, and by 1845 he was doing his full share of the million bushels of coal that annually made its way to Cleveland from the Mahoning Valley fields. By that year the first ironworks of Cleveland had been founded, and that marriage of coal and iron with consequences for the Mahoning Valley incalculably beyond the ultimate visions of Eben Gardner had been consummated. However, by the standards of the time and place, coal, the canal, and Cleveland made Eben Gardner a prosperous man.

What of the good life of Eben Gardner? The world had been

readying itself for him and for it for almost eight hundred years. The medieval journeyman become master was his remote progenitor; when that man of the Middle Ages dreamed of economic enterprise untrammeled by the regulations of the guilds he dreamed the dream of Eben Gardner. Amos Parkins the "incompleat Puritan" with his warehouse by the Thames and that wondrous set of convictions in which worldly prosperity, man's duty, and the favor of Jehovah fused into a consistent and unified whole was another progenitor, and the set of convictions to which Amos Parkins held would not have been incomprehensible to Eben Gardner. Just what might be the relationship to Eben Gardner of the three traders who met on Rotten Row is a matter of conjecture. They dealt less in commodities than in the opportunities which commodities can offer and in that sense made no such contribution to society as Eben Gardner made and indeed as the medieval master and the incompleat Puritan made, and yet their bias was as much economic as his. There is a consideration, however, that sets the three apart from Eben Gardner and at the same time sets them apart from the medieval master and the Puritan. There was something almost spiritual about the materialism of these latter three. They did not really value economic success for the material comforts that it brought, although they enjoyed them. To them the economic struggle to bring to reality a dream carried in large measure its own reward. The dream might not be the sort that inspires poets and elicits the world's admiration: to carry wool to the Low Countries, hides to the Midlands, or coal to Cleveland might be deemed prosaic dreams. But they were not prosaic dreams to those who dreamed them, nor are dreams of new and better ways to make life physically richer, better, more varied and more comfortable unworthy dreams.

There was something in the life of Eben Gardner, however, that set it apart from the lives of the young master and the Puritan. The young master had the normal apprenticeship and the Puritan started with financial backing. Eben Gardner started with an axe, a spade, a hammer, and a saw, and he made a home in the wilderness. He fought nature with the odds totally against him, and he won the fight. He left something already established in Connecticut, however little he valued its worth, and he entered the woods which engulfed him and his bride as if they never were. Like St. Paul, he spent his days in the depth of the sea. But he emerged triumphant and ended a prosperous and respected man. He had made life in the United States physically richer, better, more varied, and more comfortable by the successful fulfilment of his dream.

It was inevitable that the good life of Eben Gardner be founded in very large measure upon his business triumphs. He was a loving husband and a good father, but a loving wife and devoted children knew where a man's first interest must lie. He made up in generosity to the church what he lacked in devotion, and he never forgot the commandment that concerned his neighbor, but he obeyed it with his wallet and not his time. He lived in a time and place without civic problems as later but not necessarily happier periods have known them, but if they had existed he would have contributed generously to their solution. His strength was founded on his limitations and he built a fine career within the framework of values which he had inherited. And yet, his good life was not entirely the good life of material achievement. He stood one evening by the Cross-Cut Canal and watched a distant barge cleave a path through a field of golden grain and slowly enter the great, flaming, red orb of the setting sun. It was his field of grain, his barge, his dream, his fulfilment. His good life was not entirely the good life of material achievement.

There was in the good life of Eben Gardner a great deal of the prophecy of the good life as Isaac Bates conceived it. There was certainly the opportunity that Isaac Bates had conceived, the chance of accomplishment in a world that was fresh, new, different from the old, and untrammeled by centuries of accrued inhibitions and restraints. There was the physical achievement, as Eben Gardner worked, scrambled, and fought his way up and out of a hut in the wilderness to a comfortable home as Ohio of the 1840's understood comfort, to the financial security of fields of waving grain and barges carrying coal to a destiny as yet but dimly sensed. But that was not the dream of Isaac Bates. He dreamed in terms of human rights and human opportunity, and somehow the dream was transformed into fields of grain and strings of barges. And yet the essence of the dream was not entirely destroyed. To say that the good life of Eben Gardner was based on material possessions would be neither accurate nor fair. It was based on the sense of accomplishment that those material possessions represented, and it was based as well upon the conviction that far greater accomplishment would be possible in the years to come. If Eben Gardner was the spiritual descendant of anyone we have met, it was the medieval journeyman become master who had prepared his masterpiece for the judgment of that jury of his peers. The village at the foot of castle hill was new in a way not entirely different from the way that Warren, Ohio, was new, and the spirit of the men who followed in the footsteps of the medieval pioneers was not entirely foreign to the spirit of the men who followed after the American pioneers.

In saying this, however, one may imply something that is not quite accurate. One may imply that the physical problems of the latter paralleled the physical problems of the former. The clearings had been made in the forest and the tough sod turned long before the Middle Ages; the generation of Eben Gardner had to make the clearings and turn the sod. In a sense Eben Gardner had to do the work of both the ninth century and the nineteenth, to rough hew the logs for his cabin and to bring coal to the city where it could meet iron. Garth the swineherd did the former in the ninth century, Plugson of Undershot did the latter in the nineteenth. Eben Gardner did both. In terms of the nineteenth and twentieth centuries what Eben Gardner did was to be all but totally eclipsed by what his son did, but there was to the achievement of Eben Gardner something far greater than there was in the objectively greater achievements of his son. Eben Gardner began with an axe and an oak tree, and he ended with a substantial shipping business in a basic commodity. His son started with what his father had achieved, as did all the sons of the second generation in the Western Reserve who carried on the work their fathers had begun. The unsurpassed achievement of the generation of Eben Gardner was to bring the Industrial Revolution into the wilderness, to bring the nineteenth century into what had been before the centuries began.

And what of those who followed after them, those for whom far greater accomplishment would be possible in the years to come, who had to shoulder the duty of achieving that accomplishment to be worthy of their heritage? The answer may at least be suggested by the career of James B. Gardner, the youngest son of Eben Gardner and a man who would hold a secure but not brilliant place in the history of Minnesota if Minnesota history embraced fiction as well as fact. The start of the answer is to be found in the ancient city of Paris. By the year 1867 Eben Gardner was a man of seventy, a man of substance but a man bowed and saddened by that last tragedy which never passes away and at best softens to a quiet melancholy of resigned acceptance. His wife of nearly fifty years had died, and with her death there died the good life of Eben Gardner. James B. Gardner, then a man of thirty, and his wife brought Eben to Paris and the Exhibition of 1867. They saw many things of fascinating novelty to Americans from Ohio, things that opened the eyes and the mouth, and to some extent the mind. But the mind of James B. Gardner was open to things beyond the ken of Parisians. He stood for minutes and stared at a red, chunky substance in one exhibition case. It was labelled hematite and came from Lake Vermilion in remote Minnesota, where it was said on authority that James B. Gardner trusted to be present in great abundance. No person of culture would have stood to stare at it, but James B. Gardner was of the breed that does not understand a culture but creates one. He thought of his father's old blast furnace, the not completely successful experiments with soft coal, the string of barges on the canal, and Cleveland beyond. He thought of the proved success with hard coal that the iron masters of eastern Pennsylvania had achieved. But still more he thought of the lakes, of Erie and Huron, and that great problem at the Soo before the great shining, shimmering and icy waters of Superior reached out to draw in the setting sun. He thought of a wilderness compared to which the Western Reserve had been a

193

woodland park, and winters that curled the mercury for days in its globule of glass. And he looked again at the red, chunky substance called hematite, identified for the pedantic as a non-magnetic ore that crystallized in a hexagonal system. Two worldly, polished Englishmen strolled by, and turned to smile at old Eben's trade derivative of Ohio homespun and his son's rapt preoccupation with a red chunk of something or other. That the old man was the justification of so much of their own eighteenth century and that the young man was in a prophetic trance with the dim outline of the twentieth century tantalizing his imagination would have been light years beyond their powers of comprehension.

The next summer James B. Gardner made his way to Minnesota. He could have travelled easily and quickly by railroad through Chicago to the Mississippi and by boat from Rock Island up the river to St. Paul. Instead he went the slow, hard way up the lakes. He knew that something extremely critical to what he had in mind existed at Sault Ste. Marie and he wanted to observe it at first hand. He did so, and was satisfied that the Michigan locks were a practical link between Lake Superior and the lower lakes. He reached the head of the lake and a ramshackle place called Duluth. James B. Gardner was concerned with neither the past nor the present of Duluth, nor indeed with what many thought its future. He was told that rumors of copper deposits had made it a squatter's town and prospector's depot a decade before, and that the panic of 1857 capped by a scarlet fever epidemic had all but obliterated the place. Now it was a stampede town again, as gold-bearing quartz from some vaguely located lake in the wilderness to the north was brought down by persons of vague antecedents and fluctuating stories. James B. Gardner was not in the least interested in gold. He spent much time poring over crude maps drawn for him by persons who had prospected at Lake Vermilion, as he knew it was called, and was quite oblivious to their efforts to titillate his curiosity by ostentatiously concealing the orgin of the quartz specimens. Were it not for the plethora of eccentricity with which Duluth was currently blessed, as every bonanza town is, the days he spent studying the sandbars that form Duluth Harbor might have caused curiosity. The curiosity of the fisherman whom he hired to bring him on what turned out to be a cruise of nearly a week's duration up the northern shore of the lake was indeed aroused, but not satisfied. The tight-lipped Easterner who was paying him well for these days of aimless cruising seemed particularly fascinated by a bedraggled ghost of an abandoned settlement called Burlington Bay, but why stayed far beyond the fisherman's ken. They returned to Duluth, the fisherman was paid off, James B. Gardner went by stage down the old Military Road to St. Paul, by boat to Rock Island, and then by train to Cleveland. He had started with three certainties, that there really was a major iron deposit near Lake Vermilion, that there was coal in the Mahoning Valley, and that there was an uninterrupted water route from a point some fifty miles south of Lake Vermilion to Cleveland harbor. There was evidence enough in eastern Pennsylvania as to what can result when iron and coal are brought together.

The next ten years James B. Gardner divided between working and dreaming, working on the transportation system which his father had created in its first crude beginnings and he had built into a systematic and profitable combination of water and rail service between the Mahoning Valley and the port of Cleveland, and dreaming of a far greater and almost infinitely more profitable combination that might link the port of Cleveland with the Minnesota iron lands. He made repeated summer trips to the north country, and in the casual fashion of the time, which was more studied with him than with most, picked up thousands of acres of land in the Lake Vermilion area. Thus, when the Duluth and Iron Range Railroad came into being and its tracks were laid from the Vermilion range to that bedraggled ghost of an abandoned settlement then called Burlington Bay and now Two Harbors, where he had also casually acquired acres, his dream was ready for reality. Twenty years after he had meditated upon a specimen of hematite in an exhibition case at the Paris Exhibition he was becoming a millionaire and then a multi-millionaire because he knew how to bring together Minnesota iron and Pennsylvania coal at a place not far from the site of his father's one-room cabin in the Mahoning Valley of Ohio.

Minnesota might never have been more to James B. Gardner than a wilderness to be stripped of its hidden wealth were it not that his wife fell in love with wavelets that glinted and sparkled in the morning sun, with air like draughts of wine scented and flavored with aromatic pine, with emptiness and loneliness and birds etched in black upon a silver sky. He was a man of vision, but not of stubborness. He would leave the Mahoning Valley at his wife's desire, but he would hardly perch upon a terrace in that great amphitheater of a city, Duluth, where the rows in nature's stadium were slowly filling up. The logical compromise for a wealthy man from the East, with Connecticut in his background and propriety in his veins, was Summit Avenue in St. Paul. There he built a home befitting what he had achieved, bearing the stamp of his generation and its tastes and standards, with its arched coach gate of St. Cloud granite and its towers commanding the Mississippi in a way that our lord of the medieval fief might have envied. It was close enough to the James J. Hill house and to that glorious open area high on the bluff where Archbishop Ireland and Jim Hill planned their cathedral to show St. Paul that James B. Gardner was one of those who mattered. Perhaps it was the Connecticut in him that bred far sighted prudence as well as vision. When the Mesabi range was opened and when Rockefeller and Carnegie stepped in, James B. Gardner knew that his hour had come to step out. He would fight his equals and those somewhat more powerful than he, but he would not tilt a lance against the titans. He was content with a fortune from the Vermilion range, and did not contest the far greater fortune that lay beyond. Besides, he had another dream.

He dreamed of Montana, of fields of the best and hardest wheat that grows, of beef cattle in the lush grounds by the river, of a hill of copper, of an empire that stretched on and on across the wide Dakotas and vast Montana until it ended vaguely in the mountains, and of one last mountain top from which one might see the Pacific. Rome was once a seat of empire, and St. Paul would be. And then he had the cerebral hemorrhage, after which there remained only the memory of yesterday and the awareness that his son, who was calling himself J. Bradford Gardner and thereby irking his father for a reason neither he nor his father fully understood, would have to fulfill that particular dream.

It would be a grave misreading of the truth to imagine that the good life of Mr. and Mrs. James B. Gardner lay in their material prosperity. They started with sufficient material prosperity for any reasonable couple, he the son of a successful foundry owner and shipper and she the daughter of a Cleveland merchant. It was bred in the bone of James B. Gardner that to be content with such prosperity as he inherited would be a grave sin against the Almighty, Who expected ten talents of the man endowed with five. Work is man's destiny and his single greatest source of happiness, and the work to be done in a half opened continent was beyond any man's imagination. The iron of Minnesota existed and the coal of Pennsylvania existed. They would not have existed if God had not intended that they be brought together. If God gave James B. Gardner the vision to see how this could be accomplished, then God had laid upon him the solemn mandate to achieve it. In carrying out God's will, James B. Gardner did his entire share to build America, to bring to the use of a new and burgeoning land everything that iron, incomparably the most precious of all metals, could mean in the building of cities and their factories, the building of railroads to link the ocean of yesterday with the ocean of tomorrow, the erecting of every shrine to the nineteenth century goddess Progress that man's ingenuity and dedication could contrive. James B. Gardner did his appointed work, and that was the good life.

Otherwise his good life was that of his father. Like Eben before him, James was a good and faithful husband, a loving father, and a devoted friend when time permitted the benign and gentle virtues. He gave generously to the Congregational Church, which he attended not infrequently, and because he had a high admiration for vision, enterprise, and the power to think in broad, expansive terms, he gave generously to Archbishop Ireland's Roman Catholic cathedral that was to be, and rejoiced that the day in 1906 when the first sod was turned was warm enough for the butler to help him down Summit Avenue to observe the ceremony. He gave as well to the charities of his adopted city, but his concept of charity contained certain theological quirks that somehow were the twisted residue of the thinking of the incompleat Puritan. An object of charity was one who had borne the brunt of God's wrath, a widow, an orphan, a cripple. It was part of the good life to offset the wrath of God by aiding such, or perhaps it was part of the inscrutable design of God to make desolate the widow and orphan that His elect might cultivate charity. It never occurred to James B. Gardner to feel pity or show so much as the spirit of charity to the tall, strong, inarticulate men of Scandinavia who shivered in the cold of Bridge Square in Minneapolis and crowded its dismal flophouses in the months when the harvest was in and there was no work in the forests and the mines. They also had come to America following a dream, but they were tall and strong and therefore deserved neither pity nor charity. It was within the power of James B. Gardner to create a culture, but not to understand its workings. His mind also was a fief, orderly and organized within, but outside its limits the land was unknown and the inhabitants incomprehensible.

And yet, who will say that the good life of James B. Gardner did not make a most substantial contribution to the good life of America? His vision made a physically better life a general reality. His ability to translate into the tangible the essence of a dream is the hallmark of all those who build a culture. He accepted the stern challenge of Progress, and he met it. There was nothing mean spirited about the way in which he used his yardstick of material values. He had nothing but profound admiration for Jim Hill, whose power to dream and to achieve was so much greater than his own. He had profound admiration for Archbishop John Ireland, for whose church he felt the instinctive dread of the Puritan but whose vision and drive in a cause so alien to his own endeavors commanded his total respect and opened wide his purse. He even had profound admiration for Andrew Carnegie and John D. Rockefeller, whose might had forced him to retire from active affairs and to dream again.

The true trouble with his good life, as with the good life of his father, was its uneasy fusion of the spiritual and the material. He valued material progress and achievement, to be sure; there never has been a time when material achievement and comfort have not been part of the good life of most people. Yet neither he nor his father was a materialist; a fleet of barges hauled down an Ohio canal, an ore boat dipping below the horizon on Lake Superior, were symbols of an achievement the real rewards of which were spiritual. But in their good lives the material and the spiritual were one and inseparable, and that was not true of the ancient Athenian whose good life was service to his city, of the medieval baron whose good life was the protection of his fief, or of the Renaissance governor whose good life was service to his prince, let alone the good life of the monks of Monte Cassino, the Franciscans, or the Puritans who created Zion in America. Nothing made the fusion of the spiritual and the material possible but the goddess Progress, who always kept the dream a step ahead of the achievement. But what if the goddess should die? James B. Gardner sat on the second story porch that the sun filtering through the trees of Summit Avenue reached in the late afternoon. He watched his son, who was calling himself J. Bradford Gardner, step from that most dream inspiring offspring the iron age has ever borne, the automobile. He watched his son, and he wondered.

He had better reason to wonder than he knew. James B. Gardner felt that he was very much the son of his father, but he knew that he was not to anything like the same degree the father of his son. He had carried out his father's work, and done so in his father's spirit. The ore boat bringing Minnesota hematite to the Cleveland docks was the logical successor to the barge that brought coal to Cleveland. The difference was in the scale of operations, not in their nature, purpose, and spirit. James B. Gardner was of the second generation of industrialists who built shrines to the goddess of Progress where the burnt offerings had the white heat of molten iron and the smoke of sacrifice blackened the Ohio skies. It is not true, of course, to say that with his generation the Industrial Revolution was completed, but it might be said that it was finally and entirely triumphant. The implications of electricity were far from fully understood and nuclear power was as yet an unshaped dream, but the pattern had been established, the basic facilities of factory and transportation built, and what lay ahead would be an extension of what had already been accomplished. No future Gardner could ever do what Eben Gardner and James B. Gardner had done, and therefore no future Gardner could ever know that fusion of the spiritual and the material which preserved them from materialism if it also denied them the good life that is entirely a thing of the spirit.

James B. Gardner watched his son step from the automobile, and he wondered. He had the vision that let him realize something of the potentialities in this hybrid offspring of the buggy and internal combustion, an offspring so erratic, so noisy, so smelly, and also to a man of imagination who worshipped at the shrine of Progress, so enthralling. For the first time in human history man could move himself, free from the limitations of his own strength and the borrowed strength of animals, and free from the limitations of rails. Had his son been such in the sense that he was his father's son, he would pin his faith and his future on that queer contraption at which people laughed. But J. Bradford Gardner was a man of a different kind and a man given to different dreams. It is not clear that he himself could spell out the difference, and certainly his father could not, but he belonged not to the third generation in the Industrial Revolution but rather to its second phase. He was not a maker of machines nor was his interest centered upon the materials of which they are made and the lines of transportation by which materials are brought together. There was very little of what had given him so much for which he really cared, surely not his father's trade in iron ore or his grandfather's fleet of barges out of which that trade had grown. Yet Bradford Gardner would deny that this was true. He was fascinated by the more remote forms that economic manipulation can take, the fiscal arrangements on which business enterprise depends, the organization by which corporate structure is erected and as taxes ceased to be what they should be, a negligible consideration, and became a factor with which businessmen must contend, on that subtle interplay of profit and loss whereby loss contributes to profit and makes it greater. Eben Gardner and James Gardner were immediate builders of enterprise, but Bradford Gardner was a remote manager of enterprise. They were owners, he was a director.

The logic that brought his grandfather and his father west brought him east. There was building to be done in the East, but there was far more building to be done in the West, and so Eben Gardner and his son moved westward. It was possible to manage and direct from the West, but the sort of indirect and comprehensive management and direction for which Bradford Gardner had an instinct was centered in New York. Thus a geographic cycle was completed, and Bradford Gardner ultimately made his home in a particularly well-manicured and insulated town in western Connecticut, the state his grandfather had left almost a century before. His inherited wealth eased his way into appropriate directorships, and he enjoyed quite literally the pleasure of economic remoteness, of playing chess by telephone in games where pawns were swept aside without his ever seeing them, rooks and knights interchanged, and checkmate averted or achieved, and whose hand moved the pieces never quite disclosed.

J. Bradford Gardner was not in the final sense a materialist. There was something spiritual about his grandfather's vision of coal and its uses, and something spiritual about his father's vision of the union of coal and iron. Because a nation grew larger, richer, stronger through their visions, they had their own justification for being. But the vision of J. Bradford Gardner was of a different sort. He dreamed of power and its exercise, and whether the medium were coal, iron, or something entirely different from either was a matter of no consequence. There was something social in the very individualism of his elders, as society was the better for their personal gains, but there was nothing social to the dream of Bradford Gardner. His power grew and sometimes society was the better for it and sometimes the worse. He seldom if ever knew, nor is there evidence that he cared. There are spirits good and evil, and there was an evil spirit in Bradford Gardner which he never for a moment suspected. The sheer greed for money is a very vulgar greed and only the very vulgar have it. Certainly Bradford Gardner was not of that stamp. The greed for the power that money and position bring is more subtle and it can infect those who think themselves immune. That was the temptation Bradford Gardner faced and knew he faced, but it was a temptation against which he fought in ways that varied from the very naive to the very subtle.

J. Bradford Gardner was every bit as convinced that his was the good life as was Squire Gilbert who basked in the peace of the Augustans. As a matter of fact there was a very real similarity between their lives, with all the obvious and profound differences. Just as Squire Gilbert lived in one of those infrequent and fleeting periods when society is on dead center and the prosperous are secure in their prosperity, so did J. Bradford Gardner. Corporate America ruled the land, and the ilk of Bradford Gardner ruled the corporations. Unlike Squire Gilbert, Bradford Gardner knew no villagers but his benefactions to the Park Avenue church of his Christmas and Easter attendance would make pathetic the Squire's humble efforts at railing in the communion table. There was hardly a properly grounded charity in New York ministering to the worthy poor that did not list Bradford Gardner among its directors, and he never begrudged to such charities the attention to detail and the expenditure of thought that he gave to his merchantile directorships. His service to the yacht club and the country club was equally devoted, and when he suggested that both could use their facilities on occasion for deserving charities and eyebrows were raised, he let them be raised and he held his ground. It would be an iconoclast indeed who would question that the life of Bradford Gardner was good.

Yet there was an iconoclast within himself. His grandfather and his father alike could work hard for what they achieved, take deep and sincere pleasure in it, and then dissociate themselves from it entirely and dream of other and often very different achievements that would also make the nation larger, richer, and stronger. James Gardner's achievement was Minnesota; Montana was his dream. But somehow power does not lend itself to that sort of dream. The dream of power is like the dream of sex or liquor, the dream that tantalizes and can never satisfy. The dream of power is satisfied only with more power. J. Bradford Gardner came to know this rather soon in the game, but as an intelligent and resourceful man he learned to sublimate the dream. He had only one child, a son who was born in 1912, graduated from Yale in 1934, married in 1938, and entered the Army in 1940. He sublimated his dream of power in his son.

There was a basic shrewdness in this, and that fundamental ability to foresee which marked all the Gardners. The difference was that he foresaw in the abstractions of the business world, not its concrete terms. His grandfather could foresee the union of coal and iron, his father the union of Minnesota and Ohio. His ability was to foresee the basic trends of corporate structure. His grandfather and father alike had the power to foresee expansion; he had the power to foresee contraction. He foresaw that what Rockefeller did was merely the prelude to what American business in general would do, that the trend of the future would be toward consolidation and combination of economic enterprises, with corporate structures that became larger and more complex but steadily fewer in number. He knew that the full development of this trend would come after his time, but he believed it would come in the lifetime of his son.

Bradford Gardner came to realize very slowly that he stood upon a watershed in American economic history. He was the middle figure among the five generations of Gardners who made their varying contributions to their country and, in their diverse ways, lived the good life or attempted to live it. His personal memory did not extend back to his grandfather, but his grandfather was so totally a living memory in the Gardner household that Bradford really was unaware that he had not known his grandfather. It was as if he had been present at the building of that log cabin in the Western Reserve, at the slow and desperate struggle to gain a toehold in the wilderness, at the laborious felling of the trees and the turning of the sod. In a simple sort of ancestral memory he shared the dream that the Cross-Cut Canal made possible, the coal that was mined, the barge that was loaded, and the union of coal and iron at the Cleveland mill. He shared in a literal sense the achievements of his father's later days, the opening of the Vermilion mine, the stubby ore cars rattling down to Two Harbors, the ore boat setting the first leg of its course well to the south of Isle Royale, the impatient wait for spring at the Soo and the hectic race against winter there, the thread of passageway in the rivers between Huron and Erie with the fog that can beset it, and the treachery of which Erie is capable until the boat has made Cleveland or Ashtabula. He shared as well the baronial splendor of the Summit Avenue home, and a society of that stiff formality and starched elegance which are found only in the provinces. He was unhappy about St. Paul and he barred Minneapolis from his mind.

He had all this in his background, but he also had an awareness that it was not in him to achieve in the same way that his grandfather and his father had achieved. They had their forms of imagination and he had his, but they were not the same. His father could look at a map of Montana and see golden fields, sleek herds, molten rivers of metal, and an inland empire. He could look at the same map and see wiggles that were railroad tracks and dots that were towns. He disliked train travel and he loathed towns. His imagination was for the abstractions of economics, for concepts that his grandfather and his father never so much as entertained. They were builders, he was a manager. What he managed, to be sure, were the massive entities of American enterprise and he managed them in days when the building of the basic structure of American enterprise was finished and its management had become the task of prime importance. He became, and he knew he had become, the symbol of American business to the American people, a symbol that he knew was unreasonably glorified in the 1920's and unreasonably vilified in the 1930's. Because he had a fundamentally philosophic mind and a particularly fine one, he was not unduly impressed by the earlier decade nor spiritually crushed by the second.

Mrs. J. Bradford Gardner was of quite different metal from her husband. She was one of those whom fortune blesses with all the material blessings in its cornucopia, and then benignly guards from an awareness that such is other than their inevitable right. She had enjoyed St. Paul society and found Minneapolis exciting. Naturally all this was speedily and enthusiastically forgotten when the move was made to western Connecticut and the New York orbit. She revelled in the 1920's and adjusted quite easily to the Depression. It was not, of course, a Depression in any personal and painful sense to the Gardners, but it was a period when time had to be marked and new courses set. Mrs. Gardner made the fashionable concessions to hard times: she closed the place at Southampton and let the staff go, and she gave up the evenings at the Met which her husband's attitude had always made a hair shirt for her.

Bradford Gardner was happy that for his wife the Depression was merely a new adventure, a sort of reducing diet that simplified life without really lessening its delights. It was rather the psychic impact of the Depression upon his son, young Brad Gardner, which puzzled his father, bothered him, and in truth moved him more than he would admit. It was not so much that Brad questioned the old certainties on which the Gardner fortune was built as the fact that he seemed indifferent to them. His father sensed that there was something of the sort behind young Brad's marriage to an Italian girl, and yet she was third generation in the United States, had been educated by the Madames of the Sacred Heart, and was given a really splendid wedding, if one a shade beyond the Gardner taste, by her father the contractor. To use the sort of term that was instinctive to J. Bradford Gardner, one might say that there was in his son some sort of impending consolidation that never came off. There was the Gardner heritage, but there was the Depression mental framework. There was marriage to a girl of alien stock and creed, and yet J. Bradford Gardner had the tough realism to recognize a very close kinship of the spirit between her father the contractor and his own grandfather as he had heard him described. Then the baby was born, and young Brad and his wife had the infant christened Eben Gardner. At the party J. Bradford Gardner and the Italian contractor had a drink together, the contractor shrugged his shoulders with his native eloquence, and J. Bradford shrugged his. Both knew that the choice of Christian name meant something, but neither knew just what it was. As things turned out, they never did discover. Young Brad had entered the Army well before Pearl Harbor. He made his officer's training, in due time was shipped abroad, and took part in the invasion of Italy. On a badly pock-marked road with mud holes that would mire an ox he was struck by a piece of ricocheting shrapnel and killed. It was the road that winds to the summit of Monte Cassino.

Naturally the dream of J. Bradford Gardner was transferred to young Eben Gardner, and the dream grew as Eben grew out of Andover into Yale, and then out of Yale into his future. There was something about the boy that commanded his grandfather's respect, and respect was something he did not give lightly to those younger than himself. When he was barely in the teens he had a sort of quiet confidence, a tendency to look inward and find his answers there. He was in every sense a normal boy, Bradford Gardner and the contractor assured each other perhaps a shade more often than was necessary. A curious sort of relationship had developed between the two older men. Every now and then Bradford found himself thinking of the contractor, who was exactly his own age, as his father. The truth is that the contractor was a generation behind Bradford in his instinctive pattern of thought. He thought of housing developments as James Gardner had thought of ore ships and ore docks, but he did not think of economic enterprises in terms of consolidation and combination. Bradford dreamed of his grandson merging Steel and Telephone, but the contractor dreamed of him building a larger Levittown. Neither man knew just what the boy dreamed, if indeed he dreamed at all. He played the boyhood games, got into boyhood difficulties, flexed his mental muscles when at sixteen he discovered Literature and Art and nibbled at Music but drew back again, and offered about the normal amount of trouble where cars and girls were concerned. There was always that barrier between him and the grandfathers whom he sincerely loved, but it was hardly a barrier that he raised or could help being there. It was something in Eben himself, and if it meant that one could go only so far toward understanding him, it also meant that others could go only so far toward tempting him, or beguiling him, or leading him astray. So he went his way through Yale, played touch football for his college, did reasonably well in economics to the happiness of Bradford and in art to the happiness of the contractor, and graduated. He was ready for the road that leads to the consolidation of Steel and Telephone, or to the larger Levittown. But he did not take that road. He took two vaguely undirected years of graduate study and then joined Vista. He was assigned to work on an Indian reservation in Montana.

The night that Eben told him what he was to do was a night of strange and mixed emotions for J. Bradford Gardner. He thought of the night the telegram had come telling of young Bradford, but for a reason which he could not understand there kept coming into his mind what his father had told him of the first Eben, of the one-room cabin that at least had a chimney and his wife's one good dress that caught on the nail and tore. More obviously, he thought of his father's dream of Montana and an empire of wheat, cattle, and copper. It puzzled him that the first thought persisted rather than the second, the thought of a wedge of forest running west to Sandusky and back on the fifty-first parallel to Pennsylvania. He sensed that in some dimly metaphoric way his grandson was going, not to an established empire but to a Western Reserve.

Bradford Gardner had at his command the last and finest weapon a human being can possess, a highly intelligent and philosophic mind. He had always been aware that however much he differed from his father and his grandfather, he was closer to them than he was to his son and grandson. One side of the watershed has to be the familiar side. It is the side that has been traversed. The other side has to be unfamiliar. Bradford Gardner had long since realized that his son and grandson lived and had their spiritual being on what

207

was to him the unfamiliar side of the watershed, the side into which he could look but somehow could not enter. If either had opposed his set of values or argued their worth, he could have met him and, he was convinced, overpowered him. But neither did. Both were indifferent toward them, accepting the comforts and conveniences they offered, never spoke of them with contempt or even disrespect, but took them for granted as they took for granted health and youthful strength. In 1817, he thought, the first Eben left Connecticut to create the future to the image and likeness he desired on the Western Reserve. A century and a half later the second Eben left Connecticut to do the same on a western reservation. The values that the second Eben treasured and his grandfather vaguely sensed were not the values of the first Eben which, as his grandson, he understood. But were they necessarily invalid, or even less valid? Things are not the same on the one side of the watershed and on the other. By the values of the first Eben and his son, the decision of the second Eben to turn his back on the family tradition was the end of the story of the Gardners. But Bradford had in mind the thought that the first Eben had done the work both of the ninth century and the nineteenth, had rough hewn the logs for his cabin like Garth the swineherd and brought coal to the city where it could meet iron as did Plugson of Undershot. The second Eben had to do the work both of the fifth century and the twentieth, the work of the monk of Calabria slaving for learning's sake in a land of all but total darkness and the task that was entirely one for the strange and unprobed side of the watershed, of making the fifth century meet the twentieth. Were the values that the second Eben treasured necessarily less valid than those of his ancestor? Bradford Gardner was by no means sure that this was the end of the story of the Gardners. It might even be the beginning, come around again.

2.

The Success Story

IT has often been said that the American story is the success story. It might be said with equal truth that the American good life has been the successful life. It is not in the least difficult to say such things. What may be difficult is to say them without overtones of sarcasm or satire, righteous reprobation or supercilious contempt. No one, with the possible exception of Horatio Alger, would maintain that the success story has never deserved reprobation and contempt. On the other hand, this generation has had a superfluity of those who maintain, usually with only a dim awareness of the nature of what they are condemning, that the success story has always deserved reprobation and contempt. In the story of the Gardner family, and it is the success story, there is much that exposes itself to sarcasm and satire, but little that is worthy of reprobation and contempt.

The Gardners worshipped the Christian God in the several ways fashionable in their successive generations, but they burned their weekday incense at the shrine of the goddess Progress. The primary characteristic of any god, be it a true god or a false, is that aspiration keeps the suppliant coming to his shrine; prayer is for the future, not the past. Only a St. Francis comes to the shrine in a spirit of pure love and can say on his deathbed, "By the grace of His Holy Spirit I am so intimately one with God that I am equally content to live or die." Only a St. Francis can so completely deserve Heaven that Heaven hardly matters. The Gardners really crested in the Victorian mansion on Summit Avenue in St. Paul, and even the estate in western Connecticut that Bradford Gardner achieved was on the sunset side of the hill. Their goddess had not been Success but Progress. Progress did not entirely stop with James B. Gardner, but after him it was fitful and uncertain. Perhaps this question may be more important than it seems today: did Progress start again with the second Eben Gardner?

Progress is the goddess whose claim to divinity must be appraised. If our thesis has any validity, progress is really achieved only by those in whose thinking there is a fusion of the material and the spiritual. The good life of most of those whose stories we have tried to tell has been based on such a fusion; the material was certainly subordinated to the spiritual among the Franciscans and it was substantially subordinated by the ancient Athenian who served his city with a cheerful disregard for his physical comfort, but that was not in general true of the others. Service to one's fellow man developed out of a pattern of living among the Benedictines, as it did among the barons of the medieval fiefs and the governors of the provinces of the Renaissance in the Old World and the New. Only when we reach the Enlightenment does that fusion tend to dwindle, as in Squire Gilbert, or to disappear as among the merchants of Rotten Row. Yet in the Enlightenment it appeared again in saints like Sara Finch and philosophers like Isaac Bates. But how do the Gardners fit into the picture?

The truth is that they do not really fit into the picture at all, that in their case the fusion of the material and the spiritual was of a different sort because the material was to such a degree the spiritual itself. The first Eben Gardner faced a great, rich, varied, virgin land, a land totally potential. The Indians had lived on its surface, and often starved on its surface. The pioneers had crossed its surface and recorded it, but little more. It remained for Eben Gardner and those like him to change

210

the potential energy hidden beneath those endless forests of oak and maple into the kinetic energy that sustains, enriches, and makes more comfortable and secure the lives of many. Thus there was a vision always present in the life of the first Eben Gardner, as he slowly won the first and toughest round of the fight with nature and then moved on to win the rounds that lay ahead. The reward for Eben Gardner was never entirely in the achievement and perhaps it was not even primarily there. Much of the reward was always in the vision that the achievement evoked, the vision of the future that lay within his grasp if he could muster the forces of mind and will that it demanded. And the reward of that vision made reality was the further vision that it begot. That he should prosper in the process was only right, the logical corollary to initiative, vision, and hard work, but prosperity was never his limited goal.

The same was true of his son James B. Gardner, except that Progress made it possible for him to have more expansive visions. Where his father could dream in terms of one wedge in the state of Ohio, he could dream in terms of an entire region. Nature separated Minnesota iron from Ohio and Pennsylvania coal, reason demanded that they be brought together, and God created the Great Lakes. It was the obvious will of God that a man of initiative, vision, the capacity for hard work, and the willingness to take big financial chances should bring them together. For years James B. Gardner could dream of this, but nothing more. It was a job too big for him alone, and he could only prepare himself for its performance by buying land in appropriate locations and then biding his time in patience until his hour came. The hour came, he made the most of it, but the most of it was not the wealth that gave him the Victorian mansion on Summit Avenue. The most of it was the sight of a string of ore cars rattling down to the dock at Two Harbors, an ore boat making a symmetrical furrow in the quiet waters of the bay, red demons dancing across a velvet sky when white hot metal was poured, and there was more than that. There was the knowledge that this was the Iron Age, and that it was not the melancholy age that ancient myth had made it but rather the vibrant, living, forward-looking, forever dreaming Age

of Progress, and that he was one of the makers of it. It was, perhaps, his entirely fitting reward granted by the Almighty that
when the titans forced him to retire and a blood vessel burst-
ing in his brain spelled quietus to his active life, he had
Montana to dream about. In James B. Gardner as in his father
the material and the spiritual were one and inseparable.

Bradford Gardner did not have his father's assurance that
he was one of the makers of the age of Progress. It was not so
much that the age of Progress was over; probably it never
really ends. It was certainly central in the life of the contractor,
and his dreams for his grandson were entirely in its terms.
What had happened was that as the material part thinned out
in Bradford's life and thought to a set of abstractions, as coal
mines became shares of common stock, lands purchased became corporate bonds, operating companies became remote
and holding companies the present fact, the spiritual part
thinned out with it and disappeared. A corporate merger is
simply not an achievement in the same sense as the building
of an ore dock, and the sort of vision that goes into the con-
struction of an industry that links Minnesota to Ohio fades to
the light of common day when it becomes a matter of the fiscal
adjustments that its future may require. Bradford Gardner enjoyed his game, but it was not the game his father and grandfather had played. They had helped to build America; he made
delicate adjustments in the operating machinery.

There is little point to speaking about the position of young
Bradford in the game, and it is too early to speak of the position of young Eben. There really was a lost generation in
twentieth century America, but it was not the generation that
proclaimed itself such after the first World War. The generation that was really lost was the generation that graduated into
the Depression, was nearing or in the thirties when the war
broke out, and could see the age of forty in the not too remote
distance when the war was finally over. There were many like
Young Brad Gardner who did not make it at all. This was the
one generation in American history that went from late boyhood to early middle life without ever knowing in the true
sense the experience of young manhood. As for young Eben,

he is in the stage of the one room cabin, and it is not even certain that it has a chimney.

This much it seems possible to say about the good life of material success: it does exist, it can be achieved. It is most likely to be achieved when the material part is very material indeed, but success itself is measured by a different yardstick. So long as things of tangible value that enrich the country and improve its life come from it, its rewards are real, but its rewards have never been material. It was achieved in the highest degree in the decades when the country was being opened, but it was achieved only by those who were the builders of the country and not the manipulators of the wealth which the builders created. Because there was in it an identity of the material and the spiritual hardly to be found in the good life of any other time or place, it had within itself the seeds of its own fairly speedy destruction. Once the vision of the builder gave way to the cautious planning of the financier, achievement ceased to be its goal and power took its place. The good life of material success is most likely to be achieved in a new and developing country, and in some ways is native only to such a land.

But what is a developing country? There are other frontiers than the geographic, other trackless forests than the Western Reserve of Ohio and the Arrowhead Region of Minnesota, other stores of hidden wealth than the Vermilion and Mesabi ranges. Wherever is the horizon of human knowledge and achievement, wherever pioneers probe that horizon and those who come after the pioneers consolidate and make productive what they have unearthed, there is a developing country. Thus the developing country of this generation is chemistry, biology, medicine. The Eben Gardner of it wears a laboratory smock, spends the day probing the Western Reserve of human knowledge, and brings back from it what makes life richer, more varied, and more secure for his fellow man. And beyond there is a barely discovered country, the Vermilion range of human relations, the society that promises as much to Sara Finch and Isaac Bates as it does to Squire Gilbert and the traders of Rotten Row. The country itself is not a mirage, but to think that the equal promise it holds is material in its terms is to

213

make it a mirage. The good life is a far more subtle thing than that.

The great paradox of the good life of the individual is that it exists only in the regions of the human mind and heart from which it is resolutely banished. The great and saving grace of the Gardners in their successive generations was that by instinct they knew this truth. Old Eben and James knew it well, because they were builders and builders alone. The older Bradford was the one most sorely tempted, yet even he knew that nothing quite so surely destroys the happiness of life as the lust for power, and when he sublimated his own instinctive lust for power in the imagined career of his son, generosity slipped between his better and his worser self and strengthened the former. Young Bradford never had his chance, and young Eben is still in the depth of the sea. The good life of all the Gardners was based upon the conviction that it is dynamic and not static, that change is its enduring principle and progress is its inevitable pattern. It could be that, and it could fail abysmally and become that saddest of all mockeries of the good life, the life of sheer materialism. It was saved partly by the power to dream, but even more by the fact that others were its chief beneficiaries, that a better America was always central to its purpose. And then, with young Eben it becomes a better world, and it may yet be his destiny to prove his vision more comprehensive than any of his progenitors enjoyed. And the vision is so simple! His father lay in mud-caked blood at the base of the road that winds up to the summit of Monte Cassino. When the battle was ended, the monks of the vision filed down the mountain to bind up wounds, bring food and clothing to war's victims, calm the anguished and give promise to those sunk in despair. Young Eben Gardner may yet prove to be one of their number. The last of the Gardners may have found again the good life of Monte Cassino, may have discovered that the good life of the individual is achieved when he gives up everything, and everything returns to him with a new light lambent on it.

214

3.

Freedom and Opportunity

Miss Hargrave choked a bit and then coughed. For a moment she felt a pinch of apprehension, and then it passed away. This was the cough from dust, not the other cough that was coming more frequently, the one they say is caused by the heart. Anyone might cough from the dust in that attic. She did wonder about that old trunk, though, and she had meant more times than she could recall to see what was in it. She knew that the past was in it, but Miss Hargrave had no more fear of the past than she had of the future. Much of the past was pleasant, some of it was sad, there were parts that one would like to do again a different way but not too many of them, and parts at which an old lady could nod with determined satisfaction. She had enjoyed a good life, almost eighty-six years of it now, and she still could hold her own against the nieces who talked of rest homes with increasing regularity. The Lord would tell her when she was ready for a rest home, not her nieces, and if His methods are often rough and ready (His liking for the broken hip is notorious), at least He lets you have the last ounce of your freedom and opportunity. She was not yielding a moment of the former, nor was she totally ready to consent to the fact that the latter was over.

She made a tentative plunge of the arm through some lace

215

doilies that had been placed carefully on top, that they might yellow their way to oblivion without the danger of getting wrinkled in the process. She came up with a manila envelope so brittle that it shivered into little spears of crumbling paper. Inside was a composite photograph, the pictures of some twenty little children taken in the poses that the very young assume when the sense of humor is in the embryonic stage and the photographer with a whole school to shoot is too hurried and too harried to care. Beneath each grinning face the name of the urchin was written in what had now faded to something like brown ink but in an unmistakable Spencerian hand with the orthodox slant to the right as taught at Normal School. Miss Hargrave recognized her still somewhat girlish handwriting, recognized the children, and looked at something far beyond the sloping attic wall, at the memory of the first class she had taught, that third grade in the Daniel Webster School down on the Flats. She recalled that there were just three grades in the old Webster School, that each was pretty sure to have a new teacher almost every year, that there were three new teachers her year there, and that she got the third grade because she was two inches taller than the girl who got the first grade and an inch taller than the girl who got the second. At least that was what the superintendent of schools said when he assigned the three of them to their grades. She had believed him then and she was more than a little convinced even now that it was the truth. All three of them had had their two years at Normal School and were past their nineteenth birthdays. There wasn't any obvious basis on which the poor man could have chosen among them except height.

Miss Hargrave knew what every teacher knows, that you remember the students you teach in your first and second year far better than you remember any but the standouts among their successors, and memories of standouts can be quite grim. It was sixty-five years since she taught this third grade at the Webster School and these urchins were now in the mid-seventies, those who survived. Occasionally, when Miss Hargrave made her still reasonably brisk way down to the Women's Institute or to tea with a friend at Brumbacher's store, she would pass some elderly lady or gentleman and greet pleasantly by the first name some youngster she had had in her first years of teaching. Her elderly friend would smile back with equal pleasantness, but call her Miss Hargrave.

She looked at the picture of one little girl, Martha Dumbrowski, at a little face a shade rounder than the others, a smile somewhat more natural and failing in the natural only because it had to force its way through a barrier of shyness, and at the top of a simple little dress with a delicate lace edging that would have suggested to Miss Hargrave, if the Normal School had included such matters in its curriculum, that Poland is something like France and a touch of the elegant sometimes shows in a peasant setting. She did remember Martha's parents and the day they both came to the school with her gift for Easter; Martha's father, a great tower of a man who could have overpowered Miss Hargrave by his mere existence were it not for a smile in his blue eyes, a gentleness in his voice, and something that she was just barely old enough to recognize as culture trying to break the barrier of a foreign language, and Martha's mother with the tired look about the eyes, and the smile that somehow reached out to the heart of a girl trying to appear a grownup and a teacher and assured her that everything was understood and that Martha's parents wanted and Miss Hargrave wanted the same thing for Martha, and that all knew it.

She wondered if Martha really got what her parents had wanted for her, and what Miss Hargrave had wanted too. She was invited to Martha's wedding, and learned that there are aspects to matrimony in the Polish tradition beyond the New England ken, but learned as well that a high degree of human warmth and friendliness is among them. In fact, Miss Hargrave was by no means sure that she did not learn vastly more from Martha through the years than Martha had learned from her back at the Webster School. Martha's father, who had attended the Military Institute at Lodz, never got beyond the tannery in Southwood. Yet he made a good home for Martha and her brothers, and Martha's mother kept it clean and attractive. Martha went to business college and if only one of her brothers

217

got beyond high school, the fault was theirs and not their parents'. Martha married a Polish boy from a background indistinguishable from her own, and they had seven children. They had one early death, one great and proud success, four quiet satisfactions, and one cruel heartbreak. Now that Martha Dumbrowski was in the grave (Miss Hargrave never bothered to remember marriage names which she found quite distracting; she never knew to whom people were referring when they used marriage names), Miss Hargrave was inclined to think that she really did have what her parents had hoped for her. Miss Hargrave never would have thought so when she was forty or even sixty, but by eighty-six a new set of values has taken over.

Somewhere in the trunk, but hardly worth the effort of searching for it, was the class picture that contained Martha's brightest, little Stanley. Miss Hargrave always thought of Stanley when she thought of Martha; the surge of pride that put a tremor in the mother's voice and a light in the mother's eye when she met Miss Hargrave on Franklin Street and told her of his success in pre-medical studies, his progress at medical school, the wonderful opportunity that an internship at Massachusetts General Hospital represented, and then the hanging out of the shingle and the waiting for the first case were part of Miss Hargrave's recompense for years in grade school. His first case was an ordinary case of measles and Stanley knew full well that it came to him because he was hardly apt to charge as much for measles as an established doctor, but that did not matter. It was his first case, and in some subtle way it proved that his grandfather was right in leaving a military career at home for a tannery job in no sense its equal. When a man pulls out and heads for his Western Reserve, he does metaphorically enter the depth of the sea and he may emerge changed, but his real hope and expectation may also be that the future of his line has been changed.

Martha had a certain fierce loyalty to solid worth that curbed in a salutary way her pride in having in her brood a doctor and a learned man. The girls made solid marriages to hard working men, as time went on owned their own homes and lived to the day when working people had automobiles and those fortunate enough to have the right kind of children got Sunday afternoon rides. It was nothing out of the ordinary for Martha's daughters and their husbands to bring her for a pleasant Sunday at York or Hampton beach. One of the boys was made a foreman at the tannery rather quickly, and the one who worked for the candy company in Cambridge did just about as well. They lived the simple lives of ordinary Americans, with the simple pleasures of their kind, but they were entirely free to go where they pleased and do as they pleased within a framework of law that was so remote from them as hardly to exist, but within a framework of society that gave them a guidance so thoroughly desired and acceptable that they never dreamed of it as restrictive. Like their parents before them, they accepted freedom gratefully and deferred opportunity to their children. Miss Hargrave had a notion, from what her younger and former colleagues at the Woodrow Wilson school told her, that their children would indeed be prudent to defer in turn genuine opportunity to their children to be, and no doubt would do so. There was a strong family tie, far more than the Christmas and Easter kind, and it showed itself in all its strength when the terrible matter of Paul occurred. The Dumbrowskis, as Miss Hargrave conveniently thought of them, had faced every problem but disgrace. Now they faced disgrace, and faced it down.

It was natural, perhaps, that Miss Hargrave's thoughts came back to Stanley. Doctors were in her thoughts now more than they used to be. Naturally she had a Yankee doctor herself, but if she were Polish like her neighbors across the street, she would certainly have Stanley as her doctor. The truth is that Stanley was in a tradition so ancient that if the awareness of it ever entered his head he would be staggered and expel it in outraged disbelief. Southwood had a large Polish population, and it was Stanley's primary care and concern. It had some Lithuanians, not enough to support a Lithuanian doctor, who would swallow pride and accept the services of a good Polish doctor. It had quite a few Italians who did not seem to care about the racial antecedents of a doctor, and some Irish who

219

insisted on a Catholic doctor, with race a minor but not negligible factor. It had many Nova Scotians who were bland about the matter, and then that great number of people of such mixed antecedents and such casual disregard for the whole business of race that one can only call them Americans and let the matter rest. Stanley was their doctor.

Stanley's tradition was ancient, and it transcended medicine. His working hours would be difficult to define, although office hours of a sort were posted on his door. He worked when people were sick and needed him, and while that could mean morning or noon it more frequently meant night. His specialty was the care of the human body in whatever might beset its frail and mortal state, and although on occasion he was stuck and called for help from the more narrowly learned, relatively few people in Southwood were given to exotic diseases and inscrutable conditions. It was not the practice of medicine that made his tradition ancient, but something within Stanley himself. The Poles of Southwood depended on him almost to a family, and so did many others who were not Polish but needed care and understanding. Stanley assumed a great and serious responsibility when he hung out his shingle in Southwood, and never for an instant did he think of his life as belonging to himself. It belonged to the people of Southwood, his town, his care, his responsibility. He prospered, of course, as well he should, but his triumphs were the child saved from that grim, forgotten killer diphtheria, the mother and baby both brought through safe and sound in a delivery that beaded Stanley's forehead with great globules of sweat, the broken hip gingerly nursed along until an old man walked again, and the woman with cancer brought as gently as possible to the grave as Stanley played chess with pain, deftly advancing and withdrawing the drugs that made its checkmate possible. It was his solemn duty to do these things and to put them before everything else, and that included his wife, his children, his home, his natural inclinations and desires. He was of the tradition of the Athenian citizen who gave the best hours of his life to the service of his city, of the baron who guarded his fief and its last and least inhabitant, of the governor in the service of his king and

220

warden of his people. He was in the tradition of the Benedictine monk who bound up the wounds the Ostrogoths inflicted, of the Franciscan friar who sought out the lepers, of the Puritan divine who left security in the name of faith and the salvation of souls, of the timid little Methodist who cared for the child of the mother with smallpox. He never suspected this, of course. He thought of himself as a family doctor practicing in an ordinary New England town and hardly known in the next town, which had its own doctor.

Stanley's brothers and sisters admired him, but they had their own lives of limited but genuine satisfaction. Like all the world's simple, humble people in times and places that give people freedom and opportunity, they enjoyed the present but lived in the promise that the future held for their children. Actually their children had limited ability, but in a sense that did not matter. Stanley's brothers and sisters thought of the good life to be, the life that their children would enjoy, in terms of its material comforts and satisfactions, quite oblivious of the fact that the material comforts and satisfactions they enjoyed were not at all the essence of the good life to them. They were kindred of the simple folk of Athens, the dwellers on the fief, the townsmen of the Middle Ages and Renaissance, the flock of the Puritan divine. They had their sense of wonder, and what is more important, they had the sense to wonder. Their wonder concerned simple, tangible things like the automobile and later the radio, and their children in turn would wonder about that parlor genii that suddenly takes shape out of the zigzags that flash across the glass of television. Their sense of wonder concerned these matters, but they also had the sense to wonder about what genii might eddy out of the bottles of the future, and how their children might be readied to profit by their visions. In their simple way they also were convinced that life tomorrow will be better, richer, finer than it is today and that their earthly destiny was to prepare their children for this mystical tomorrow. All immigrant Southwood was Stanley's care, their own little families were his brothers' and his sisters' care, but the difference was in extent and not in kind. As always and everywhere, the good life of Martha's brood and

221

their families was the life lived for others, and the sacrifice of self was at its heart.

Had Miss Hargrave been in the mood she might have woven in her mind the life stories of other children on that ancient picture, and the life stories of their children. There was little Timothy, with the hills and glens of Kerry in his face, whose star was the policeman's badge his father wore and he would wear when his time came. Miss Hargrave often saw Timothy on matters quite foreign to the professional concern of a grade-school teacher but not yet within the professional concern of a policeman. When trouble is brewing in a home a teacher often knows it first, and when a policeman knows it it is apt to be too late. Miss Hargrave was a lioness where the welfare of the third grade was concerned, and Timothy hated trouble. They conspired more than once, and a quiet word from Timothy to a man who was drinking too much or an ominous word to a man seeing another man's wife too much more than once protected one of Miss Hargrave's children and warded off the trouble that Timothy hated. Timothy had never heard of Portiuncula, nor for that matter had Miss Hargrave, but he was one of its sons. And there was little Susan whose face was old and serious even when she was a third grader. She went her mousy way through grade school and high school to her job in the assessor's office at town hall, and from there to her grave at the age of sixty-nine. The suggestion would have put her in a tizzy and in all seriousness have been unkind, but without her ever suspecting it she really ran Southwood. She was the one who had been at town hall time out of mind, knew everything about the town, and would never dream of saying what should be done but could say what always had been done and so was done now. Susan ran Southwood, just as there are Susans who run the United States of America and every country in the world that really is a country and has stability and strength. In Southwood law and order was neither a slogan nor a challenge. Law was Timothy and order was Susan. There was nothing more to it than that.

And what of Miss Hargrave? For fifty-one years she built three generations of Southwood, and she built well. Most human beings read and write, do simple arithmetic, entertain some relatively simple ideas about life and its values, and try to make out of life what they can. Miss Hargrave taught reading, writing, and simple arithmetic; she read stories to the children that illustrated simple and sound morals; she taught them "America the Beautiful" and told them about George Washington and Abraham Lincoln; she stressed honesty and kindness, and made a real issue out of cleanliness. Most of her third-graders in the early years went to work in the tannery or in Boston after grade school; later they went to work after high school. Some went to college; one became a United States Senator and another a Superior Court judge, but greatness was not a common visitant to Southwood. Even the Senator and the Judge who did much reading and writing had no call for anything beyond simple arithmetic, and Miss Hargrave taught them this. If all the children whom Miss Hargrave taught could somehow trace to their first origins the knowledge and the skills they habitually used in their daily lives, from the Senator and the Judge down through Martha and her husband, Stanley, his brothers and sisters, on to Timothy, Susan, and the rest, they and possibly all the learned world would be surprised at how much they brought from Miss Hargrave's class and the classes of the girls two inches and one inch shorter than she, and the classes of all the other teachers in the Webster and the Woodrow Wilson Schools, and how little really stemmed from high school and from college years. The good life of Miss Hargrave was the good life of Southwood, but the two were so inseparable that no human perceptivity could say where the one ended and the other began.

Miss Hargrave had a dim sense that was so. From time to time she would look at the picture of some class of many years ago, and let her mind wander. Some little faces did not belong in the developing picture, but others did. The picture developed, expanded, took on new dimensions. A town grew as families grew, and in a town where the good life was the good family life the influence of Miss Hargrave was like a benign presence that is felt only when it is removed. For fifty-one years Miss Hargrave helped to build Southwood, and for sixteen years after her retirement she watched her work develop. In a way her good life and Stanley's good life were similar, the life of dedication to the town. It was true even more of her than of Stanley, since Miss Hargrave had no spouse and no children except the children of others, and as time went on no family except some nieces whose concern it was to insure their own peace of mind with knowledge that Miss Hargrave was safely stowed away in a rest home. As it turned out their peace of mind was safe. After phoning for two days and getting no answer, they came over and found Miss Hargrave slumped on her chair in the attic, the picture of the third grade at the Webster School still on her lap and her forefinger resting on the round, shy little face of Martha Dumbrowski. At the funeral service they gave and received consolation in the thought that after all Miss Hargrave never had to go to a rest home. But she had gone to a Rest Home.

4.

The Human Story

BY the yardstick of external achievement the annals of Southwood were brief; it takes more than a United States Senator and a Superior Court Judge to make an Athens or a Rome. On the other hand, it requires only a Martha Dumbrowski to to make the good life. There is a sense in which her vision was the vision of Eben Gardner and James B. Gardner, except that her children were her Western Reserve and her Vermilion Range. She had a good and loving husband and a comfortable home; present comfort and a reasonable share of the world's good things have always been part of the good life. Just as present achievement was part of the good life of the older Gardners but the vision of the future was the spiritual part, so with Martha Dumbrowski except that the field of her vision was more limited and love and not achievement was its point of focus. Her son Stanley was her Vermilion Range, the other children her Western Reserve, but flesh and blood command a higher value than coal and iron. That she dreamed of the good life her children would enjoy in terms that were tangible and material in no way diminishes the essentially spiritual nature of her dream. We have to envision the spiritual in terms that are material; the Holy Spirit inevitably is a dove. The essential point is that in the vision of the Gardners the material and the spiritual were one and inseparable, whereas in the vision of Martha Dumbrowski they were not. For that precise reason the vision of the Gardners had within itself the seeds of its own fairly speedy destruction, but not the vision of Martha Dumbrowski. Not coal and iron but human love was the raw material from which her dream was wrought. It is of the nature of coal and iron that they be mined, made part of the active life of men, and wear away; it is of the nature of love that it continue to live deep in the heart where it vitalizes the hidden life.

Therefore the human stories of Southwood are not to be measured by the standards used for the success stories of the greater world. It was the great achievement of Martha Dumbrowski and that man we have so sadly and inexcusably neglected, her husband, to create a strong, united, wholesome family life, and that is certainly the oldest, firmest, most unchanging form the good life can ever take. Its presence is obvious in every generation, and it is merely the accident of literature which sometimes stresses it and sometimes fails to stress it that makes it seem more important in one era than in another.

The good life of Stanley, family doctor to immigrant Southwood, was simply the good life of his parents writ large. The Lord had given him five talents just as truly as He had given five to James B. Gardner, and his duty to make them ten was just as peremptory. He did it by making a large segment of a New England town his responsibility. He denied himself much pleasure, but took his compensation in the form of great happiness. He soon learned what every doctor learns, that you don't win all the time and you must learn to roll with the punch of fate, and that it never eases another's agony to share it emotionally. He learned efficiency of method and economy of time, and the knack of transmitting sympathy and understanding with a look, a pat of the hand, a minimum of words. By giving to each what each needed and could employ, he was able to give to more, and Southwood always had its Oliver Twists who needed more. He drove a Cadillac and let those down on the Flats who chose to murmur because Martha Dumbrowski's son drove a Cadillac do so to their hearts' content; he was a Cadillac doctor and he knew it. On his rare vacations he and his wife wallowed in luxury at Nassau, Palm Beach, or Palm Springs. He thought he was a sybarite, never suspecting that he was a Franciscan.

Miss Hargrave would indignantly deny that there was any self-sacrifice in her life, and fundamentally she would be right. To give is one thing, to sacrifice is another. Miss Hargrave gave to the little children of Southwood for a half century, but it was never a sacrifice but a labor of love. There is, of course, the selfish viewpoint from which any giving to others is sacrifice of self. Miss Hargrave was thoroughly aware of this particular heresy, and had her favorite set of parables adapted to the third grade to illustrate the principle involved. Furthermore, since Miss Hargrave was an old China hand with the third grade and knew that you can't be too explicit and direct when you instruct third graders, she enforced generosity where the sharing of candy was concerned with the autocracy of a Charlemagne. It was the great good fortune of Southwood that she brought into the twentieth century uncorrupted by modern pedagogic theory the nineteenth-century axioms for the teacher imparted to her at the Normal School in her eighteenth and nineteenth years, and they stood three generations in Southwood well. Not for a moment did she live in a world of memories, not even as a lady of eighty-six avoiding the rest home, but she had a world of memories for winter nights. Rather she lived in modern Southwood, took part in its activities, upbraided its corporate errors and applauded its corporate advances, and had a sense that in no small measure the town was what she had helped to make it. Just as James B. Gardner could look at the ore docks of Two Harbors and Cleveland, Miss Hargrave could look at the town of Southwood, but with the fundamental difference that the ore docks belonged to him but the town did not belong to her. He had built for himself, and so for him the material and the spiritual were one and inseparable. She had built for others, and so the vision and the fulfillment were distinct. Her good life was a modest structure, but it rested on bedrock.

Was the fact that Southwood was an American town of any significance? It would seem that it was of great significance, although it would be chauvinistic to deny that it could have been a Canadian town, or an Australian town, or a town in one of certain smaller and perhaps therefore happier European countries. For one thing, Southwood did not stand at the foot of castle hill. It was, in the happiest of possible senses, almost entirely a law unto itself. Its people abided by the law, although they would be hard put to define the law by which they abided. Most of them were content to let Timothy and his associates define the law on the rare occasions when it needed to be defined, knowing the justice, wisdom, and indeed mercy, of any definitions likely to issue from Tim. Because the law was really the general pattern of living by which people abided, there was a pervasive freedom in Southwood far more genuine than the sort of freedom embodied in that often truculent word *rights*. Out of that pervasive freedom arose the sort of opportunity that Southwood offered, the sort that challenges a man's character as well as his ability. It offered Stanley the opportunity to become a tower of strength for immigrant Southwood, and it offered his brother Paul the opportunity to ruin his life. It offered Miss Hargrave the opportunity to prepare three generations for opportunity, and it found the proper niche for Susan, with her genius for organization, operational procedure, and personal obscurity. It did all this with no need for a baron to guard it against its neighbors or a governor to marshal it in the service of a sovereign. It did it with a minimum of limitation on initiative and yet with a warm awareness of a town's responsibility where life's tragic victims are concerned. It did it without caste or class, without heredity and within one pattern of environment, and yet with no self-consciousness when it drew obvious and inescapable distinctions between Yankees and Poles, Irishmen and Italians. Since the distinctions tended to favor one side about as often as the other and when the chips were down and neighbors needed neighbors the distinctions disappeared, they did no harm to Southwood life and really gave it a bit of spice and flavor. At least the Thanksgiving Day football game between East High, on the edge of

228

the Flats, and West High School up on the hill translated ancestral divergences, theological differentiations, and economic distinctions into bone rattling tackles and earth shaking blocks, and when it ended with nothing worse the relief of two high-school principals was visible, audible, and fully shared by mothers gray and haggard at the sight.

The picture is idealized and nostalgic? It is, of course, idealized. The good life itself is an ideal. It is less certain that it need be deemed nostalgic. One is nostalgic for the past only when one is certain that it is past and that it was better than the present. But the vital truth about Southwood is that it belongs to neither the past nor the present. Southwood used to exist, but it still exists. It exists as a town in New England and in Old England too, and in every state of the union and in every country of the western world. It exists in the heart of great cities, wherever there are neighborhoods conscious of themselves as neighborhoods, where people share the same pattern of life based on the same set of values, live by modest standards, live peaceably and aim at modest goals. The person who goes on the conscious search for Southwood will never find it, but the person who lives by Southwood values may find that he has always been in Southwood. Stanley's shingle hangs on the house at the corner, Miss Hargrave teaches at the local school, Timothy sees her children across the street, Martha Dumbrowski lives two houses down, Susan is behind the desk in city hall.

Epilogue

IT is no more possible to analyze and classify the components of the good life in itself than it is possible to analyze and classify the unimaginable myriads of dreams and aspirations that have entered the human heart. All that one can do is ascertain what have been the dominant concepts of the good life at significant stages in human history, and then to find the common denominator, if there be one, in these concepts. It can be affirmed, however, that every society knows one prevailing pattern of living to which it gives approval, and that this pattern is what the society considers the good life.

That pattern can develop from circumstances quite without ethical or moral foundation. The topography of Greece is like the topography of a piece of paper crumpled into a ball and then casually opened, a topography of mountains and valleys, isolated harbors, great arms of the sea, and arms of the land probing far out to sea. It is by nature a land of isolated settlements and the Greek city state was implicit in the topography of the land itself, and so was the sort of localized patriotism the Greek city state engendered. That patriotism which was so fundamental a component in the Greek ideal of the good life was paralleled by another fact of an entirely different sort. The Greek genius evolved a mythology of unequalled richness, a treasury that has poured out its riches to artists in all the creative arts for three millennia, but the Greek genius never evolved a theology. Hellenism, to borrow Matthew Arnold's meaning of the word, is a spirit of incomparable aesthetic richness, but one must turn to Hebraism for morality. The ancient Greek had no Hebraism to which to turn, and therefore Greek ethics and morality had to be induced from human reason and worldly values. Stoicism and Epicureanism had to stand stead for religion, and Plato and Aristotle be the Greek Moses and Isaiah. Therefore the ancient Greeks derived their ethics and morals from philosophy and found their deepest responsibility and richest opportunity for service in the welfare of their cities. Civic life has never since been so large a component in the good life as it was in ancient Greece.

The Middle Ages, on the other hand, were more oriented to the after life than the dark ages that preceded them or the ages of perhaps increasing or perhaps illusive brightness that have followed them. To medieval man the salvation of the individual immortal soul was the only final responsibility, but to him as to all men in whom the spirit of religion dominates, the love of God merged with the love of neighbor. It may be seriously questioned if the modern welfare state has ever achieved the efficacy of charity, let alone the spirit of charity, that the Middle Ages attained in its choicest spirits, times, and places.

The ancient and the medieval patterns of the good life are in the fundamental sense of objective the most antithetical of the patterns we have considered. On the other hand, in the highly important sense of the good life of personal relationships and in the not inconsiderable sense of the physically good life they had much in common. No society has ever quite so exalted the abnegation of self and the dedication to the social order as did the ancient Greek. What other societies have considered man's natural, primary concern, his family and his livelihood, seem to have dwindled and almost disappeared in the Athenian citizen as they did in the medieval monk. The Athenian arose from his straw cot in a house of sun-baked brick, wrapped himself in an oblong length of cloth and fastened it with a safety pin, ate some pudding and a bit of fish, put some change in his mouth, and left to make his contribution to a philosophy of the state that has given the western world its fundamental structure and to do so in a public building that is still the deathless glory of the human race. The medieval monk did the same, except that his was the service of the Lord and the care of the Lord's people, and he perpetuated a structure he deemed not of man's hands in a building that is another deathless glory of the human race. Athens lives and Chartres lives, and both live not by brick alone but by the conviction that the good life is the life of service to the city, be it the city of man or the City of God.

After the Middle Ages the polarization between time and eternity which makes antiquity and the Middle Ages so antithetical tends to disappear. In the Renaissance, at least in England, the good life of the individual was largely sublimated, in the code accepted by the finer spirits, in the good life of the nation. On the other hand, the Reformation was an aspect of the Renaissance, a rebirth at least in purpose of the form and spirit of the early Church. Again the focus is on eternity and not on time. Thereafter the temporal trend becomes pronounced. The eighteenth century in the English-speaking world was the most self-centered of centuries and therefore the century in which the prevailing pattern of the good life was most nearly grounded on individualism unabashed. Yet even this generalization is partially false. The eighteenth century saw appear first in France and then in America a spirit that somehow blended the ancient preoccupation about the City and its welfare with natural law concepts and Christian principles. Out of it came the most philosophic, firmly grounded, and enduring formal codification of the good life within the social pattern ever achieved, the American Constitution.

It is true in general that as we pass from the Renaissance into the modern age individualism becomes a respected philosophy and the good life of the individual a concern seemingly greater than in the earlier periods. A number of factors conspired to make this especially true in the United States. The first was the pattern of living imposed by the frontier. The very definition of the word makes the frontier the natural home of individualism, and successive waves of immigrants from Europe and also waves of native born Americans followed the instinct for the west with a faith in progress, opportunity, freedom, challenge, and service somehow distilled in the alembic of

233

American life into the American spirit. The second was the physical wealth of an unopened continent; for decades beyond the Western Reserve was the Vermilion Range, and beyond Minnesota was Montana. The result was a factor in the American spirit not to be found in the other societies that we have treated, a unique fusion of the material and the spiritual made possible by the fact that each stage of material achievement opened new vistas of possible achievement ahead, and the related fact that each stage of material achievement was quickly and visibly translated into a richer, more comfortable, and more varied life for the American people. The third was the American pattern of living itself, as codified in the American Constitution. It provided not only a legal maximum of individual freedom but what was vastly more important, a pervasive atmosphere of individual freedom in which the individual might achieve. This atmosphere of freedom was often shamefully abused, and yet so rich was the unopened continent that even those who abused it often made their contributions to the physical good life of the American people. Nor can the significance of this third factor be disregarded in the light of the richness of an unopened continent. There is a similar richness in southern Siberia, but the spirit of progress, opportunity, freedom, and service has never been allowed to meet the challenge. Somehow that spirit belongs to the instinct for the west, not the instinct for the east.

In the United States the instinct for individualism and the tradition of individualism reinforce each other. Two recent national administrations, one of them the longest in American history, have symbolized themselves in terms suggestive of the corporate good life, the New Deal and the Great Society. We may pass by the purpose of the Great Society with a quiet *requiescat;* it was consumed in the napalm of foreign war and racial strife. The New Deal, on the other hand, was a long and intensive effort to change the prevailing American concept of the good life from the individualistic to the social. In this its failure was complete. The most constructive and best designed of the New Deal employment ventures, and there were such

234

along with the others, never really seemed to the American people other than a temporary palliative of the welfare sort. A third administration had a different concept, at least if one can read a concept behind the symbolism of a title. President Kennedy symbolized his aspiration in the name New Frontier, and the most striking of his public utterances and the phrases that already have clustered about his name in popular memory concerned what the individual could do for his fellow man.

With this we approach the common denominator, the heart of the matter. Beneath all the surface differences that time, place, and society can generate there are certain areas of agreement visible in man's concept of what comprises the good life. Let us consider the negative areas of agreement first. No vital and enduring society has ever equated the good life with the physically comfortable life. To say that much is merely to voice a truism. What is more to the point, no society has ever totally eliminated the physically comfortable as a component of the good life, not even the ancient Greek. Asceticism is the deliberate curtailing of the physically comfortable in the name of a higher motivation than the temporal. Asceticism would have no point if society in general did not consider physical comfort an aspect of the good life. Once the equation is made complete, however, and the life of comfort is deemed the good life, the degeneration of the society, or of the individuals in society, is well advanced. Every vital and enduring society has agreed on this point.

The second negative consideration concerns the relationship between the good life and happiness. In the concrete pattern of daily living, there may or may not be a relationship between the good life and what is commonly considered happiness. Only to one austere enough to equate happiness with the satisfaction of duty performed, or should one say pessimistic enough to expect no greater happiness than that, is there a necessary relationship between the two. The person who deliberately leads a good life, or does so instinctively, never does so in the spirit of hedonism. As for happiness, much depends upon the individual himself and his personal interpretation of happiness. One thing, however, is certain: neither the good life nor true happiness is attained by deliberate hedonism.

This brings us to the affirmative, and to a principle sufficiently pervasive to make one consider it a permanent and integral part of the good life itself. The principle is that some men, usually a very small minority, lead the good life of service to society at large, but that most men who lead the good life do so in terms of their personal stations in life. The welfare of the entire fief was the concern of the medieval baron, the safety of the county and beyond that of the country was the responsibility of the Renaissance governor. Honor, prestige, wealth, authority, all were prerequisites of position, but they did not comprise their good life. When the last and least beggar on the fief was cared for, when the last and least child in the county was secure, the life of the baron and the governor was the good life. In the ultimate analysis, political democracy is the attempt to achieve this concept of the good life within a social framework. It may be pure democracy as it was in Athens, or it may be representative democracy with every conscientious representative assuming the same austere role. It would be equally naive or cynical to assume that every American President and governor, or no American President or governor, has led the good life that *noblesse oblige* dictates. The fundamental point is that the good life of the minority called to posts of authority and responsibility is the good life of service.

What is true in the secular realm is true in the religious. The Benedictine monk who came down to rebuild the road to Caserta, his brother who stayed on the hill copying the manuscript of Aristotle, the Franciscan who sought out the lepers in the caves across the ridge, the Puritan divine who helped to hack a toehold in the wilderness that the gospel might be freely listened to and obeyed, the Methodist band leader who brought to the eighteenth century a light very different from that of the Enlightenment, every man and woman of God who has worshipped in the stillness of his heart even as he has brought help and hope to the afflicted have led the good life of service. The youngster of today who is trying through his

Peace Corps service to bring something of today into the lives of those bemired in a hopeless yesterday, and the oldster of today not too old to do the same in city streets through Vista service, are of their company. The service of God and the service of one's fellow man are not really one nor are they inseparable. The essential point is that they are one in spirit, and the latter is the handmaid to the former. The good life of religion, be it formal religion or that kind of secular religion so difficult to distinguish in spirit from the formal kind, is always and everywhere the life of service. *Noblesse oblige* inspires the religious life, in every form, at every level, in every age.

And the people of Southwood. The father whose good life centered about his family must have lived in ancient Athens quite as truly as in modern Southwood. It is simply that literature, that aristocratic art, does not record his presence. The parents whose good life lay in the promise of their children lived at the foot of castle hill in the Middle Ages. Artists did not put them on canvas, since canvas is for the tortured Christ, His grieving mother, St. Sebastian with the arrows sticking out and St. Lawrence beatific on the griddle. The doctor whose good life was the welfare of his patients did his dedicated if feeble and insufficient best in the Renaissance. Lawyers led good lives in the name of justice in the nineteenth century and businessmen made possible the physically better and richer lives of their fellow men, but they are economic and social forces as viewed by modern social scientists.

Southwood never fares too well when books are written. Literature ignored it until very late in the eighteenth century; no glory of the Romantic Movement is greater than the discovery by Burns, Blake, Wordsworth, Crabbe, and Lamb that Southwood exists. In the twentieth century literature again has largely turned its back upon it, preferring as subject matter life in its discordances and abnormalities to life in its normal patterns. But every father whose good life centers about his family, all parents whose good lives are lived in the promise of their children, the doctor whose good life is the welfare of his patients, the teacher whose good life is the future of his students, the lawyer whose good life is dedication to justice, the business-

237

man whose good life is the physically richer and better life his enterprise makes possible, every last human being and every least human being who lives in the sacrifice of self for the benefit of others and as if by sheer accident finds happiness is an individualist living the good life of the individual. The good life of Southwood is the good lives of a host of individuals and the good life can be achieved quite as well under the philosophy of individualism as under a philosophy that exalts service to society. Individualism itself is not an evil; it is the spirit that can motivate individualism that must be questioned. The secret of the good life of the individual is the same as always: the search for happiness can never be conscious nor self-centered, and succeed. The good life, like happiness itself, is an abstract by-product of a concrete pattern of living. That, at least, is what history seems to say.

DATE DUE

GAYLORD			PRINTED IN U.S.A.